Suburban Crime
The Interplay of Social, Cultural, and Opportunity Structures

Sanjay Marwah

LFB Scholarly Publishing LLC
New York 2006

Library of Congress Cataloging-in-Publication Data

Marwah, Sanjay.
  Suburban crime : the interplay of social, cultural, and opportunity
structures / Sanjay Marwah.
      p. cm. -- (Criminal justice recent scholarship)
  Includes bibliographical references and index.
  ISBN 1-59332-145-7 (alk. paper)
  1. Suburban crimes--United States. 2. Crime--Sociological aspects--
United States. 3. Crime--California--Los Angeles Suburban Area. I.
Title.
  HV6791.M363 2006
  364.10973'091733--dc22

2006019398

ISBN 1-59332-145-7

Printed on acid-free 250-year-life paper.

Manufactured in the United States of America.

Table of Contents

Acknowledgments

I would like to acknowledge the intellectual contributions of Robert K. Merton, Mathieu Deflem, Mark Colvin, and Robert Dudley to my work. I also owe the later two along with other members of my dissertation committee, Frank Fukuyama, Kingsley Haynes, Roger Stough, and Catherine Gallagher, a special debt of gratitude. There are countless others to thank that would require more detailed specification; they know who they are. Thank you to all!

CHAPTER 1

Structural Analysis and Crime Research

Introduction

Scholars and policymakers have ignored the influence of general and contextual factors behind the scale and distribution of traditional crime and violence rates in large U.S. metropolitan areas. Crime and violence result from and contribute to the development (or lack of development) of a metropolitan region. Explaining crime rates as compared to the incidence of crime across individuals requires structural frameworks that account for both the development of a metropolis and its crime and violence problems. This study applies an encompassing framework to examine and explain property and violent crime rates across suburban municipalities within the five-county Los Angeles metropolitan region. This framework operates through the notion of opportunities borrowed from criminological research and function and status from urban sociological research. The major thesis is that opportunities, when conceived as both resources to achieve objectives (related more strongly to status) and as physical targets or property (related more strongly to function), in combination with functional and status differences help to explain the scale and distribution of property and violent crime rates across municipalities. Opportunities are strongly related to functional and status aspects of suburbs and suburban stratification. Crime and violence require both targets and/or motivated actors who usually lack resources. The distribution of resources and

1

targets which result from the operation of multiple structures, is critical for explaining the distribution of crime rates across the metropolis.

Opportunity Structures and Crime and Violence Rates

The major theoretical conceptualization of opportunities derives from the work of sociologist, Robert Merton, on anomie-and-opportunity structures and the work of criminologists developing and applying routine activities theory. These two major frameworks have different conceptualizations of opportunities. Merton's (1956, 1968, and 1995) conceptualization sees opportunities as resources to achieve goals and objectives widely accepted in the metropolitan region and broader society and generally, to maximize various types of status. Resources derived from conditions in opportunity structures are accessible only to individual and group actors through their positions (status) in social structures. Traditionally, existing research views Merton's theory as explaining property crime as a rational utilitarian process whereby structurally motivated offenders lacking opportunities seek to achieve the culturally induced goal of material success (Vold et al. 2002). Others have insisted that strained individuals who lack opportunities are frustrated and these frustrations lead them to commit crimes (Agnew 1992, 1995). Merton has challenged this perspective by arguing that his focus is on the range of conforming and deviant behavior, on the achievement of a range of many goals not limited to economic success, and more specifically, that there are no arguments in his theory regarding the social-psychological states of actors (Merton 1956, 1995).

The theory remains useful in explaining property crime rates, however, when considering the location of motivational elements behind the decisions to commit crimes and their concentration in and across suburbs. However, Merton's conceptualization seems better suited to explain violent crime rate differences across different type of suburbs. Violent crimes often involve the seeking of resources through generally considered illegal and deviant means. These status goals and objectives can be specific to particular situations and contexts and/or broader in focus and orientation. Resource deprivation may lead to increased motivations for individuals and groups to consider crime as an alternative to maximize global and local status. This is the crucial factor in why particular types of violent crimes, assaults for example, involve conflicts between similar status individuals and groups trying to obtain local and extra-local resources. The newest element of Merton's anomie-and-opportunity structures paradigm, the concept of opportunity structures, is theoretically important as the objective situations (the conditions of action) influencing criminal and noncriminal choices and behavior directly operate in the paradigm. Merton adds opportunity structures to social and cultural structures already incorporated, which allows the paradigm to specify all elements underlying human choices and actions. Briefly, the paradigm includes elements of structure and agency - resources (derived from opportunity structures – the conditions of action) and ideas and values (from cultural structures) - influence actor (located in multiple social structures with particular statuses) choices.

The second conceptualization, which views opportunities as physical targets, is better suited to explain property crimes (Brantingham and Brantingham 1984; Warr 2001). The value and type of physical targets across suburban jurisdictions offers different degrees of attraction to potential offenders who seek to obtain the highest value property from their crimes (Cook 1986). Existing research on suburban crime and violence has found support for the routine activities perspective in explaining property crimes (Stahura and Hollinger 1988; Stahura and Huff 1986; Stahura and Sloan 1988). Such research also supports the concentration of wealth and status or resource abundance as a critical explanatory factor, which is also consistent with an anomie and opportunity structures framework (Stahura and Sloan 1988). It can be argued that increased property crime being a result of affluence and prosperity may be an unintended consequence of purposeful actions by various actors to maximize their individual and group status. Resource abundance therefore may lead to increased attractive targets, which motivated offenders seek to obtain such as money and goods. If it coincides with resource deprivation, increased motivations to consider crime as a means to achieve particular ends are pertinent as well. The uneven distribution of resources and targets across the metropolitan region necessitates examining both factors in explaining rates of crime and violence. In both perspectives, crimes result from choices made by individuals and groups, but with different elements structuring these choices. The largest differences between theoretical perspectives studying crime concern the factors influencing these choices and the constraining and/or facilitating forces that structure these choices. The scope and domain of these and other theories differ as they attempt to answer different questions and explain different types of deviant behavior, including property and violent crimes.

Robert Merton's conceptualization is broader than the routine activities perspective and should be used as a basis for combining elements from the later perspective. Merton's generic concept of opportunity structures refers to both physical and nonphysical conditions. There are no limitations to incorporate physical environmental features, which scholars examining crime as an event criticize the discipline for ignoring. Merton emphasizes the structural patterning and location of criminal and noncriminal adaptations, statuses, and access to resources. Resources derive from various environments and particular conditions present in these environments provide various contexts and situations in which actors make choices.

One of the critical differences relates to the importance of both structure and actor considerations in the Mertonian framework. The routine activities perspective puts considerable emphasis on offender decision-making in isolation from other decisions by these offenders (or other offenders and nonoffenders) and ignores the underlying stratification of individuals and groups. The perspective also disproportionately focuses on the features of the particular targets and less on the broader environmental and nonphysical considerations influencing crime and violence. The greater emphasis is on offender choices and less on how different structures and processes distribute targets, motivations, and resources. Routine activities theory and theoretically similar perspectives have unduly ignored and underemphasized motivational aspects behind crime and violence (Miethe and Meier 1994). In contrast, Merton (1936) sought to explain the location and distribution of crime adaptations across and within various types of social structures and argues that motivations to crime and violence distribute in a nonrandom fashion across the social strata. Further, criminal and noncriminal choices and actions can involve different motivations, but they can be both be explained partially by the pursuit of higher status.

The similarities in these two types of actions lie in similar processes of decision-making and achievement of goals and objectives by individual and group actors, but the differences may lie in the availability of resources or means to achieve particular goals and objectives. Particular types of crimes are more prevalent not only because they are structurally possible, but also structurally motivated. Violent crimes, as defined by the broader society, are more heavily concentrated in that lower-status individuals and groups are both victims and offenders. Property crimes are more widespread and bifurcated with victims from all status levels and offenders generally from lower status levels. The more affluent locations and individuals in society are more attractive targets than the lower level locations and groups because of the higher value of such targets. However, property crimes may be higher in particular locations and groups from the lower strata for other reasons, despite the lack of attractive targets. The major constraint may be the lack of direct access to attractive targets and the availability of these targets in less affluent locations, but targets of varying quality are widely available in all types of locations. White-collar crimes are less likely to be prevalent for these later groups and concentrated in higher status groups.

Motivations for crime vary across society in terms of their intensity and content. Status considerations are important for many different types of behaviors and actions as they are for crime. Achieving and maximizing status requires resources. The generation and distribution of resources result from the organization of important social, economic, and political structures and the differential positioning and access of individuals and groups in these structures. Targets are more widely distributed than resources across these structures, albeit the quality and potential attractiveness of such targets varies considerably. However, positioning in and access to the same structures relevant to the distribution of resources also apply for targets. Consequently, targets are means used to maximize status and invariably involve motivational considerations. The distribution of both targets and resources is more easily incorporated into the Mertonian framework and distributional considerations are more narrowly defined as targets from the routine activities perspective. Further, the ability to provide safety and increase guardianship (both formal and informal) is dependent on resources, monetary and nonmonetary. The relationship between guardianship and targets is contingent upon the quality of resources used to respond to criminal and deviant actions. Lower quality resources or reliance on formal responses to crime and violence may be ineffectual, especially if high crime and violence rates are concentrated in such areas (Bursik 1988; Reiss 1986).

Structures and Crime Analysis

Merton's broader framework also incorporates the influence of structures on human behavior (Crothers 1987, 1996). The original paradigm centered on social and cultural structures. The book argues that Merton's framework is important to apply for several reasons. First, it brings a macro perspective to examine crime patterns and environmental influences currently dominated by micro-environmental theories of crime (Meier 1989). This follows the tradition of Durkheim and purposively focuses on explaining crime and violence rates rather than the incidence of individual and/or group deviance. This focus on rates is a source of confusion in current criminological and sociology of crime research as many have interpreted and applied Merton's theory at the individual and/or group levels. A systematic approach is needed to be developed at the macro-level and is a necessary supplement to more micro-oriented approaches examining patterns of crime and violence (Miethe & Meier 1994). Micro theories ignore the non-physical environments that play a role in influencing the patterning of crime. Macro theories are inherently interested in the organization of society and its members and the effects of such organization on human behavior.

Second, Merton emphasizes the non-random nature of crime and violence and the location of such behaviors in society's multiple structures. Merton (1968) explicitly focuses on patterns of behaviors including deviant behavior and identifying and analyzing the forces responsible for such patterns. Crime and violence patterns are distributed across the metropolis in particular ways that require explanation. These patterns are not randomly distributed, but have distinct profiles, spatial and in other dimensions such as political organization, economic conditions, and social differentiation. All these profiles are linked and result from the interplay of multiple structures. Prominent criminological and sociological theories have stressed the importance of ecological and organizational examination of crime rates (Cullen 1983). However, past research has not adequately laid out the factors responsible for organization of ecological areas and how they link to crime patterns and trends (Meier 1989, 2001; Reiss 1986). Merton's approach links multiple structures and their effects through the addition of opportunity structures. The later structure is where resources are derived for use by individuals and groups to achieve different goals and objectives. In this regard, resource distribution is critical to Merton's paradigm. Further, the distribution of resources is inevitably an important part of any explanation of non-random patterns and their location in any society.

Individuals and groups are located in these multiple structures in numerous ways, some directly and others indirectly. The most relevant and direct location of individual and groups occurs in social structures. Merton (1968, 1995) specifically emphasizes the interplay of social and opportunity structures through the location of individuals and groups in social structures. Shared location of individuals and groups increases the likelihood of exposure to and influence by similar structural conditions and similar choices/adaptations to these conditions. In Merton's analyses, this is always a probabilistic process and structures never determine agent choices.

In other structures, such as cultural, economic, and political ones, the location of individuals and groups is more indirect so that extra-individual units and/or non-human phenomena are the relevant elements of examination. These include the organization and distribution of non-material entities such as norms and values in cultural structures and corporations and interest groups in economic and political structures. Of course, only individuals and groups give credence to these values, obey norms, and operate political and economic structures - so that incorporating individual and group elements is critical to any social science analysis. However, in order to make generalizations about structures and for the effects of structures on individual and group behavior, one can abstract from the limited cases examining a limited set of individuals and groups to shared environments of all types including physical and non-physical environments.

The resulting patterns of behavior are more likely to be non-random because they occur due to the operation of multiple structures reinforcing a distinct organization and distribution. For example, crime and violence rates are distributed in the social structure due to the interplay of the social structure with opportunity structures and the cultural structure. This book deals mostly with the interplay of social and opportunity structures as the data on suburban crime and violence rates as well as data in suburban function and status are relevant for these two structures. Data on the cultural structure is not directly collected or analyzed. However, consistent with Merton, one finds that the pursuit of material success and maximizing status are important values in metropolitan regions across the United States for both individuals and groups as well as for suburban municipalities. Thus, it is not unreasonable to argue that suburbs compete for resources, monetary and non-monetary, and this competition reflects the broader American culture and the organization and distribution of major values, norms, and interests in this culture. The cultural structure plays a vital part in the production and distribution of crime and violence rates, but its effects are only examined indirectly in this study.

Third, Merton's approach is integrative and incorporates elements of both structure and agency (Barbano 1968). Despite the common misconception popular in the fields of criminology and sociology of crime that Merton's approach is offender focused, the focus on structures and agency is accomplished through the study of situations. (Barbano 1968) Situation lies at the intersection of structures and human agency. Merton's structural analysis is different from others that focus on examining society as a large system (such as Talcott Parsons). The subjective definition of the situation is not ignored in the approach (Barbano 1968). Merton stresses the structural contexts or situations for which empirical data must be collected. Each situation results from different combinations of structures, or more properly, the conditions of these structures.

There exists a tendency for most approaches to favor either structure or agency in their analysis (Henslin 1988). Aside from Marxist and critical theories (which many critics point out have not been empirically tested), criminology has tended towards dominance by individual theories and most empirical work in the field uses data on individual attributes. These micro theories are important for the advancement of the discipline, but there need to be further incorporation and testing of macro theories (as pointed out above) as well as integration of theories that allows for development of reliable and valid datasets for macro-level attributes. Merton's paradigm and theories put greater (if not most all) emphasis on structural sources of human behavior. This study does the same and focuses on environmental aspects of property and violent crime rates and suburban municipalities.

Finally, Merton's approach emphasizes the importance of resources and the distribution of resources as critical explanatory factors in explaining human behavior. While many approaches consider such factors, Merton's contribution is unique as it brings together the multiple structures and processes that produce the relationship between resource distributions and patterned human behavior. Most theories look at a limited set of structures and processes and argue that these are more influential than others. Merton recognizes that is the totality of conditions in individuals' environments that influences their choices and these choices in turn influence the resulting conditions. Individuals and groups compete for status and access to and accumulation of resources. Structures are organized and developed with a focus on resources - resource capture/extraction, production, preservation, enhancement, and distribution. While institutions specialize in a particular function with regard to resources, issues of resource distribution (and generally distribution of anything, e.g., values) are critical in explaining the resulting patterned and located behavior. Further, resource distribution issues permeate multiple structures and institutions as well as many types of human behavior. The nature and state of multiple structures, that is their conditions, is the very source of these resources to be used by individuals and groups to meet their goals and objectives.

Suburban Places and Opportunity Structures

This book directly links and tests opportunity structures and resource distributions to the distribution of property and violent crime rates. The major general hypotheses are that i). suburbs with greater resources (resource abundance) tend to have lower rates of both property and violent crime, but can have elevated rates of property crimes with greater levels of employment and retail activities and ii). suburbs with lower amount of resources (resource deprivation) have higher rates of violent crimes and may have higher levels of property crimes with concentration of employment and industrial activity. The types of property targeted and concentration of motivated offenders and resources to achieve certain goals and objectives differ across suburbs as well. These relate to differences in functions and status levels across jurisdictions.

The nature and process of suburbanization is directly relevant to explain property and violent crime rate differences (Sloan and Stahura 1986; Stahura and Sloan 1988; Skogan 1977). Suburbs are highly differentiated providing different physical and nonphysical environments more or less favorable for the occurrence of crime. The particular configuration of conditions, populations, and businesses unique to each suburb contribute to their particular crime problem. Suburbanization is a selective process and suburbs vary along multiple dimensions. The development and growth of suburbs differs considerably, with each suburb seeking to use its available resources to prosper in the suburban hierarchy (Bollens 1987). The stratification of suburbs is multifaceted and structured by numerous mechanisms. Suburbs specialize in function, hosting populations and businesses of various types and strata and differentiate by the status of these actors. Ideally, every suburb and its residential and employment populations seek to maximize status. However, suburbs stratify by both function and status in complex ways. The result is considerable suburban diversity and inequality.

Research on suburbanization has recognized that its impacts have not been homogeneous for different groups and places. Two major models have generally explained the growths of suburban populations and suburbanization relating to place characteristics (Hwang and Murdock 1998a, 1998b). Both models assume that individuals and groups attempt to maximize their shelter, work, and quality of life needs. These needs are then ranked in terms of desirability and status. The first model, the spatial assimilation model, explains group differences in population by different racial, ethnic, and socioeconomic groups as the outcome of the ability to translate their socioeconomic achievements towards assimilation into desirable suburbs. According to this perspective, the abilities of groups differ and reflect the general racial and socioeconomic inequalities existing in society. From this view, minority assimilation and suburbanization are products of both individual abilities and group inequalities, with individual factors as primary. Over time, spatial assimilation occurs with the movement of lower-status individuals into higher quality residential suburbs. The growth of minority suburbanization is used as direct evidence of assimilation by individuals and groups into the mainstream institutions of society. This perspective does not address the stratification of places or consider status differences between places as having influence on minority suburbanization.

The second perspective, place stratification, emphasizes the importance of stratification of places as well as stratification of racial and ethnic groups in explaining the degree of assimilation. Collective actors, particularly higher status groups having higher levels of a range of resources, use their resources to maximize their statuses including residence in more affluent suburbs. This perspective recognizes the selective nature of residential suburbanization and the uneven assimilation of racial/ethnic groups into the suburbs. Asians and Anglo suburbanization rates are found to be higher and black suburbanization the lowest with Hispanic suburbanization higher than that for blacks. Black suburbanization and the suburbanization of low status and resources groups are limited and channeled through various land use and zoning mechanisms and racial discrimination in housing markets. Individual and group characteristics are also translated from the micro level of individuals in these models and examined in terms of their fit with the general characteristics and outcomes for places in terms of desirability and exclusiveness. Despite focusing on the stratification of places, empirical testing using the place stratification theory ignores the distinctive characteristics of places and focuses on explaining outcomes of individuals and groups into suburban residence. Place employment characteristics are not examined nor the functional and status attributes specific to places underpinning the suburban hierarchy. The place stratification perspective, when modified and combined with existing views of the functional and status attributes of suburbs, is useful in linking suburban stratification to property and violent crime rates.

Differences in the function and status of jurisdictions offer different environmental and resource conditions implicated in the behavior and actions of both residents and employers in these jurisdictions. These in turn provide the contexts and environments in which crime choices and actions are influential to individual and group adaptations. Viewing a metropolitan region as having multiple social, economic, and political structures, one can view choices made by individuals and group actors differentially located and distributed in physical, economic, political, and social space (Weiher 1989; Williams 1971). Thus, these choices directly link to the overall environmental and contextual conditions existing in each suburban jurisdiction as well as across these jurisdictions. These choices exhibit considerable interdependence, as do the different conditions existing in the suburbs and the location of these conditions (Friedman 1994). Specialization in function also demonstrates the interdependent nature of metropolitan development.

Higher status suburbs are better able to mobilize their resources and act collectively to capture and extract resources from various structures. They have shared interests to maximize individual and collective status and to accumulate resources over time to maintain and improve their statuses (Burns 1994). Lower status suburbs, in contrast, are less likely to able to obtain resources and offer chances for their residents and employers to achieve both individual and collective goals.

This reflects their reduced abilities to collectively organize and mobilize their resources and to fully match individual interests with collective interests (Danielson 1976).

Suburban Stratification and Rates of Property and Violent Crime

Changes in the nature of urban form and structure have accelerated in the post World War II United States. The suburbanization of housing and employment has rapidly changed the nature of economic and social activities in modern metropolitan systems. While the number and types of suburbs have increased, differences in status levels and degrees of homogeneity along racial, ethnic, and socioeconomic dimensions persist. In the past, traditional urban economic and sociological research focused on questions of mobility, accessibility, and location that were more specific to neighborhoods in central cities. In the past, neighborhood analyses were necessary. These concerns now extend to contrasting central cities and suburbs as well as examining heterogeneous suburban areas themselves. In current metropolitan environments, pressures for suburban expansion and changes in metropolitan form signify a focus on suburbs and other related jurisdictions is essential.

In this study, the primary units of analysis are suburban municipalities (i.e., cities and towns) in the five county Los Angeles consolidated metropolitan statistical area (CMSA). Municipalities are distinct actors in metropolitan regions that play important roles in creating and modifying the environments that underlie the distribution of crime and violence rates. Through their land-use and revenue powers, jurisdictions are critical for creating the landscapes of metropolitan regions. Numerous sorting mechanisms, including ethnic and class segregation, separation of land uses, and generation of status and power, involve municipal level decisions and choices (Weiher 1989, 1991).

The Los Angeles region is chosen for multiple reasons. The region has been examined by a variety of researchers across many social science disciplines and has been more recently contrasted to the prominent Chicago School. In fact, an emerging L.A. School that challenges the model of the older and dominant Chicago School has influenced substantial research (Dear & Flusty 1998, 2002). As the second largest metropolitan region in the United States, Los Angeles exhibits considerable intra-metropolitan variation. This will allow for in-depth analysis of the properties of suburban places along multiple dimensions. Past research and analysis on suburban crime have generally grouped suburbs from many metropolitan regions; a separate examination of each metropolitan region is necessary to fully comprehend the reasons for the particular distribution of crime levels and types across these suburbs.

A significant amount of research suggests that the causal factors explaining property and violent crimes (and rates) are different in many types of environments. The disciplines of criminology and criminal justice have tended to de-emphasize these different etiologies in search for a general (universal) theory of crime and deviance. For these and other reasons, many different types of theories have developed that emphasize different facets of what generally, and is commonly, called deviant behavior. Unfortunately, theorists have not paid specific attention to specifying the scope and domain of different theories. Application of any theory seems to be limited to particular types of environments, situations, and types of crime and violence. Most criminological theories are more readily applicable and useful at particular levels of analysis and for particular questions. The theories in the field have been differentiated along macro-micro and structure-process lines, but it is still common practice to assert that theories are applicable for all types of situations and crimes. Other related problems include distortion of theories and the resulting misapplications and failing to acknowledge the contextual nature of crime and violence. These tendencies also exist in the literature on suburban crime and violence, where theories borrowed from early historical periods and for dramatically different environments are applied to newer settings. More attention is needed to refine existing theories and develop newer ones more useful in studying current societal and metropolitan contexts.

By ignoring the inherent complementarities and necessity of using multiple theories, the field has not addressed the need to develop and apply theories that incorporate broader changes in the society. Single cause and 'context-less' approaches are unable to account for the complex set of factors related to crime and violence. While ecological models of crime stress such factors, they have been developed without concern for how environments are externally created and organized and the implications of such stratification in the etiologies of property and violent crimes.

This study develops model specifications for specific offenses. As there are multiple suburban crime and violence problems, with each suburb having a unique mix of supplemental offenses, an offense-specific approach is warranted. Additionally, it is expected that suburbs differentiated on function and status provide different targets and resources with distinct effects on particular offenses. Property crime offenses are more target-specific and generally are higher in suburban employment centers. Violent crimes are more status-specific and generally are higher in lower-status suburbs. This study strongly supports crime, target, and status specific models to explain the diversity of suburban crime and violence.

Contributions of the Study

The study contributes to the fields of criminology, sociology (theory in particular), and urban studies by applying major theories in examining the structure of metropolitan environments and resulting patterns of crime and violence. These metropolitan environments provide the basic contexts in which choices and decisions are either constrained or facilitated for various actors. The application of the anomie-and-opportunity structures paradigm along with a typology differentiating suburbs on function and status are relevant in understanding and explaining multiple and diverse outcomes in large metropolitan environments. This study provides an important examination of Merton's anomie-and-opportunity-structures paradigm that is currently not available in criminological and sociological research. Through these efforts, the relevance of the paradigm in explaining suburban property and violent crime rates is established. Further, the paradigm is compared to existing theories of crime and violence along multiple criteria most notably the paradigm's incorporation of contextual and environmental aspects of crime and violence and its acknowledgement of the probabilistic nature of any explanation of human behavior. Many existing theories focus on identifying the essential cause(s) of crime and violence regardless of the underlying environmental contexts within which such behaviors are located and tend to be deterministic in tone and substance.

This study also provides an important extension of existing research focused on suburbanization, suburban typologies, and suburban heterogeneity. Currently, most analyses focus on the impacts and effects of either function or status separately, which ignores the interdependency between these two dimensions in creating the suburban system. It also corrects a common tendency to ignore suburban status differences because of data availability and other concerns with data. The empirical orientation of most existing research is on individual and group attainment and not on place level profiles along multiple dimensions. The methodologies used in this study are at the level of suburban municipalities, which is the proper test of place stratification theory as well as being critical in explaining the distribution of suburban property and violent crime rates.

For the most part, suburban crime and violence research has been sparse and limited, and more importantly, lacks a theoretical base. This study meets this gap with the application of Merton's anomie-and-opportunity-structures paradigm to the Los Angeles metropolitan region. Further, the book examines multiple sub-types of property and violent crime offenses in suburbs. Earlier approaches have been more limited in examining multiple types of offenses.

CHAPTER 2

HISTORY AND RELEVANCE OF OPPORTUNITY STRUCTURES

The Evolution of the Opportunity Structures Paradigm

Robert Merton's theory of anomie and deviant behavior is revisited with explicit attention to introducing and extending the concept of opportunity structures. Since this new concept underpins much of mainstream structural sociology, Merton's conceptualizations and their usefulness in explaining crime and violence in metropolitan America are examined. Other criminological traditions and theories are examined theoretically with attention to their differences with Merton's opportunity structures and crime framework. These theories work at distinct levels of analysis and use particular units of analysis. Contrasting theories helps to demonstrate the overall relevance of the anomie-and-opportunity structures paradigm for studying crime and violence in metropolitan regions and shows the different types of questions and phenomena these theories seek to answer. Newer theories of crime like routine activities/lifestyle victimization theories will also be contrasted to the newer opportunity structures theory. The scope and domain of these different theories determine their ability to explain property and violent crimes as well as different types of such crimes.

The flexibility of Merton's approach is highlighted and its inherent complementarities with particular theories and concepts are stressed.

A History of the Paradigm: From Anomie to Opportunity Structures

The evolution of the anomie-and-opportunity structures paradigm spans almost six decades, beginning with Merton's classic 1938 article and culminating with Merton's (1995) elaboration of the concept of opportunity structures. The dominance of the paradigm in sociology and criminology was associated with Merton's earlier work, and even its revitalization in these literatures starting in the 1980s, concerned clarifications of his earlier work. Consequently, the majority, if not all, theoretical and empirical research on his paradigm has ignored the opportunity structures concept. Nevertheless, a fuller understanding of his current paradigm necessitates presentation of his earlier work. Further, clarification of Merton's paradigm and its applicability to studying crime and violence requires examining the history of its own internal revisions, major criticisms and responses to these criticisms, specifying the concept of opportunity structures and opportunities, and examining its relevance to studying suburban crime and violence rates. The evolution of the paradigm must be seen as having undergone numerous attempts of clarification by Merton and others (many of whom were his students) to help determine the applicability of his paradigm to study crime and deviance.

Early Manifestations
In the earliest version of his thesis, Merton (1938) began by distinguishing a sociological perspective of crime and deviant behavior from prevalent positivistic biological, psychological, and even, social-psychological approaches to studying deviance and crime. One of the most dominant theories in the sociology of crime and criminology that emerged later, social control, shares features with these individualistic approaches. These later approaches posited for man a human nature rooted in nonconformity, a Hobessian state of man against man. Bernard (1995) discusses Hirschi's social control theory in the same vein, humans are described as isolated and self-interested who are

naturally prone to deviance unless they are controlled or attached to society. Social order and control were the primary functions of society and were oriented to restrain such innately self-interested and biologically driven individual needs. From the positivistic perspective, criminals and deviants were considered drastically different than non-criminals and deviants, who had abnormal features and characteristics. Deliberative attempts to ensure social order such as allowing designated authorities to control problem populations ensured social order. These approaches had obvious elitist undertones and reinforced the sharp inequalities existing in such societies during those times.

Merton sought to interject a sociological perspective that went beyond just individuals and abnormalities and presented objective (cultural and social) conditions external to individuals that shaped and influenced their behaviors in earlier versions of the paradigm. From the onset, Merton made clear that his approach attempted to answer questions that individualistic approaches had traditionally ignored. Instead of explaining the incidence of deviant conduct and behavior in individuals, Merton's approach attempted to explain rates of various types of deviant behavior within society and its multiple social structures and overarching culture (the focus on rates would come in his own work after the 1938 article). Groups and individuals within society shared a culture and its goals and objectives, but faced different pressures to meet goals valued by this culture. Different adaptations by differentially placed individuals reflected sharp differences in the conditions facing them and the situations typically confronted by them. The aggregate cases of similar adaptations were juxtaposed against the stratification of these individuals and groups making these adaptations, thereby explaining their likely responses. Nevertheless, even at this early juncture, Merton did not suggest that individuals were controlled completely by their circumstances, but rather were the ones responding to such situations and conditions. Merton emphasized that shared location of individuals and groups explained their propensities to consider deviance from prevailing norms. The sociological flavor of Merton's social structure and anomie approach and many of the key concepts derived from the perspective of Emile Durkheim. Durkheim sought to develop a science to study society with a vision of this new field of sociology as dramatically different than then established disciplines. This sociological vision purposefully counters a psychological and individualistic approach that took individuals' states of mind as reflecting entire states of societies. This later approach placed prominence on a Hobessian view of society as composed of isolated self-interested persons with little natural needs for social relationships.

Rather, for Durkheim, social phenomena were social because individuals relate to each other and influence each other in numerous ways. After all, society depends upon cooperation by individuals for daily existence and strong interdependence in many spheres is a pertinent reality. Fundamentally, individuals and groups differentially related to each other and these multiple relationships formed the underlying basis of society and social order. In different types of societies, these relationships involve shared ideas and values, rituals and practices, and even a division of labor consistent with emerging modern societies. Durkheim's view of human nature was more dualistic than a Hobessian one, allowing individual interests to ensure social order in that individuals in society obey the rules and laws because of their inherent dependencies and relationships with each other (Bernard 1995). It is essentially in the interest of societal and group members to obey the law and every society relies on this source of social order to maintain itself over time. In times of rapid social change and chronic conflicts, such as the transition to capitalistic and democratic societies and conflicts between labor and capital, the normal regulatory forces of society served by individuals obeying the laws break down, resulting in anomie, i.e., deregulation of man's passions by society (Deflem 1989). As others have pointed out (Deflem 1989; Orru 1987, 1990), Durkheim differed from Merton in emphasizing the inability of society to regulate man's goals and not the means to reach these goals.

Consistent with Durkheim, Merton proposed a framework to examine the social and cultural origins of deviant behavior and particular conditions leading 'normal' individuals to respond normally with actions considered deviant from the prevailing norms. These conditions existed in society, and being properties of societies and their social structures, may be abnormal for society and individuals and groups existing with their boundaries (anomie being an important societal level condition for both Durkheim and Merton). Durkheim had earlier promoted a science of sociology that focused on explaining social facts and societal conditions with other social facts and conditions. Further, social facts could not be equated with their individual manifestations, but a represented reality of their own, *sui generis* (Deflem 1989). The basis of Merton's framework shared with Durkheim the sociological emphasis on exteriority and constraint. These conditions were external to individuals and constrained them by influencing their choices and actions (Merton 1934). The link between conditions and action is critical, as shown below, because conditions are objective, external, and beyond the control of a single individual or a few individuals.

In order to determine the non-biological, non-psychological, and generally non-individualistic features of society implicated in deviant behavior, Merton proposed incorporating elements of social and cultural structure at the cultural level or plane and individual adaptations as responses to the social situations prevailing at the cultural and social structural levels. The role of culture in this framework was twofold. A society's culture provides the goals, values, ends, and interests for individuals and groups as well as prescribes the legitimate institutional means or procedures to achieve these goals.

Cultures are organized with a hierarchy of values. In this regard, particular goals and values given greater prominence than others and associated norms (organized and expected ways of reaching these goals) promoted through institutional mechanisms are characteristics of cultures. Individuals and groups ultimately give credence to these values and culture by being influenced by them and orienting their behavior toward achievement of ends through the institutionally prescribed means. Anomie is essentially a cultural phenomenon for Merton, at the level of society, social structures, and groups with differential consequences for different strata (i.e., large number of individuals):

> There may develop a disproportionate, at times, a virtually exclusive, stress upon the value of specific goals, involving relatively slight concern with the institutionally appropriate modes of attaining these goals. The limiting case in this

direction is reached when the range of alternative procedures is limited only by technical rather than institutional considerations. This constitutes one type of cultural malintegration…Of the types of groups which result from the independent variation of the two phases of social structure, we shall be primarily concerned with the first, namely, that involving a disproportionate accent on goals. (Merton 1938, pp. 673-674).

The effects of anomie are differentially consequentially for Merton, although this particular point was not explicitly stated in the earliest
version of the paradigm. Merton then argues that many groups do not see the value of the proscribed institutional means and rules so that these means become deinstitutionalized, literally out of the control of the larger society, social structures, and culture. Merton (1938) here crucially distinguishes his approach from more individualistic approaches by pointing out that antisocial behavior originates in the broader culture and social structures:

> Fraud, corruption, vice, crime, in short, the entire catalogue of proscribed behavior, becomes increasingly common when the emphasis on the *culturally induced* success-goal becomes divorced from a coordinated institutional emphasis. This observation is of crucial theoretical importance in examining the doctrine that antisocial behavior most frequently describes from biological drives breaking through the restraints imposed by society. The difference is one between a strictly utilitarian interpretation which conceives man's ends as random and an analysis which finds these ends deriving from the basic values of the culture (pp. 675-676).

This is consistent with a dualistic Durkheimian perspective of human nature as individuals are motivated by their own self-interest as well as values of their groups, communities, and the broader society (Bernard 1995, p. 89). Continuing with the focus on individual and groups as actors and bearers of culture through their actions, Merton develops a typology of alternative adaptations. The five categories include conformity, innovation, ritualism, retreatism, and rebellion. Each category of adaptation references individuals' acceptance, elimination, and/or rejection (the rebellion adaptation being dramatically different than the other four adaptations, involving substitution of new goals and standards) of the broader cultural goals of their society and/or institutionalized means considered legitimate and prescribed. As role adjustments not tied to specific or single situations, Merton points out that these adaptations will differ within individuals depending on the social activities in question. The retreatist and conformist adaptations are the least and most common adaptations respectively in the typology and consequently, not a primary focus for Merton.

Individual responses from Merton's perspective invariably reflect personality characteristics particular to the individual, but also reflect the particular cultural background in which individuals exist. As culture-bearers of society, their acceptance or rejection of goals and means are adaptations subject to the cultural demands of their groups and society and the specific means available to them, depending on the common situations faced by differentially located individuals in multiple social structures. For example, all three of the adaptations of interest (innovation, ritualism, and rebellion) result from disassociation between means and ends and result in different personality adaptations brought on by the broader culture and social structures as contexts for individual adaptations. Thus, individuals are still the primary actors in such situations. They may be differentially subject to such pressures, and even facing the same pressures, may respond differently. Further, as *the means for individuals* are differentially distributed across and within multiple social structures, one can expect certain adaptations to be more prevalent in particular situational contexts. Merton argues that innovation, being the most closely linked with crime, is more likely in American society not only because of the strong emphasis on achievement of goals such as material success, but:

It is only when a system of cultural values extols, virtually above all else, certain *common* symbols of success *for the population at large* while its social structure rigorously restricts or completely eliminates access to approved modes of acquiring these symbols *for a considerable part of the same population*, that antisocial behavior ensure on a considerable scale (Merton 1938, p. 680).

Then Merton shifts his analysis back to anomie turning from individual adaptations to consequences of antisocial behavior for the broader cultural and social structure. The widespread use of illegitimate means would attenuate the already anomic culture as individuals and groups would focus on out-competing each other and be less concerned about using the legitimate means. According to Merton, anomie can become even more prevalent as the society is not able to coordinate or balance the means-ends aspects of its culture and social structures. Not organized to provide an equal distribution of means with ends, society loses its control over individuals and groups. Anomie magnifies because pressures to succeed stressed in the culture lead individuals and groups to use illegitimate means and constraints over means become ineffective:

"The end-justifies-the-means" doctrine becomes a guiding tenet for action when the cultural structure unduly exalts the ends and the social organization unduly limits possible recourse to approved means. Otherwise put, this notion and associated behavior reflects a lack of cultural coordination (Merton 1938, p. 681).

Merton comes full circle from culture and social structure to individual adaptations to culture and social structure - that is from the organization of society and its culture, their effects on individuals and groups, and back to the organization of society and its culture. Cultural (the way the society is organized in terms of ends and means) coordination and anomie exist in society and this anomic culture can become even more anomic. Mainly by failing to control the means, society presents social situations to individuals where goals are given even greater prominence by these actors over the means. Their responses are to abnormal conditions existing in their society and they have little ability (or perhaps, desire) to change these conditions by themselves. The 1938 article ends with an extensive agenda for research to expand, elaborate, and clarify Merton's framework. The list is prophetic, in that much of Merton's own revisions of this scheme, ones by his students and colleagues, and by even his own critics, are explicitly stated.

Conceptual and Theoretical Clarifications
In later work, Merton expanded on his classic article through numerous revisions and extensions. Merton (1949) sought to distinguish his framework by the types of questions and explanations it best answered. Additionally, this explicit statement was to counter, once again, biological and psychological approaches to deviance that emphasized abnormalities:

> If we can locate groups peculiarly subject to such pressures, we should expect to find fairly high rates of deviant behavior in these groups, not because the human beings compromising them are compounded of distinctive biological tendencies but because they are responding normally to the social situation in which they find themselves. Our perspective is sociological. We look at variations in the *rates* of deviant behavior, not its incidence. Should our quest be at all successful, some forms of deviant behavior will be found to be as psychologically normal as conformist behavior, and the equation of deviation and abnormality will be put into question (Merton 1949, p. 277).

Merton quotes Edward Sapir in a footnote to this quotation, where a distinction between social science and psychological data and problems is made. These former types of data involve abstracting from individual characteristic to examine what individuals (and groups) share interpersonally or structurally. Clarification of rates is important, as it suggests that individuals differentially located in society's social organization and social structures would be subject to different pressures and strains as well as differentially exposed to the effects of a society-wide state of anomie. Merton wants to emphasize that his framework is from the perspective of the social structure of society and the sources of such pressures derive from the society they exist in and the manner in which it is organized:

> Most generally, the basic proposition set forth in this paper is that some unknown but substantial portion of deviant behavior does not represent impulses of individuals breaking through social controls, but, on the contrary, represented socially induced deviations-deviations which the culture and the social organization conjoin to produce (Merton 1956, p. 29).

Aspects of the social and cultural structure are sources of deviant behavior and differential rates of different types of conforming and deviant behavior are the result of these sources. Using one common differentiation of individuals and groups in society, class strata, Merton points out that:

> The underlying premise here is that class strata are not only differentially subject to anomie but are differently subject to one or another type of response to it (Merton 1968, p. 217).

The focus on the 'social topography of anomie' (Merton 1956, p. 44) also helps us to understand the concepts of patterned exposure and response, which are again sociological rather than psychological. Merton (1956) states:

> It is the patterned exposure which is the psychological correlate of social structure. Individuals in various groups are consistently exposed to this discrepancy between what the culture enjoins and access to institutional avenues for meeting those requirements. A second point which would distinguish the two approaches: Horney deals primarily and usefully with the responses of individuals to socially induced pressure situations whereas the sociologist is concerned also with the effects these situations have on the normative structure itself (p. 37).

Patterned exposure and response are non-random with structural sources being important for these patternings. For Merton, the distribution of goals and means within society, aside from their organization, are critical in terms of non-random exposure to the society's social structure. Goals uniformly distribute across the class strata, for example, but these same goals differentially distribute in the broader culture (a hierarchy of values and goals). Means, on the other hand, differentially distribute across and within social structures. Patterned exposure to differential means is then critical for the individual adaptations. This leads Merton to suggest that innovation is itself patterned:

Now let's look at structural situations in which there is greater difficulty in living up to those normative requirements. And further, let's look at types of adaptations to contradiction between norms on the one hand and the patterned social situations on the other. Just as it is a relevant question to ask what produces varying degrees of anomie in different sectors of society, so it is relevant to inquire further into the varying adaptations to anomie, the types of adaptation, which can be distinguished.... Those persons who maintain the culturally validated objectives but, for social structural reasons which I attempted to indicate, are less likely to be able to approximate them have a greater tendency to engage in a type of adaptation which I designate by the neutral term "innovation," without prejudging whether it will be socially valued innovation or a socially devalued innovation, such as delinquency and crime (Merton 1956, p. 45).

The consequences of patterned deviant adaptations apply to particular, and not general, normative systems. Such consequences can enlarge anomie, if deviant behavior within the social system (not the entire society) and being more prevalent in some groups, is actually rewarded. Merton (1968), again speaking of innovation, seems to suggest that this results in formation of subcultures where there are groups (and more limited social structures) controlling and responding to individual deviant behavior:

In some proportion of cases, again dependent upon the
control-structure of the group, these departures from
institutional norms are socially rewarded by 'successful'
achievement of goals. But these deviant ways of achieving the
goals occur within social systems. The deviant behavior
consequently affects not only the individuals who first engage
in it but, in some measure, it also affects other individuals with
whom they are inter-related in the system. A mounting
frequency of deviant but 'successful' behavior tends to lessen
and, as an extreme potentiality, to eliminate the legitimacy of
the institutional norms for others in the system. The process
thus enlarges the extent of anomie within the system so that
others, who did respond in the form of deviant behavior to the
relatively slight anomie which first obtained, come to do so as
anomie spreads and is intensified (p. 234).

Another important, but often overlooked, distinction made by
Merton concerns the social environments and situations that individuals
face. Again, he sought to differentiate the social structure and anomie
approach, but this time from psychology and social psychological
approaches. The later fields tended to view social environments of
individuals as limited to their immediate and particular surroundings
and relationships (i.e. the milieu) and/or individual definitions of the
situations. This was problematic for Merton because it ignored the
structural sources of individual behavior. Additionally, situations
described narrowly, not in reference to broader features of society,
ignores how these situations themselves distribute and their locations in
particular strata in society. Broadening the view of situations and
examining the structural sources of strain (or pressures) allow for
examination of the different social contexts and situations faced by
groups and individuals:

But the social contexts of such an individual, depending on
whether he is on one group or another, may differ radically (at
least so it seems so to me) and greatly affect the pressure and
his reactions to the pressure. The contexts which are provided
by this change in the largest aspects of the social structure, and

through intervening stages to the particular situation which any particular adolescent faces, can be detected only if a systematic efforts is made to deal simultaneously or serially with three levels of analysis (Merton 1956, p. 42).

The three levels of analysis referenced here are structural, contextual, and situational (particular situations). Rates of deviant behavior cannot then be seen as resulting solely from identifying individualistic and situationally close factors, but have to be identified through structural sources as well. Clearly, Merton desires to differentiate his approach, but does not want to suggest that non-structural factors are unimportant. Rather, these factors are intervening ones that influence the particular behaviors in question. In general, sociological approaches tend "to concentrate on observing repetitive behaviors involving large numbers of people..apt to be less sensitive to the highly individualized, idiosyncratic aspects of what he has observed " (Merton 1956, p. 79).

Another critical extension was specifying the nature of the anomic culture and how American society typified such a culture. Cultures promote certain goals and values (as well as norms) over others. One views culture with two components in hand, the goals and the prescribed means. The best methods to demonstrate the hierarchy of values in a culture would be to look its non-material aspects and to examine the transmission of this culture through its major institutions. Merton spends extensive amount of space in his later revisions and extensions with precisely these ends in mind. Describing the importance of monetary success as given relatively higher prominence in the scale of American values, Merton asserts:

Prestigeful representatives of the society reinforce the cultural emphasis. The family, school, and the workplace-the major agencies shaping the personality structure and goal formation of Americans-join to provide the intensive disciplining required if an individual is to retain intact a goal that remains elusively beyond the reach, if he is to be motivated by the promise of a gratification that is not redeemed (Merton 1949, p. 283).

Culture is itself patterned, meaning goals are arranged and present in a non-random manner. Merton pulls instances from influential documents and statements from prestigious representatives in American society to illustrate the patterned emphasis of goals and means (Merton 1968, pp. 190-193). Referencing the lofty goal of monetary success, Merton finds "there flows a continuing pressure to retain high ambition…coupled with this positive emphasis upon the obligation to maintain lofty goals is a correlative emphasis upon the penalizing of those who draw in their ambitions" (1968, p. 192). The role of society and its culture is also to discourage use of substitute goals and auxiliary values by reinforcing the emphasized goals. This includes deflecting criticisms of prominent goals from individual and group members. Accumulation of wealth is not possible for many in American society, yet the society through its culture devises ways to encourage its members to continue to strive towards this goal, to point out that failure is only temporary, and that its members must not withdraw ambition (Merton 1949, p. 286). To illustrate, Merton (1949) states:

> In sociological paraphrase, these axioms represent, first, the deflection of criticism of the social structure onto oneself among those so situated in the society that they do not have full and equal access to opportunity; second, the preservation of a given structure of social power by having individuals in the lower strata identify themselves, not with their compeers, but with those at the top (whom they will ultimately join); and third, the providing of pressures for conformity with the cultural dictates of unslackened ambition by the threat of less than full membership in the society for those who fail to conform (pp. 286-287).

Interestingly, culture and anomie in society now were subject to change as well. Merton alerts us to this specific qualification by stating that "this process making for anomie need not, however, continue unimpeded. Under conditions still to be identified, countervailing tendencies may develop." (Merton 1968, p. 223). Further, Merton was clear that this framework for cultural and social structural analysis was not limited to only the emphasis on a few goals, i.e., wealth or material success, but could be broadened to include other achievement goals (Merton 1968, p. 220). It is critical though to point out that the institutionalized prescribed means derived from a culture are not equivalent to the actual means available to individuals in society. That is, the ideal (culture) is different from reality (social structural arrangements of society). Individuals and groups seek to achieve the ideal, but do so from different positions in multiple social structures.

Having clarified the focus of his approach in terms of rates not individual incidence, on the structuring of environments, contexts, and situations, and a fuller delineation of culture and patterned exposure, Merton turned to detailing individual adaptations. Merton now directly orients his approach to asking which adaptations are more likely of persons and groups differentially located in the social structures of a society and its culture (Merton 1968, p. 193). A greater effort is made to describe the most common adaptations likely for different groups and strata in society. With regard to the non-conformist adaptations, Merton describes each in terms of its psychological and sociological states. For example, innovators, who reject the institutionally prescribed means, but accept and assimilate the cultural goal(s), tend to be risk-takers.

Sociologically, innovators tend to be located in the lower strata of society and feel greater pressures to adapt through innovation than those from the upper and middle strata of society (Merton 1949, pp. 290-291). Even though it seems obvious from a logical perspective that pressures are quite equally distributed, Merton's logic suggests that higher occupational (and on other bases) strata individuals get away with more deviance because they are not detected or responded to (Merton 1949, p. 291; Merton 1968, p. 198). According to Merton, unlawful behavior is quite common across society, but for various unspecified reasons, these acts of deviance remain undetected or escape punishment. Middle-class strata individuals feel less strain from Merton's perspective because they have greater relative means than individuals from the lower strata. This is true only of particular societies, where an anomic culture exists, egalitarian ideology holds sway, or achieved statuses given greater prominence. In these societies, almost by default, there will exist noncompeting individuals and closed access by social structures to means to reach such goals (Merton 1949, p. 294). American society fits this prototype. The fact that businessmen, who reached the top through unapproved practices or other illegalities, are unlikely to be viewed in a negative manner in this society, leads Merton to make the following comment:

> Goals are held to transcend class lines, not to be bounded by them; yet the actual social organization is such that there exist class differentials in accessibility of the goals. In such a setting, a cardinal American virtue, "ambition," promotes a cardinal American vice, "deviant behavior (p. 294).

Among the above clarifications, there exist others with greater clarity that illustrate the role of social structure in influencing deviant behavior. Under a new heading (The Strain Toward Anomie) and with changed language, Merton (1949, pp. 308-309; 1968; pp. 211-212) identifies social structure as the producer of anomie and deviant behavior. This social structure is unevenly organized and thus, the strain toward anomie, is also unevenly distributed. Merton (1949) writes:

> This strain toward anomie does not operate evenly throughout the society. Some effort has been made in the present analysis to suggest the strata most vulnerable to the pressures for deviant behavior and to set forth some of the mechanisms operating to produce these pressures....But the central tendencies toward anomie remain, and it is to these that the analytical scheme here set forth calls particular attention (p. 309).

Unfortunately, Merton does not directly define social structure in his writings on social structure and anomie, but the definitions can be located throughout the large corpus of his wide-ranging work on structural analysis, sociological theory, and other social concepts. This is true also of his explications of reference groups and manifest and latent functions, among many others. This can probably explain partly why many scholars and others have consistently misapplied his work. Merton presents a clearer conceptualization of social structures consistent with the anomie-and-opportunity-structures paradigm in the latest evolution of his paradigm (shown below).

Merton's Opportunity Structures Extension

The evolution of the paradigm leads us to its latest revisions and extensions and introduces us to the newest concept in the paradigm, opportunity structures. Merton (1995) presents this new concept in his review of the social structure and anomie paradigm. Merton organizes his discussion from a sociology of knowledge perspective by stressing the diffusion of theoretical ideas and the nature of knowledge building in the social sciences and physical sciences. Our purposes relate more closely to the opportunity structures conceptualization and the specification of the anomie-and-opportunity structures paradigm.

The focus here is on how the original concept of "differential access to opportunities" included in the earliest version of the paradigm evolved into the different, yet linked, concept of opportunity structures (Merton 1995, pp. 8-23). Differential access to opportunity, often overlooked by scholars in comparison to the disassociation between goals and means, ties directly to social structure:

> Central to the first, 1938, formulation of SS&A paradigm in print was the sociological idea of a continuing interplay and frequent tension between the cultural structure (the distribution and organization of values, norms, and interests) and the social structure (the distribution and organization of social positions or statuses). This, of course, has been generally recognized in the ensuing critical examination of the paradigm. However, a correlative structural idea has often been overlooked. As some of the papers in this volume recognize, the hypothesis of the social distribution of adaptations to the interaction between culturally defined goals and institutionally acceptable means is closely linked to the basic structural concept of differential access to opportunities among those variously located in the social structure (Merton 1995, p.6).

One should note that in the above quote, Merton has now defined the social structure as the organization and distribution of status (positions) not institutionalized means. Compared to the earliest versions of the paradigm, the newest version places the production of means within opportunity structures (seen below) with the distribution of or access to means still dictated by the social structure. This change is revealing. Merton now separates positions from means and locates the production of these means in a differential structure or organization. This may be an analytic distinction, but its importance lies in that Merton sees the necessity of including the production and distribution of means into separate realms, each subject to different dynamics and with different sources. In the older versions of the paradigm, the distribution of means awkwardly mixed with the production of means and seemed to relate with the social structure in unclear ways.

Before describing the latest (and major) evolution of the paradigm, Merton provides fuller guidelines on applying earlier versions of the paradigm, which have direct implications for the newer paradigm. For that matter, these are consequential for structural sociology and the type of theorizing and research that are possible with this approach. The first is that access to opportunities does not entail actual utilization and realization (Merton 1995, p. 8). Importantly, this guideline helps us to understand that acting individuals and their definitions of the situation (e.g., the opportunities perceived and used by them) are important for ultimate outcomes such as deviant behavior. Merton has chosen to place the individual dead and center in his paradigm, despite his emphasis on structural factors and extra-individual environments. Sociology of the structuralist variety has been subject to intense criticisms on precisely this point. For Merton, it reflects a recognition that any theory of behavior has to involve individuals and groups as actors. Structures are theoretical and analytical abstractions that are unable to operate without real actors. Nonetheless, abstractions are useful to help understand the organization and relationships between actors and the creation of objective situations and contexts in which actions occur.

The second guideline relates to how differential access to opportunity is a probabilistic, not deterministic, concept (Merton 1995, p. 8). Besides reinforcing the earlier guideline's emphasis on acting individuals, it introduces us to Merton's brand of structural sociology whereby "the correlative concepts of structural constraints and opportunities provide for individual variations among socially structured alternatives"(Merton 1995, p.8). The role of structures of any kind in Merton's paradigm are in shaping and influencing actor behavior and choices, they do not determine absolutely the ultimate choices and outcomes. For example, the existence of anomie in the broader society, does not determine the choice of adaptations by actors, but only increases the likelihood of this adaptation under these and other related conditions (e.g., uneven distribution of means for example). The implication is clear for both the newer and older paradigms; these paradigms are fully probabilistic in their abilities to explain social phenomena such as deviant behavior or crime. Merton's acknowledgement of probabilistic theorizing is dramatically different than for some criminological as well as sociological theories; which have a tendency to be deterministic in tone (see below).

Merton also presents a distinction relevant for the anomie-and-opportunity structures paradigm and for studying deviant behavior. In the typology of adaptations developed earlier, Merton now differentiates rebellion, called nonconformist behavior, from innovation, ritualism, and retreatism, termed aberrant behavior. The later type of adaptations involves more self-interested conduct, not necessarily rational-utilitarian behavior, as "aberrants try to hide their violations of social norms even as they regard the norms they violate as legitimate…As result, their rule-breaking is socially defined simply as an effort to satisfy their personal interests in normatively unacceptable ways" (Merton 1995, p. 12). The critical part of this differentiation is that aberrants, unlike rebels, do not challenge the existing values and goals of a society or group's culture, but rather seek to satisfy their own personal needs. These are precisely the types of persons who are innovators accepting the broader goals, but using illegitimate means to achieve these goals. For whatever reasons specific to them or factors derived from the social and cultural structures, it is no longer in their interest to obey the law and/or norms.

The 1995 piece also links the anomie-and-opportunity structure paradigm with many correlative concepts. Among the most important for our purposes are unanticipated and unintended social consequences of purposive social action and social dysfunctions. With regard to the first of these, Merton (1995) suggests that social structures themselves are subject to change by individuals and groups (as the actors), but also change from unintended consequences. The crucial link with the paradigm in question is that social structures (along with the culture) are not functional for all groups and individuals, but that the arrangement and organization of society is unequal, resulting in potential deviant behavior being concentrated in particular strata of society. Such realities of restricted access result in realities of high levels of wide variety of deviant behavior. Individuals and groups in these strata are unable and/or unwilling (as shown above with the distinction between rebels and aberrants) to change these arrangements, even if they are unfavorable to them. These are realities, regardless of their moral implications and evaluations, resulting from the realms of possibilities and not solely through deliberate planning (Merton 1995, p. 13). Function simply defined as being able to meet various needs of individuals and groups. These realities and possibilities directly relate to social practices and the arrangement of society being functional for some and dysfunctional for others. Merton (1995) states:

> The normative doctrine of universally accessible opportunity known as "the American Dream" may be functional for substantial numbers of those with the social, economic, and personal resources needed to help convert that Dream into personal reality just it may be dysfunctional for substantial numbers of those with severely limited structural access to opportunity. Under those latter restrictive conditions, it invites comparatively high rates of the various kinds of deviant behavior-socially proscribed innovation, ritualism, and retreatism-set out in the SS&A typology of adaptations (p. 16).

Merton then presents the concept of 'opportunity structures as an overlooked (even by him) component of his original social structure and anomie article and the subsequent revisions to it. This is a retrospective examination of the concept, but an oversight that Merton feels strongly obligated to correct. Merton (1995) presents a paradigm of action for many types of behavior involving acting individuals and groups that desire to achieve goals and objectives (referenced as outcomes from an actor perspective). The behavior and actions of actors shaped (not determined) by the objective situations they confront, as well as their own goals and objectives formed by the values and norms of their groups and the broader society, make up the composition of this paradigm of action. Animated structures of all types require actors and cannot operate without them. However, given the multiplicity of actors in society, one individual actor or group is unlikely to determine the operation of even a single structure.

In Merton's paradigm, opportunity structures are distinct from both the cultural and the social structure. Merton was interested in how locations in the social structure (socio-economic status) relate to differential access to society's opportunity structures, defined as the interplay between structural context and individual modes of behavior (adaptation). Opportunity structures, thus, are used to understand the distribution of choices across individuals and groups located across the social structure:

> Opportunity structure designates the scale and distribution of conditions that provide various probabilities for acting individuals and groups to achieve specifiable outcomes. From time to time, the opportunity structure expands or contracts, as do segments of that structure. However, as indicated by the correlative concepts of socially structured "differential access to opportunity" in the original paradigm of SS&A and of "structural context" in the paradigm for functional analysis, location in the social structure strongly influences, though it does not wholly determine, the extent of access to the opportunity structure. By concept, then, an expanding or contracting opportunity structure does not carry with it the uniform expansion or contraction of opportunities for all sectors of a socially stratified population, a familiar enough notion with diverse implications (Merton 1995, p.25).

The critical part of this definition of opportunity structures relates to how Merton defines this structure distinctively from cultural and social structures, defined above. For both social and cultural structure,

Merton is generally interested in the organization and distribution of goals and positions. With opportunity structures, the *scale* and distribution are crucial. Merton (1995) also adds 'character' to the above definition of opportunity structures:

> It would also register the further theoretical idea that not only were there socially structured differentials in access to the opportunities that then and there did exist but that the scale, character, and distribution of those opportunities which formed objective conditions affecting the probability of successful outcomes of choices were subject to varying rates and degrees of structural change that differentially affect those variously located in the social structure (p. 28).

Although not explicitly stated, scale refers to the level of conditions, not opportunities. Access to opportunities applies to individuals and groups and is in reference to actors. Further, the distribution of opportunity structures really concerns the distribution of conditions. Conditions are given significant theoretical significance by Merton, as they refer to the particular objective (not subjective) situations faced by acting individuals and groups. This is consistent with Merton's perspective that actor choices occur within particular contexts and conditions serving as the objective situations confronted by these actors. Conditions create (provide) the opportunities for acting individuals and groups to achieve certain goals. Because actors do not directly experience, confront, and control all objective conditions, one can suggest that these are more circumscribed and particularistic (even though they are created at higher levels). These conditions can be broken into situations more specific to particular actors and groups. It is useful and more appropriate to state that conditions approximate objective situations and contexts that individuals confront. Further, these conditions may be regarded functionally, in that they facilitate or constrain, the ability of individuals to achieve particular goals and objectives. These conditions can be concretely defined as particular large-scale trends that influence individuals' abilities to obtain social, economic, and/or political resources.

These opportunities are produced and created for acting individuals and groups by conditions in this schema. Opportunities, derived from conditions, refer to the means as in the earlier paradigm. For acting individuals and groups, opportunities are important in achievement of their goals. However, they may be fruitfully conceived as resources, which are organized (structured or patterned) so that there are differences in the levels and distribution of such resources for differentially located individuals and groups. Being beyond the control of individuals and not determined by them, these condition-created-dependent resources are differentially accessed by individuals and groups.

There exists a strong interplay between the social and opportunity structures. Since access to the opportunity structures and resources relates to positioning in the social structure, changes in the social structure affect changes in the opportunity structures and vice versa. One should be cautious in applying opportunity structures as they do not necessarily refer to a single situation or condition, but may involve multiple conditions, situations, and consequently, multiple resources. Further, these opportunity structures and objective conditions shape and influence access to these resources by individuals and groups and are in turn shaped by social structures. The paradigm now, as stated, has become a theory of situations and actors. Characterized by prevailing values or goals, conditions, and potential resources, the differences in situations and actors are contextualized, where the concentration of particular situations is accompanied (associated with) by particular classes of actors and particular types of behaviors. Cohen (1965) describes the nature of Merton's overall paradigm:

> His dramatis personae are cultural goals, institutional norms, and the situation of action, consisting of means and conditions. Deviance is an effort to reduce this disjunction and re-establish an equilibrium between goals and means. It issues from tension; it is an attempt to reduce tension. Roles figure in this theory as a locational grid, They are the positions in the social structure among which goals, norms and means are distributed, where such disjunctions are located and such adaptations carried out (p.12).

Importantly, the anomie-and-opportunity-structures paradigm does not imply a structuralist-deterministic perspective that neglects the role of human agency and individual selection. Instead, perception of opportunities or meeting expectations of particular roles will vary across individuals, demonstrating the importance of subjective and individual-level factors. Merton (1995) therefore recognizes that any sociological account of social behavior and phenomena is incomplete and can be complemented by an analysis of individual-level processes. However, as a sociologist, Merton's interests are to explain deviance as a social phenomenon, that is, at the macro level, in particular the effects of various structures (cultural, social, and opportunity) on the patterning and distribution of choices and adaptations. That aspiration lay at the very foundation of the development of Merton's project (Merton 1938, p. 672).

In Merton's paradigm, opportunities and opportunity structures are generic and apply to all kinds of social phenomena. For our purposes at hand, Merton's concepts also refer to the features of all types of environments, social, economic, and physical. For example, Merton (1995) points to the multiple types of environments influencing the formation of friendships and interaction patterns in a worker's housing community:

> As has been noted, we had found that social, spatial, and architectural configurations provided unintended and unrecognized opportunity structures affecting the probabilities of forming social ties (such as local friendships) with particular kinds of significant others leading to patterns of homophily (i.e., friendships among social similars) and under determinate conditions patterns of heterophily (i.e., friendships among social dissimilars) (p. 29).

Opportunity structures, also, are not necessarily fixed or immutable. Merton's theory underscores the importance of context, whereby some level of contingency is always operating and influences outcomes or behaviors. Already in his original typology of adaptations in the 1938 article, Merton makes clear that countervailing forces, whether at the aggregate or individual levels, exist. These forces can mitigate or, alternatively, accentuate existing individual-level or structural processes (Merton 1938, p. 676).

Of special interest to the study of deviance, Merton also connects the anomie-and-opportunity-structures paradigm with complementary conceptions such as 'the accumulation of advantage and disadvantage' and 'structural constraints'. The former highlights how socially based structures (especially the socio-economic structure) are created and maintained. As the adaptation of innovation, for instance, tends to be more prevalent among the lower classes, Merton sees processes of disadvantage operating to stratify and distribute opportunities so that lower classes have a difficult time achieving the widely accepted cultural goals through legitimate means. As a result, the structural strain towards anomie will be more common for these disadvantaged groups (Merton 1949). Further, these disadvantages imply the possibility of the accumulation of more disadvantages and fewer resources. Conversely, those with advantages are able to accumulate more resources and further their status in social structures. The social structure system based on status or social positions ensures that this operates through structuring access to the opportunity structures (and resources).

The link between structural constraints and the anomie-and-opportunity-structure paradigm makes sense inasmuch as strains and stresses at the structural level affect rates of deviant adaptations. In societies where socio-economic conditions constrain particular groups more than others, the possibilities of alternative legitimate options and means to achieve culturally approved goals are limited and will influence deviant adaptations. Merton also discusses how motivations derived culturally and structurally play a role in such behavior:

> Although the term structural constraint is often construed to mean that the social structure only places limitations upon individual choice, it was emphatically argued in the introduction to the 1949 extension of SS&A paradigm that this structural mode of "functional analysis conceives of the social structure as active, as producing fresh motivations which cannot be predicted on the basis of one's knowledge of man's native drives. If the social structure restrains some dispositions

to act, it creates others." [A]s...Peter Blau has noted, in contrast to Durkheim's fundamental and strongly sociologistic concept of "structural determinism," which puts aside such psychological concepts as motives as irrelevant, the mode of structural probalism represented by the SS&A paradigm conceives of culturally and structurally induced "motivation as an intervening mechanism through which structural constraints usually become effective (with a) theoretical focus on the structural conditions as the crucial explanatory concept to account for social relations and conduct." (Merton 1995, p.17).

Consistent with Merton's emphasis on rates and aggregates of behavior, constraints and opportunities from various structural sources concentrate certain types of dispositions in different social positions. These dispositions are not absolute in character, but more like tendencies associated with these social positions (Blau 1990, 1994). Motivations, like opportunities, are still structural in character with structural properties. The distribution of anomie in a Mertonian sense works through these processes so that the cultural structure is also implicated in emphasis of particular goals and approved 'institutional means' in society at large.

The anomie aspect of Merton's paradigm, although not talked about in detail in his recent retrospective piece, is also important with regard to explaining the presence and strength of cultural goals and the importance of the cultural structure. Thomas Bernard (1984, 1987) in this respect makes an important point in suggesting that Merton's theory comprises distinct structural and cultural propositions. The structural arguments (on the differential access to legitimate means) should be tested within particular societies, while the cultural arguments (on the diffusion of cultural goals) are more appropriately tested cross-culturally or nationally. Additionally, Merton's concept of anomie cannot be tested at the individual level and is instead conceptually tied with (and explicitly based on) Durkheim's notion of social morality (Merton 1938, pp. 672-673; see Deflem 1989). Indeed, Merton chose to focus on American society where, he argued, anomie was widespread (and more prevalent in comparison to other nations), but not uniformly distributed across society, as Durkheim's would suggest. The concept of anomie in Merton's paradigm, in reference to the American Dream and the premium it places on monetary success, signifies that norms may lose their power more (or less) in distinct socio-economic strata. Despite the attempt to attribute culture as the source of strain and deviance in Merton's theory (e.g., Kornhauser 1978), it is preferable to suggest that the cultural structure is where anomie is produced so that cultural goals and the norms to achieve them (institutional means) are given legitimacy and credence. These goals, means, and interests are created and maintained through diverse processes, but mediated through institutions, groups, and individuals. In any case, Merton's conception of widespread consensus on these cultural attributes throughout society is subject to empirical examination (as are alternative perspectives).

Major Criticisms and Responses

Given the wide scope and unfinished nature of the anomie-and-opportunity-structures paradigm, Merton's paradigm and theories have been subjected to numerous criticisms and revisions (Besnard 1990). An evaluation of some of these criticisms in light of broader efforts is needed to assess the validity of the anomie-and-opportunity-structures paradigm as a framework for research and analysis of deviant behavior. In particular, the following revisions are discussed:

      a) Appropriation of Merton's theory for a micro, individual-level theory of deviance;

      b) Assertion that the cultural structure alone explains the rates and distribution of deviance;

      c) Identification of Merton as a structuralist who neglects human agency; and

      d) Establishment of Merton's theory as a deterministic structural model rather than an integrated cultural-structural model.

Many of these criticisms of Merton's theory have misinterpreted and even disregarded some of its central aspects. These criticisms profess ignorance of Merton's attempts to develop a structural sociology that emphasizes the interplay of human agency in practice and structures of various types operating in real-life contexts (within particular conditions).

Application of Merton's Theory at the Micro Level

In criminology and criminological sociology, Merton's theories have particularly been challenged by social control and social disorganization theorists. With regard to the validity of some of the propositions and applicability issues, critics have focused on 1) the limited utility of Merton's notions of shared goals and their distribution across society; 2) whether one is measuring aspirations or expectations; and 3) whether strain and anomie refer to phenomena at the individual, group, or societal level (see Bernard 1984 for a detailed discussion).

Despite some exceptions (e.g., Messner and Rosenfeld 1995), most of the direct empirical testing has focused at the group and individual levels and on understanding juvenile delinquency. Cloward and Ohlin (1960) and Cohen (1955), for instance, focused on strains for juveniles in gangs in lower class areas and the resulting patterns of delinquency. Since many of the criticisms have come from social control and, to a lesser degree, social disorganization theories, applicability questions focus on empirical testing and research at the level of individuals. But such a focus on individuals is problematic, not only given Merton's explicit sociological orientation, but also given the significance of contextual effects on crime and deviance. Yet, one of the underlying assumptions of social control and social disorganization theorists (as well as newer routine activities/lifestyle victimization theories) is that individuals motivated towards deviant are spread throughout society and any real explanation of crime and deviance must aim to explain conformity rather than deviance.

Most social control theorists assume that differences in context are not relevant in explaining deviant behavior and that individual-level factors play a more prominent role (Hirschi 1969; Gottfredson and Hirschi 1990). Social disorganization theorists, especially more recent revisionists, do emphasize the importance of social contexts, but nevertheless work from the viewpoint that communities not organized to control its members are more prone to criminal and deviant behavior (Bursik and Grasmick 1993). Messner and Rosenfeld's (1995) institutional-anomie theory is consistent with social disorganization inasmuch as they also regard institutions as the master variable in explaining crime and deviance. Institutional anomie has been noted to de-emphasize the focus on the stratification of society underlying Merton's approach (Bernburg 2002). In Merton's approach, individual and groups are located in social structures and the stratification occurs due to the distribution of resources, a product of the distribution of favorable or unfavorable conditions. In the institutional-anomie model, however, economic institutions dominate, while for social disorganization theories, the lack of institutions and organization and resulting disorganization are the major reasons for deviance.

Critics from these camps miss out the important contribution made in the anomie-and-opportunity-structures framework, highlighting structural location and differential access to opportunities as important institutional parameters. Organization by communities or the importance of non-economic institutions is dependent on their competitiveness levels and relative access to resources. Further, communities are not organized solely for the purpose of control of its members, but also compete in the broader society and economy. For social disorganization theorists, competition is natural and involves distinct pathways and processes. But for Merton, competition is clearly social in terms of status and resources. The concept of opportunity structures highlights the importance of stratification of institutions and ability to organize and compete. Additionally, institutions in social disorganization theories seem more oriented towards internal organization and stability, but do not adequately highlight the external sources of stability and organization.

A central misinterpretation of Merton's model is its application to the analysis of individual deviant behavior (Cullen 1988). Newer strain theories such as general strain theory (Agnew 1992, 1994) rewrite Merton's theory in social-psychological terms to explain that strained individuals are frustrated and therefore commit crimes. While Merton has given some credence to the related notion of 'anomia' (Merton 1964), he is otherwise quite clear that he is primarily interested in studying crime rates, their distribution, and structural strain (Merton 1959, 1995). Hence, since even the analytical scope and domain of theorists from general strain theories and social control theorists using

Merton's theory are different, a dismissal of Merton's theory seems premature on these grounds alone.

Cultural Structure as the Source of Strain

Ruth Kornhauser (1978) has popularized the notion that Merton's strain and anomie theories use only cultural structure to explain the presence of strain and deviance. For her, Merton's conception of strain derives from the broader culture, which Merton assumes to be largely uniform throughout society. Kornhauser maintains that this uniformity of culture implies that strain is constant and most individuals are strained, so that strain does not provide any real explanatory power. She also suggests that Merton actually uses a 'control' variable to explain the concentration of innovation among the poor and lower classes. This refers mainly to the defective socialization to cultural values producing anomia in these classes. For Kornhauser, strain seems to be inherent in human nature (in that insatiable needs and their gratification exist for every human being). Any strain model for her is incomplete as it only looks at the positive benefits of crime and deviance, not their costs. Cohen (1997) perceptively argues that social control theorists focus on the costs of deviance and Merton emphasizes the costs of conformity. Kornhauser, like social control theorists, deny that deviance benefits the deviant, who is ultimately the one with motivations to commit these acts. These motivations derive from structural sources as well as individual factors in Merton's paradigm.

Kornhauser focuses on culture in a fashion similar to what she depicts as the logic of cultural deviance models: culture explains everything. Ironically, a stable social structure preventing disorder and crime in Kornhauser's conception of social organization requires a strong culture, albeit grounded and embodied in the same social structure. As mentioned before, social disorganization theories accord prominence to the institutions of control, but the conception of such institutions is oriented towards a universal process of establishing structural stability. Stability and organization exist if members of communities are referenced to cultural differences between communities in terms of structural characteristics (Kornhauser 1978, p.75). Poorer, more heterogeneous, and more mobile communities tend to have less controls and more deviance because they lack the ability to realize their common interests and values. Controls are developed for the major purpose of ensuring cooperative outcomes and maintaining order. But as this often requires a common morality and a specification of structural roles and obligations, this argument becomes circular and tautological.

Such notions of cultural strain that attributed to Merton's theory seem to be misguided and *a priori* motivated by a desire to dismiss Merton's strain theory entirely. But Merton never suggested that structural strain or anomie were equivalent to individual strain or anomia. Also, Merton argues that the cultural structure and the presence of anomie, not strain, are representative of American society in general. His interest was in explaining structural strain. The cultural structure is not the source of any strains to deviance in particular groups. In societies where the cultural goals are overemphasized, Merton did foresee high levels of deviance across the board, but the form and concentration of deviation always remains dependent on variable positioning in the social structure and differential access to opportunity structures. Thus, Merton stresses distributional forces that in the anomie-and-opportunity-structures paradigm are mainly tied to the social and opportunity structures. The attribution of cultural determinism to Merton's paradigm seems far-reaching given that the critics emphasizing the problem of the constancy of strain could be similarly accused of being structural (and surprisingly, even cultural) determinists.

The Neglect of Human Agency
Another re-occurring criticism of the anomie-and-opportunity-structures theory focuses on the neglect of human agency and individual-level factors. Douglas Porpora (1989) argues that macro models too exclusively concentrate on uncovering law-like generalizations about social facts at the expense of intervening, psychological processes involving human actors (Porpora 1989, p.198). For Porpora, a 'sociological holist view' represents structures as external to individuals and as operating in a mechanical and independent manner, divorced from human interests. Porpora does not cite Merton's theories explicitly, but criticisms have been developed against Merton in similar terms (Gottfredson and Hirschi 1990).

Porpora's criticism highlights a vital aspect of the Mertonian paradigm, namely the significance it attributes to the purposive nature of human behavior. In the anomie-and-opportunity-structures paradigm, despite the importance given to structural strain, the specification of cultural goals and norms, and the structurally variable modes of adaptations, the impact of structures is clearly acknowledged to be mediated by human agents. Still, human behavior (actions and choices) involves structurally influenced (not determined) motivations to achieve goals and make choices for particular purposes. In the case of deviant behavior, as with other types of behavior, these purposes are individual but achieve the level of a structural property through the concentration of strain for similarly located individuals. Of course, persons in similar positions and locations are bound to make similar choices, but only in a probabilistic sense. Once the structural property is achieved, the persistence of different structures only reflects the strength of the choices and adaptations of individuals and groups within the society. Because human beings develop interests and give credence to values, the anomie-and-opportunity-structures paradigm is consistent with a conceptualization of structures as produced and reproduced through the actions and choices of individuals. Thus, Porpora's non-deterministic conception of social structure, which holds that "people are motivated to act in the interests structurally built into their social positions...," is in actuality not far removed from Merton's notion (Porpora 1989, p. 200). Specifically, Porpora's conception is similar to the anomie-and-opportunity-structures paradigm in emphasis of structurally induced (cultural and social) motivations or interests as being critical in understanding structural strain:

> However they act, individuals affect the structural relationships that bind them in intended and unintended ways. Thus, according to this conception, there is a dialectical causal path that leads from structure to interests to motives to action and finally back to structure. The structural relationships and the various, often conflicting interests they generate are both the material conditions motivating action and the intended and unintended consequences of such action (Porpora 1989, p. 200).

However, a crucial difference lies in the addition of opportunity structures in Merton's paradigm, while opportunities to achieve specific goals or outcomes are lacking in Porpora's conception. Indeed, its is precisely the opportunity structures component of the Mertonian paradigm that renders the deterministic critique mute. Through the interaction of all three structures (cultural, structural, and opportunity) the anomie-and-opportunity-structures paradigm conceives of human behavior (including deviant behavior) as having structural properties and structural origins in a probabilistic sense only. Factors of human agency intervene in the actualization and perception of opportunities (and actors recognizing these properties) (Cohen 1985).

A Deterministic Structural Model?

Although Merton's paradigm is less deterministic than most structural models, there exists the view that structural sociology can never adequately stress the importance of culture in human behavior. Rubinstein (1992, 1993, 1994) uses Merton's anomie-and-opportunity-structures model as an exemplary of such tendencies in structural sociology. In his view, these perspectives tend to neglect human agency and ignore the role of culture at the individual level. Rubinstein (1993, 1994) suggests that sociologists and economists share this tendency of using structure to explain human behavior. As both fields in his characterization tend to ignore how human actors have cultural predispositions and a will to make choices (moral or otherwise), these disciplines are deterministically favoring structural or exogenous explanations. The difference between economists and sociologists is that the later view social order based on competing groups exercising power, while the former view order as composed of disaggregated and competing individuals.

For Rubinstein (1993, 1994), sociological and economic efforts to make human actors featureless downplay the importance of human will and human culture. Both will and culture for Rubinstein are individual properties and in this, his model of human behavior and action is closer to the rational actor models of the economists. Further, Rubinstein (2001) views any structural level theories as wholly incomplete and ideological in their convictions of the influence of opportunity structures on individual outcomes. Although he is less clear and silent on this, Rubinstein seems to think that structures cannot exist because human will is primary to human action. More importantly, Rubinstein clearly does not accept the existence of a cultural structure like that in the anomie-and-opportunity-structures paradigm.

While Rubinstein clearly does not sufficiently explore Merton's integrated cultural-social-opportunity structural model, in which human agency and actor choices result from both actor traits and the influence of objective situations. Further, there is no appreciation for Merton's emphasis on explanations of structural (not individual) strain. Merton's paradigm is clearly not psychological as such approaches center exclusively on individuals and their characteristics. Nevertheless, any individual cultural model poses an important limitation to Merton's paradigm. The subjective element of opportunity structures (referenced and relative to the cultural and structural levels) suggests that the paradigm remains mostly a probabilistic model (Merton clearly recognized and incorporated this point). As opportunity structures are unlikely to be effected by or controlled by the action of individuals and groups, they represent the objective situations faced by individuals and groups. However, access to resources and use of resources is under the control of actors. If individuals select opportunities in different ways, the persistence of structural effects through the three structures in the paradigm seem to limit the explanatory power of the paradigm. However, the anomie-and-opportunity-structures paradigm does have the advantage of not being dependent as individual level models are in trying to explain motives and actions based on psychological and mental processes.

Many of the misattributions of researchers outside the paradigm instead demonstrate the weaknesses of their own approaches with respect to many of the issues they raise. Social control and social disorganization theorists gave overriding importance to institutional factors. The former theoreticians ignore contextual factors, such as socio-economic conditions. The latter tend to be structural determinists, and surprisingly, move towards being cultural determinists.

The realist-Marxist conception of social structure used by Porpora (1987, 1989) is very similar to the one used in the anomie-and-opportunity-structures paradigm, except that the latter paradigm incorporates cultural and opportunity structures as well. Given that the anomie-and-opportunity-structures paradigm does incorporate or at least acknowledge the importance of human agency in social science behavior, future models using this paradigm will have to acknowledge up front the probabilistic nature of any structural modeling. Nevertheless, structural properties of behavior do exist and the anomie-and-opportunity-structures paradigm goes further than most existing models in describing the parameters making up different structures.

The criticism of Rubinstein against structural models of ignoring cultural human will seems to pose an important challenge to future structural paradigms (Rubinstein 2001). However, individual-centered approaches have their own limitations, mainly arising from their downplaying the existence of all extra-individual structures and especially, the existence of cultural and opportunity structures. These approaches explore the psychological and mental processes of individuals but are subject to problems of making any generalizations across individuals. It is clear that Rubinstein and anyone adhering to his criticisms about structural sociology do not share and approve of any research showing the importance of structural effects on human behavior, particularly the role of power and stratification underlying conceptions of cultural, social, and opportunity structures. If Merton's *oeuvre* is to have any meaningful impact in the future of criminology and sociology, it should at least be its legacy as a truly sociological contribution. Further, because of the powerful insights in Merton's theoretical project, these shortcomings should not prevent the developing and testing of a Mertonian theory of deviant behavior. On the contrary, a visionary sociological paradigm of anomie-and-opportunity-structures underlies Merton's contribution to the study of deviance. As such, efforts must be made to think with, rather than against Merton, an endeavor which itself follows Mertonian aspirations (Merton 1949).

Contrasting Notions of Opportunities

The situational and opportunity structures aspects of Merton's paradigm need to be made clearer and compared to existing criminological theories. This section explores such linkages with explicit attention to opportunities in major theories.

The common medieval adage 'opportunity makes the thief' seems to be very prophetic and relevant for modern day criminology and sociology of crime theory and research. In this statement, it seems the situation rather than the characteristics of the thief are more pertinent for the occurrence of crime. One of the most prominent myths in the discipline is that most crime theories are offender based, while only a few are oriented towards analyzing situations linked to criminality and crime as an event. The major argument of this section is the fallacious nature of this assertion. Especially since most, if not all theories of crime, describe situations where offenders, victims, and institutions of control have different roles in producing, responding, and controlling crime. Situations broadly defined are the relevant environments and contexts influencing both criminality (how individuals become criminals) and crime as an event. In this view, all notions of opportunities incorporated in these theories really concern which situations are more likely to lead to more crime and criminality. Whether a lack or abundance of opportunities influences crime and criminality, many theories assert that opportunities play a role in certain situations. So in fact, the thief can also make, or at minimum take advantage, of the opportunity depending on the situation. The different notions and uses of opportunity, however, are severe limits on being able to evaluate and test theories.

Two of the major traditions in criminology, differential association and routine activities theories, have maximized use of this adage and its inverse to understand, explain, and predict criminality and criminal events. However, even between these two theories, there exist varied conceptions of the meaning and significance of opportunity. In Sutherland's theory, opportunity essentially refers to learning opportunities, whereby individuals learn from other individuals the various skills and tools to commit criminal acts. Sutherland's conceptualization of opportunity, though not formalized, heavily influenced Cloward and Ohlin's concept of illegitimate opportunities. Sutherland viewed opportunities as generally outside of his theory, but recognized their importance:

> It is axiomatic that persons who commit a specific crime must have the opportunity to commit that crime. On the other hand,

opportunity is not a sufficient cause of crime, since some persons who have opportunities to embezzle, become intoxicated, engage in illicit heterosexual intercourse or to commit other crimes do not do so. Consequently, opportunity does not differentiate all persons who commit a particular crime from all persons who do not commit that crime...Second, the opportunity to commit a specific crime is partially a function of physical factors and of the non-criminal culture (Cohen et al. 1956, p. 32).

The reference to the non-criminal culture is consistent with Merton's approach while the reference to physical factors is consistent with both Merton and routine activities theorists. In routine activities, opportunities are considered solely as physical targets, which are differentiated by their attractiveness for motivated offenders and existing criminals. In differential association, opportunities are critical insofar as without cultural transmission, criminality would not be possible. In Cohen and Felson's theory, opportunities are the master variable that explains why criminal events cluster and concentrate in certain locations and why crime has increased rapidly even in times of affluence (Felson and Clarke 1998). Rational choice and routine activities theorists criticize traditional approaches for focusing exclusively on offenders and not the criminal event. Cohen and Felson strongly advocate that their approach best explains the rise of crime and violence in times of prosperity and affluence, at least in the post World War II environment. They view theorizing and research as a competition, whereby their theory comes much closer to the truth than other competing approaches (as well as being more policy relevant).

Sutherland is more humble and suggests that he focuses on a specific phenomenon, group delinquency. Cohen and Felson overextend the applicability and relevance of their theory and stretch their conception of opportunity. Sutherland has been careful to specify the domain and possible uses of his theory and recognizes that opportunities are necessary, but not sufficient causes of crime and criminality (Cohen et al. 1956). The use of opportunities by theorists and practitioners reflect differences in the nature of theorizing and research in the field of crime and violence.

These differences seem not to be that important if one views these theories as revealing parts of the truth and having general relevance to understanding and explaining some, not all, aspects of crime and criminality. If one can consider them as complementary rather than competing (Merton 1976), perhaps we would come up with more integrated and refined theories. Unfortunately, these theories are seen as competing and mostly proponents (rather than the originators) of these theories have tended to suggest that their theory or theories are better than others in explaining crime and violence. Further, some go as far as to test these theories as if they are suited for all aspects of crime and violence from juvenile delinquency to property crimes to crimes of violence and from offender motivations to physical location of crimes. Some theories are not comparable in the sense of being able to test them against each other; they have different domains of focus. In other cases, even if they are comparable to some degree, it is hardly of any benefit to try to develop a general theory of crime and violence through elimination of theories by testing a theory against another. Crime and criminality are multi-faceted phenomena, hardly amenable to explanations using a single theoretical proposition or a single variable.

Each theory usually has distinct and specific limits in what can be explained, works on different questions and levels of analyses, and has different assumptions about human nature and which behavioral processes apply (these have been called 'problematics'). If they are competing for attention and adherents, theorists in criminology cannot pretend that their theory is a general theory of crime; rather, they must humbly accept that middle-range theories must be further developed in order to develop general theories of crime and violence (Lynch and Groves 1995).

The varied conceptions of opportunity and opportunity structures in the major theoretical traditions of criminology and sociology of crime and violence theory and research complicate their useful applications. On the other hand, the different concepts of opportunities and opportunity structures used in these theories are a useful way to understand the scope, domain, validity, and utility of these theories. A review of the different criminological traditions and their use of opportunities demonstrate that all theories are situational in orientation and have specific aspects of crime and criminality as their focus. Falsification and certain types of integration do not seem to be viable methods to compare and evaluate theories. From this perspective, the anomie-and-opportunity structures paradigm has many elements of a more pragmatic approach to analyzing crime and criminality. Briefly, the ideal features of the paradigm are its probabilistic orientation, critical focus on individual and group choices and actions as crucial processes in crime and criminality, view of choices and actions as responses to conditions and situations, and the more direct involvement of non-criminal elements in the study of crime and criminality. There is a need for integration with balanced theories and making theories complementary rather than contradictory. There has to be a basis for such integration – this is what must be strived for.

Opportunities in Major Crime and Violence Theories
Not all criminological theories make explicit the use of opportunities and opportunity structures concepts. The three major explicit uses of opportunities, opportunities as legitimate means or resources, opportunities as learning of illegitimate means, and opportunities as physical targets, are associated with the strain/anomie, differential association, and routine activities theories respectively. Additionally, some other theories closely allied with these theories share similar uses of these three conceptions of opportunities, often less explicit or considered central. Of these three conceptualizations of opportunity, the physical target conceptualization of opportunity is widely perceived as the most accurate and intuitively appealing. It is considered as better oriented to examine situations most conducive to explaining the rise of crime in times of affluence – thus, avoiding explanations of crime using simple concepts such as strain, social disorganization, and differential association. This relates to these other theories in their inability to provide reliable and valid measures and tests of their concepts, their concentration on offenders and motivations rather than situational and foreground factors closer to crime and violence, and lack of provision of policy guidance on crime prevention. Rather, offender-based theories are seen to provide unrealistic, indirect, and impractical ways to reduce crime (Brantingham et al. 1976). Portrayed as responding to

environmental conditions, the key actor in routine activities theory is the individual offender. Other theories consider deviance as a group process with groups collectively making choices or groups influencing the choices of deviant actors.

However, most theories do not incorporate any explicit and clear conceptualization of opportunities or opportunity structures. This is surprising because crime and criminality are not completely random and/or dispersed – facts that most theories acknowledge and take to heart. Without some notion of 'opportunity' in any theoretical model, it would be hard to explain criminality and crime. Criminality and processes of becoming predisposed to commit crime depend heavily on the occurrence of conditions, contexts, and processes (or their absence as posited in social control theories). All of those structural and process type causes and/or effects of crime and violence embody individual and group responses and actions, which in turn imply use of some sort of opportunities to achieve control or to meet objectives and/or goals. Even communities must have resources to control their members – social organization invariably involves some criminal elements and conditions conducive to crime just as social disorganization has a mix of non-criminal and criminal elements.

Social control and conformity involve interactions between individuals, groups, and institutions - individuals and groups will become less attached and exhibit fewer bonds with institutions because there are fewer opportunities to build these bonds and attachments. No behavior or condition occurs in a vacuum, it is a result of different actors confronting objective situations, some of which they share with others and others are different. Fortunately, there are some implicit notions of opportunities that can be inferred – which help one to understand basic differences between major theories. Some individual-centered theories do not require the use of opportunities as there are no interactions and responses towards structural conditions incorporated in these theories. For this reason, these are not discussed here.

Any incorporation of opportunity and opportunity structures concepts in criminological theories and models requires four key elements: a). specification of relevant environmental and/or structural conditions; b). critical processes in articulation of opportunities; c). major decision choices by key actors; and d). meaning of opportunities for key actors (see Warr 2001). The first two elements often define the constraint or opportunity sets that apply for the key actors in making their choices and ensuring desired objectives. These also relate to the concept of opportunity structures, which can be thought of as at higher level of aggregation than individuals and compromising processes of the creation, distribution, and production of resources.

The later two elements concern the basic choices that actors make and how these fulfill their individual goals and objectives as well as in some cases, the goals of their groups, communities, and the entire society. The critical differences between theories lies in the scope conditions that translate opportunities of different kinds into achievable outcomes. As Table 1 shows, the types of opportunities that are generated work at distinct levels and involve distinct processes. These opportunities are generated with some key processes consistent with the theoretical framework employed and result in specific kinds of opportunities for actors in terms of influencing crime and criminality. The outcomes themselves are different in each theory due to selective attribution of structural influences and processes deemed critical from the perspective of the theory. These theoretical traditions are not grand theories, but rather middle-range theories, focused on specific questions, concepts, and processes. There are no universal causes or effects of crime and criminality, but rather the focus on each theory is on specific situations leading to particular crime and criminality outcomes. Then, each theory speaks to how these specific situations are likely to be influential and/or determining crime and criminality at individual, group, or other aggregate levels. In this regard, it is obvious that different questions are being answered by each theory. This is one of the major constraints in being able to falsify or integrate theories and is reflected in the use of different notions of opportunity.

It is useful to think of some of the major elements differentiating theories in general to illuminate how these crime theories are essentially poor targets for falsification and integration. Theories are used for purposes of understanding, explaining, and predicting specific phenomena. They can be considered as simplifications of reality. In the case of theories of social sciences, it has been difficult to simultaneously incorporate all potential causes and effects of behavior

Table 1. Opportunity Concepts in Major Criminological Theories

Theoretical Tradition	Types	Levels/Properties	Processes	Outcome(s)	Main Dependent Variable	Choice or Constraint Focus
Routine Activities	Physical	Individual & Population	Routine Activities; Motivated Offender Perceptions	Targets	Clustering of Crime Incidents/ Events	Offender Choice
Lifestyle Victimization	Lifestyle	Individual & Group	Structural Constraints & Role Expectations; Victim Choices	Risk/Exposure Profiles	Victimization Distribution	Balanced – More Victim Choice
Social Control	Control	Individual & Group	Institutional Control; Individual Bonding	Integration/ Conformity	Individual Criminality	Individual Choice
Social Disorganization	Organization	Communities /Systemic	Community Mobilization; Internal Community Dynamics	Cohesion	Crime Rates	Community Choice
Differential Association	Interaction	Individual & Group	Group Interactions; Individual Learning	Learning/ illegitimate Means	Group Criminality	Individual Choice
Strain/Anomie	Social, Economic, & Political Conditions	Modal Adaptations & Structural	Structured Probabilities To Achieve Goals /Objectives; Actor Utilization and Perception	Legitimate Means/ Resources	Crime Rates & Distribution	Balanced – More Structural Constraints

and outcomes. Each theory usually makes some assumptions in order to focus on particular behavioral processes or outcomes (Gibbs 1985). Testing and empirical validation of theories occurs at the level of hypotheses and theoretical propositions.

Even if there are contradictory hypotheses posited by different theories, empirical testing between these theories can be hampered if these theories work at different levels of analyses and with different units of analyses. Additionally, most theory testing works with variables (supposed to represent specific concepts), which may not be able to fully capture the phenomena to be examined. While falsification has been the principle most advocated for theory testing and integration to allow for increased variance, one can also stress that theories should be judged for their ability to interpret facts and relationships between variables. This concerns how theories are used to interpret reality, rather than for their accuracy or predictive power only. Theories differ tremendously on these interpretations of simple relationship between variables mostly because they ask different questions and focus on specific situations and instances of phenomena under examination.

Four general criteria can be used to differentiate theories (Bernard 1987):

a). scope or scope conditions – boundary and situational conditions of a theory usually specific to certain analytical levels and units of analyses. They can be considered as a set of universal statements in a theory, which define the class of circumstances where one can make knowledge claims (Cohen 1989). Delineating scope conditions allow one to understand the key theoretical propositions in theories in terms of where theories apply. Instead of suggesting that conditions apply universally, scope conditions are needed to develop empirical tests of theories because they suggest that conditions are not applicable in all situations. As theories usually develop in specific historical periods and circumstances, the scope conditions of a theory are historically derived. Substantial modifications and application of theories to different domains is possible within the framework of most theories. For the most part, this depends on whether conditions as well as methods to examine such phenomena have drastically changed. The scope of a theory refers to structures and processes and how they set up conditions for which certain actors (units of analyses) play roles in producing and creating the phenomena to be studied.

b). <u>domain</u> – refers to (in this case, types of crime) the types of phenomena to be studied. Inherent in the specification of a domain of a theory is a classification scheme that develops categorizations of a phenomena into different types with different attributes. Although general theories may have a large domain, testing these theories usually work on more specific and smaller domains. For the study of crime and violence, different domains have included property, violent, delinquency, gangs, individual criminality, criminal events, victimization, and so on.

c). <u>validity</u> – measured by how accurate a theory is in explaining the phenomena in its domain. Most social science theories are judged on their ability to explain specific hypotheses and/or theoretically based propositions. Considerable effort has been placed on refining methodological tests and measurement of theory constructs and concepts. Unfortunately, it has been difficult to obtain adequate indicators for many concepts. This is especially true for measures of cultural factors. Both theoretical falsification and integration are seen as to strategies to measure and increase validity.

d). <u>utility</u> – measured by whether the domain is rare or widespread and/or the degree of relationship between the domain and the general phenomena to be studied. For example, if delinquency is considered as widespread and central to studying crime and criminality, theories with a focus on delinquency would have greater utility than a theory of only gangs. However, utility and validity are independently judged and a theory with little utility can have high validity.

Each of the major crime theories are summarized below with regard to these four general criteria and how concepts of opportunity are used that reflect on these criteria (Vold et al. 2002 is the major text used to describe these components). For the first objective, only general statements will be made with regard to scope conditions, domain, validity, and utility as a full assessment would require detailed analyses of empirical research and applications of each theory. For the second summary statements, the type and operation of opportunities in these models will be described. In no sense is this summary exhaustive and complete.

Routine Activities

Developed by Lawrence Cohen and Marcus Felson, routine activities theory focuses on changes in routine activities of individuals and populations, such as their work, home, education, child rearing, and leisure activities, which are seen to be responsible for the increase in criminal events (Cohen and Felson 1979). The scope conditions concern how dispersion of these routine activities away from the family and household and increased portability of goods create situations where motivated individuals are able to obtain goods and achieve their expressive goals more easily. Opportunities are mainly increased targets and the key process is how motivated offenders perceive these targets in terms of their value, inertia, visibility, and access (Felson 1987, 1993). The theory is consistent with rational choice and environmental criminology theories of crime where the probability of detection and perception of offenders in terms of target selection and offender mobility play key roles in clustering of criminal incidents. The domain of study is property crimes primarily, although some have extended it to study violent crimes in high-crime physical locations such as bars and public housing (Miethe et al. 1987). The theory is considered as valid in that it accurately depicts availability of target dependent crimes, it's major domain. The utility of the theory may be considered as high as property crimes are seen as widely distributed throughout societies and the strong relationship between physical opportunities and increased property crime rates has been found in many empirical studies.

Routine activities increase physical opportunities and motivated offenders act upon these increased opportunities. Both these processes, one at the macro and one at the individual actor level, are needed to explain clustering of criminal incidents (convergence across space and time). Although routine activities are rooted at the macro level, situational factors closer to the offender's frame of reference are stressed in these theories (Felson and Clarke 1998). Only the motivated offender uses the opportunity to achieve his/her goals and/or objectives, but routine activities are created through individuals and populations finding their own niches in the 'ecological' structure of society.

Lifestyle Victimization
This theory shares many conceptualizations with routine activities, but focuses on explaining differences in victimization risks across social groups (Cohen et al. 1981). Variations in lifestyles, which are individual and group routine vocational (work, school, keeping house, etc.) and leisure activities, are related to differential exposure to dangerous physical locations, places, and times – which are situations that have higher risks of victimization. The scope conditions of this theory have less to do with dispersion of activities from family and home, but rather center on similar situations that people with different lifestyles face in meeting various role expectations and/or structural constraints. In this theory, victims and non-victims are seen as to be motivated by status considerations and adopt certain lifestyles to maintain particular statuses. The domain of the original theory was primarily personal or violent victimization, but has been adopted to study property crimes. The theory is seen as valid in that different groups having different lifestyles, such as younger males who are unmarried, poor, and blacks, have higher risks of personal victimization than other groups in society. The utility of the theory can be viewed as high for the simple fact that it considers a victim perspective. Violent victimizations are more common today and have increased for particular groups in society as well.

Lifestyle opportunities are group specific and opportunities to pursue lifestyles are linked to achievement and maintenance of particular statuses. Lifestyles are mostly an individual decision. But, group and structural processes play an important role in defining available and feasible lifestyles for individuals. Victims make their own choices given structural constraints with regard to exposure to crime situations, but larger structurally induced processes create lifestyles.

Social Control
These theories are wide-ranging and deal with both formal and informal institutional sources and processes of social control. They share with each other the emphasis on explaining why individuals and groups conform, rather than in explaining deviance (Pfohl 1985). The absence of controls leads to natural instincts of men and women to commit crime and violence. Opportunities for control depend on how

individuals and groups integrate into the major institutions of society: family, peer group, school, work, and so on. The conditions leading to greater conformity are ones that promote integration of individuals and groups into the major societal institutions. Such situations tend to be closer to individual and group dynamics. The domain of the theory has been associated with delinquency and less serious forms of crime and violence (Vold et al. 2002). Social control theories are considered valid in that stronger bonding by individuals and groups leads to fewer natural motivations to violate societal norms. The utility of the theory is enhanced, as integration with institutions is important and central to many forms of delinquency and subsequent drifting toward criminality.

Control opportunities obviously strongly relate to the strength of institutions of social control. These opportunities for control are dependent on provision of incentives and rewards for individuals and groups to conform to accepted morals and values. However, individuals are considered as the central actors in taking advantage of these control opportunities and in many instances, create their own opportunities to be integrated into major societal institutions. The breakdown of major institutions can also lead to fewer control opportunities for integration and conformity.

Social Disorganization
These theories are generally focused on the role of communities in creating social cohesion and greater opportunities for control (Vold et al. 2002). Although they share the notion of social control, the emphasis is on how communities organize to achieve common-purpose goals and objectives, one of which is conformity. Organized communities are better able to control and integrate their members to work together to achieve common goals including fighting and preventing crime. The scope conditions of this theory have been linked to urban ecological processes differentiating communities in terms of their socio-economic attributes, race/ethnicity profiles, and strength of networks and relationships within their borders (Bursik 1988). Mobilized communities will be better able to control deviance and ensure conformity by creating shared interests and values. The domain of these theories is heavily oriented towards urban juvenile delinquency, property crime and violent crime rates, especially violent

crimes in more recent applications. Original social disorganization theories were applied to examine juvenile delinquency rates in large metropolitan cities. The theory is considered valid in that it emphasizes mediating processes between structural factors and concentration of criminality in disorganized communities. The utility of the theory hinges strongly on how crime and delinquency tend to be concentrated and widespread in unstable communities and links with the broader ecological processes existing within urban areas. Opportunities in these theories apply to communities and their internal processes. Although there have been recent attempts to extend social disorganization theories by focusing on external factors responsible for differences in community crime rates (see Heitgerd and Bursik 1987), internal opportunities for cohesion are deemed critical for communities. If a community can organize, there will be greater opportunities for conformity and control. In situations where organization and mobilization are limited, crime rates are expected to higher. Mediating factors and processes condition the effects of any structural factors on opportunities for both integration and crime.

Differential Association
Differential association theory, which was developed by Edwin Sutherland, focuses on techniques for learning and motivations and attitudes toward crime by individuals and groups. Associations with other individuals and the meanings given towards by the individual experiencing certain social conditions are crucial processes in explaining delinquency. The scope conditions of this theory derive from social learning, interaction, and cultural transmission as group processes (Matsueda 1988). The domains of the theory are individual criminality, but it is highly consistent with group delinquency, gang behavior, and crime as learned behavior. Although testing of the theory has been plagued by ambiguities in key concepts and constructs (such as definitions favorable and unfavorable to violating the law), the validity of theory has increased through studies examining the role of delinquent friends and the importance of ideas and beliefs and criminal behavior as a learning process. The utility of the theory hinges on the importance of delinquency as a learned process and the role of cultural factors and beliefs as mediating any responses to social conditions

(Heimer 1997). Delinquents are seen as to be in similar situations of sharing ideas and beliefs towards using illegitimate means to achieve their goals. They may not be necessarily responding to the same situation, but attach meaning to similar situations and experiences towards violation of laws. Opportunities are produced through interaction processes in this theory and apply to individuals in their decisions to violate laws and norms. Opportunities are learned and incorporate explicit criminal techniques and ideas and beliefs. More importantly, opportunities have to be given meaning by individuals to be helpful in explaining individual and group criminality. If there is no meaning that can be attributed to individuals from committing crimes, it is unlikely that one can understand how individuals are motivated to violate the law. Individuals living in similar situations and circumstances are more likely to share both learning opportunities and responses to their shared experiences. However, this theory is best suited to examine individual and group level structures and processes.

Strain/Anomie
In the spirit of using the same criteria to differentiate theories of crime, we subject Merton's paradigm to the same evaluation as completed for theories mentioned above. The major thrust of the theory is in examining the structural sources of strain towards anomie and the various modes of adaptations by individuals striving for high status societal goals but with different structural means to achieve these goals. For Merton, anomie was higher in societies with cultures that stressed particular highly valued goals, but did not stress institutional means to achieve these goals at the same level. The high crime rate in America compared to other societies for Merton was due to this cultural imbalance between goals and institutionalized means. The strain aspect of the theory has to with the distribution and frequency of crime in groups with less access to approved legitimate means, mainly those in lower classes. There has been a lot of controversy about strain theory in terms of whether it is a social-psychological theory and can be applied at individual levels. Merton (1995) in a retrospective piece – examined in previous sections - stresses that his theory looks at frequency of crime (crime rates) rather than its incidence (individual criminality).

The scope conditions of his theory are cultural and structural conditions, structurally induced motivations and created opportunities, and individual adaptations. The domains of his theory are technically both conformity and different types of deviant responses and adaptations to structural conditions. Merton was interested why even conformity to approved goals in American society could lead to deviant adaptations. For the most part, his theory is seen as fruitful in examining property and other utilitarian crimes and has been modified to study delinquency and gang behavior. The validity of the theory has been primarily been ascertained at the individual level of testing, despite his and others assertions (Bernard 1984, 1987; Merton 1995) that the theory does not apply at this level. It is considered valid in that empirical tests have found links between social conditions and various forms of criminal behavior, especially the concentration of crime and violence in lower-class groups and particular racial/ethnic groups (Burton & Cullen 1992; Hannon 2002). The theory's utility has also been enhanced in that it explains the social and cultural influences on crime rates and their distribution in American societies as well as differences in levels of crime and violence in America compared to other countries. This study suggests that Merton's theory is valid in explaining violence through resource deprivation. The competition for resources associates with higher probabilities of disputes ending in lethal outcomes. The lack of resources may increase the possibilities of individuals and groups to make criminal adaptations to achieve various types of status, monetary and non-monetary.

In summary, each of the major criminological theories examined above clearly differ in scope, domain, validity, and utility. Further, the different conceptualizations of opportunity in these theories reflect these aspects of their theories. More importantly, embedded within each of these theories are different theories of action, where different types of opportunities as well as structures and processes are seen to provide situations for individuals, groups, and communities to move towards committing crimes and deviant acts (Bernard 1983; Lynch and Groves 1995). The situational aspects of these theories are reflected in the different scope conditions and domain aspects of these theories. Different actors at different units of analyses respond to situations outlined in the different theories by perceiving and utilizing the opportunities embodied within the different situations. Violent crimes are less likely to be explained by physical target conceptualizations of opportunity because routine activities theory does not clearly specific how motivated offenders would view persons as violent targets. At the analytic level, it is conceivable to argue that easy targets for violent crime are necessary opportunities for motivated offenders, but it is less convincing to argue that these targets are sufficient in explaining clustering of violent victimizations. Also the intervening variables or lack of them in given theory are important aspects that define structured situations for action. It is also clear that the meaning of these opportunities and the key decision choices for actors are different in each theory.

Coupled with differences in the type and level of structural constraints incorporated in these theories, these different choices and their meanings make it increasingly different to conduct comparative tests and evaluations across theories. The constraints, choices, and types of behavior in each theory are not easily incorporated within existing comparative methodological techniques. Whether one chooses to falsify theories by empirical testing or attempts integration of theories, these attempts will be of limited value if the theories are so different (Bernard 1990). Modifying or distorting theories to make them compatible for falsification and integration are obvious options, but then the unique contributions and interpretations provided by each theory are bound to be lost.

Up to this point, the focus has been on describing different conceptualizations of opportunities in major criminological theories. It has been hinted that these different conceptualizations do not bode well for falsification and integration strategies to reduce theories and to use valid and more useful theories. While falsification is difficult to achieve given that theories stress different locations of independent variation and directions of causation (see Bernard 2001), integration of theories has been a viable strategy for some time. Taking two different theoretical traditions and key concepts including concepts of opportunities (in the case of Cloward and Ohlin's differential opportunity theory) in these traditions are the basis for some established theories and empirical tests. Integration between compatible theories (those with similar scope conditions and domains) seems to be fruitful to some extent. But even these integration attempts have been limited because of distortion and misapplication of theories. Bernard (2001) has been the most articulate and detailed about the integration debate in criminology, especially in relation to improvement of integration strategies and understanding multiple aspects of crime and criminality. He proposes a 'risk-factor' approach, which explicitly deals with structured situational probabilities, focusing directly on variables to assess the strength of relationships predicted by different theories. Using the developed typology in that research, theories are divided into major categories based on the dependent variable being studied (individual criminality and crime rates): a). individual oriented theories provide observations suggesting that some persons are more likely to engage in crime than others regardless of the situations they are in; and b). structure/process theories argue that crime rates will be higher in some situations than others regardless of the characteristics of individuals within those situations. Interestingly, a review by Bernard and Snipes of crime theory and research on these two categories (Bernard and Snipes 1996; Vold et al. 2002; Bernard 2001) placed risk factors associated with social control, differential association, lifestyle victimization, and routine activities in the individual oriented theories and strain/anomie, social disorganization, and one version of social control in the situational oriented theories. This is consistent with the classification of the research here for the most part (scope & domain of the theories). However, I would argue that even individual oriented theories focus on situations increasing exposure to risk and situation oriented theories specify which individuals and their characteristics are most likely to increase risks. Perhaps, it is a question of degree so that individual oriented theories focus on choices for the most part and situational theories focus on structural constraints and situations. Thus, the typology may be forced into a categorization that limits appreciation of both situational and individual choice elements existing in most criminological theories. Interpreting relationships between variables associated with theories is often difficult and confounded as many theories are consistent (or can be made) with the same variables.

The key differences between theories seem to be varied specifications of which situations and processes apply and which actors make choices. Not all of these theories are applicable to the situations and decision choices in other theories. In the case of routine activities theory, situations are created by changes in routine activities and individual (motivated) offenders perceive the created targets and make choices to obtain the targets for their own purposes. In strain/anomie theory, both criminal and non-criminal actors make adaptations in different situations that are structured by the resources available and the status positions and roles that these individuals fall in. Both theories would predict that lower-class individuals and groups would be more likely to commit crimes and one can use the same variables (such as unemployment rate and percentage of the population that is poor) to represent the same structures and processes in each of the theories. The situations and processes described and deemed relevant in these theories differ substantially. One of the reasons is the different conceptualization of opportunities in these theories.

Another critical dimension on which theories differ is in the relative emphasis on situationally structured constraints and actor choices. As Table 1 shows, one can conceive all theories except lifestyle victimization and strain/anomie emphasize choice elements of different actors. This attribution of choice to these theories is developed by assessment of key theoretical propositions in the theories to what factors cause structural situations and how much weight is given to key actors in making choices given the different situations. If one grants that all of the theories use a theory of action emphasizing the choices of actors within structural constraints, the emphasis in these theories of choice is on actor decision processes as critical for crime and criminality. This is not to argue that none of these choice theories focus on situational constraints, but that the scope, domain, validity, and utility of these theories is intimately tied to actor choices. Lifestyle victimization and strain/anomie are considered as more balanced in their specification of choices and constraints as they emphasize both factors are necessary and sufficient to explain victimization and criminality. However, for the former theory, lifestyle choices are relatively more important than structural constraints, while in strain/anomie theory, structural constraints are stressed over choice elements. Distortion and misapplication of all these theories with different emphases on constraint and choices than originally specified in these theories will lead to faulty attributions, testing, and evaluation of these theories.

Theories stressing either the choice or constraints dimensions of crime and criminality tend towards being deterministic in orientation. The focus becomes less on explaining variation and using variables; instead theories hold either constraints or choices as constant and let either choice or constraint factors determine crime and criminality. For example, routine activities theory argues that opportunities are necessary and sufficient for crime to occur because motivated offenders choose targets not because they are otherwise constrained.

In social disorganization theory, communities choose to control crime; while structural factors distinguishing communities are incorporated in these theories, they are secondary to organizational ones in explaining variation in crime rates. Labeling theory, which is not discussed here, tends to focus on constraints almost exclusively, arguing that labels attached to deviants determine their criminality. There is a need for balance between choice and constraint aspects in crime theories and empirical research based on them. One of the more balanced approaches required in crime theory and research is a theory that emphasizes both choice and constraints equally. Further, crime theoreticians must caution against being deterministic by directly acknowledging the focus and limitations of their theory (what are they are trying to study and what situations apply); stressing that any theory can only be probabilistic at best (cannot explain everything); and directly pointing out that the scope, domain, validity, and utility of their theories are closely tied with their testing and evaluation.

While these may be lofty and impractical objectives, such type of theorizing does exist and is possible. The anomie-and-opportunity structures paradigm is properly specified with regard to scope, domain, validity, and utility aspects than most other crime theories. Merton is very clear about the probabilistic nature of his theory; clearly describes in what situations his theory applies best; points to the limitations of the theory in explaining the incidence of crime; and acknowledges that both constraints and choices play a role in criminality and crime rates. Further, his theory stresses how both criminal and non-criminal actors make choices and face constraints (and so there is not only one response to the constraints in his typology of adaptations and theory) and that actors are responding to broader situations and conditions not just to specific and narrowly defined circumstances. The discussion above described the major differences between theories of crime and violence. Unlike past research, it has been found that most theories are situational and have distinct scope, domain, validity, and utility profiles. Opportunities and opportunity structure concepts are incorporated in these theories and differ with regard to these profiles. All theories invoke a theory of action, where both choice and constraints play a role in producing criminal behavior and crime events. Most theories stress the choice aspects as being critical for producing criminality and/or control of crime. Different actors with different goals/objectives in these theories are making these choices. Because the structured situations also differ across theories, it becomes necessary for more balanced theories to study crime and criminality. Theory falsification and integration will be less successful without more emphasis on providing balanced theoretical frameworks and theories. Balanced theories stress both choice and constraint aspects behind crime and criminality and also stress the probabilistic nature of crime and criminality models with distinct scope, domain, validity, and utility profiles. Being be more explicit about the purposes and limitations, testing and integration of theories must not only be with variables, but on the unique interpretations provided by different theories.

Theory integration in the study of crime and violence will still require examining variables and their relationships. However, single variables cannot represent entire theories as many theories can be considered as consistent with many of the same variables. Less emphasis must be placed on testing and evaluation through amount of variance explained, but more efforts must be placed on integrating theories by giving both structure and agency equal balance (Fuchs 2001a, 2001b). Further, it will be fruitful to view causation as a generative process (Goldthorpe 2001) – one where hypotheses are developed with the intent to explain why variables are related. These generative processes and empirical testing on them will not provide complete verification of theories, but rather to help improve upon clearer specifications and details about both situational and choice elements in criminal behavior and actions. This would be consistent with reconciling structural and subjective approaches to the study of crime and violence (Groves and Lynch 1990). Further, it would stress the importance of the contextual nature of crime and criminality choices (Findlay 1999;Short 1998). At minimum, recognition must be made that crime theories are complementary not contradictory. As Merton (1976) once said, "In place of an exhaustive and exclusive theory of deviance, there is, and will no doubt continue to be, a plurality of theories" (p.31).

The Relevance of the Anomie-and-Opportunity Structures Paradigm

The anomie-and-opportunity structures paradigm is relevant to study and explain suburban crime and violent crime rates and patterns. One of the reasons indicated above suggests that the paradigm's scope and domain is well suited to study rates of crime and violence across extraindividual units. This section provides other reasons for the importance of the paradigm in studying metropolitan opportunity structures and crime. In particular, the paradigm recognizes variation in crime and violence rates across suburbs is context-specific. Ignoring issues of contextual applicability risks falling into development of general theories of crime that do not acknowledge that real life phenomena involve actors situated in particular settings at particular periods of time.

<u>Contextual Applications and the Importance of Context</u>
Major criminological theories have poorly understood or ignored the basic situational components of their theories. Individualistic theories are more prone to such mistakes, as they hold constant the situations in which crime takes place. However even with theories with strong situational foci, single situations are posited as being critical for crime and criminality. Rational choice theories are examples of such theories because they argue that their theories are applicable in all contexts. Cruickshank (2000) discusses such a faulty tendency by pointing out that all individuals are placed in homogeneous categories and react in identical ways to external stimuli in such theories. He also points out rational choice theories are essentialist:

RCT is a form of essentialism. A theory may be described as 'essentialist' if it holds (implicitly or explicitly) that individuals' behavior can be explained by reference to some 'essential property/ies' which determine/s behavior. With essentialism, therefore, it is not possible to have new knowledge, because one already knows the essential properties of the social realm, and observation will only verifications of one's theories of essential properties, rather than opening up new questions (p. 77).

Fuchs (2001b) argues against essentialism in the same manner as "it posits polar opposites, instead of gradations and empirical continua" (p. 9).

Ignoring contexts leads to stereotypical descriptions of the effects of situational factors. Theories often characterize the generation of crime and violence in a highly stylized fashion, ignoring the contingencies and limits of their theories. These factors are said to effect particular actors in all times and settings. Situations cannot be described universally as this does not allow for nuanced explanations. These tendencies tend to be true for general theories and result in highly abstract and decontextualized theories:

> In attempting to accomplish these goals, general theories differ with regard to the universal cause(s) of crime they specify. Sometimes the cause is found in human nature (e.g., crime is caused by the unbridled pursuit of pleasure), sometimes in drawn-out historical processes (e.g., crime is caused by modernization or industrialization) that are decontextualized or made abstract by the claim that the same process occurs everywhere, and sometimes in abstract principles (e.g., crime is behavior that promotes interpersonal insecurity). Regardless of the specific assumptions concerning crime, general theories favor interpretations that are "quintessentially transhistorical" (Kohn 1987: 729), lacking culturally grounded or historically specific qualifiers (Lynch and Groves 1995, p. 369).

Conditions and structural forces are thus historically contingent and shape the formation and influence of particularistic situations and actions.

Further, these theories discount how these situations derive from structuring of motivations and resources for offenders (and non-offenders as well). Additionally, they ignore that these situations and environments for acting individuals and groups distribute in a non-random manner. Rather, following Mertonian notions, these situations are patterned. Many structures and processes are location dependent, location referred to in physical, spatial, and even, social structural terms. Kelly (1995) describes human behavior as being "..toponomical, that is, dependent on physical and social location" (p. 215).

There is a need to stress the important linkages between situational analysis and specification of the contexts within which these situations are more likely to occur. Specification of contexts is useful as it allows for understanding the meaning of certain practices from a structural or system perspective. Rubinstein (1977) describes the utility of describing social contexts:

And as Wittgenstein demonstrates, a proper understanding of individual actions requires knowledge of the overarching social context in which it takes place. For the meaning of action is not a property of 'mind' but of the system of social practices. If social structure is defined as a system of action, and if meaning is seen as a property of that system, the demands of objectivists and subjectivists dovetail. The study of meaning and the study of social structure become interdependent and complimentary tasks (pp. 319-320).

The meaning of a crime and violence in one context is not necessarily the same in other contexts. As Fuchs (2001b) puts it "what something means, for example, depends on a host of variables, including context, situation, and place" (p. 3). The correlatives of crime and violence are often context-specific. Different types of crime and violence are more or less prevalent in different contexts, but one cannot view these as being the result of the same factors. Further, differences in motivations and situations can result in the concentration (or lack of concentration) of particular crimes in particular settings. Findlay (1999) presents one of the most convincing arguments for contextual analyses of crime and violence. He argues that Western crime theories are largely deterministic (as he puts it, they see either features of the environment or individuals as the essential explanations). Essentialist thinking involves dichotomous distinctions and fixes the categorization of characteristics deemed important in explaining behavior. By defining such behaviors as outcomes of natural properties, essentialist approaches also set a few limited contexts as determining diverse and varied behavior. He further contends that these theories largely ignore or underemphasize the contexts where actors, behaviors, and labels are located. As societies have become more differentiated, understanding these actions, behaviors, and labels requires understanding their dependency on their settings or contexts. For Findlay (1999), crime is at heart a "social phenomena involving people, places, and institutions" (p. 6). This underscores the importance of specifying the contexts of crime and violence:

> Crime can neither exist nor make sense without its particular social context...It locates crime within actual relationships and real social settings (Findlay 1999, p. 6)

Context is favored over notions such as community, society, and culture because these later concepts are artificial. When taken in their extreme manifestations, these later abstract notions often ignore actors and their agency, represent large units such as society with a single dimension, and represent ideals rather than realities. These artificial concepts become more useful when one avoids essentialist or dichotomized analyses. For example, instead of using dichotomies such as socially organized versus disorganized communities, it may be more fruitful to suggest differences in the degrees and kinds of organization and disorganization between communities. Similarly, qualifying culture and society, one should employ distinctions that alert us to the contextual nature of their influences on action such as highly individualistic societies or highly stratified societies. Differences are in degree and in kind and not always just in kind; this point would be lost with use of essential thinking. Presentation of contexts also allow for the development of models that work against single cause or indicator models of crime choices and adaptations. Findlay (1999), studying the development contexts of crime cross-nationally, formulates this issue:

> Again, this is where the connection between crime and development holds out a potential to recognize common social indicators without an overreliance on unconvincing models of causation. For instance, development may lead to marginalization, and contexts of marginalization may stimulate and order preferences for crime choices. This is not to say that either development or marginalization causes crime. Rather, it is a recognition of the interaction of certain social influences in the way to making a crime choice. Any sophisticated analysis of such a transition will appreciate other commitment levels of social influence at work on crime choices which emphasize the complex and interactive causes of crime, cautioning against an overly simplistic or single-cause approach (p. 68).

Rather, it is the interaction of different factors (at structural and agential levels) and location of these factors that result in outcomes of crime and violence adaptations. These interactive analyses tend to be sensitive to locational concerns and more readily depict the realities in particular situations and settings.

More importantly, contextual analyses are consistent with viewing crime as a choice, where the contexts partially represent the external constraints on actors. Choices to deviate are conditioned by the specific contexts in which potential offenders operate. Findlay (1999) suggests crime adaptations as seen from the offenders' perspectives are responses to their environments or situations:

> The relationships of crime which tend to eventuate out of marginalization, and the social disorganization with which it is associated, tend to reveal the 'choice' dimension of crime in more detail. This is a dimension which exists and operates

through relationships rather than the moral or rational predispositions of the 'individual' out of context. Choice is not conceived of here in terms of classical theory, reliant on 'free will' and rationality to explain choice. Rather it occurs within a range of contextual determinants, only one of which (but not essentially) may well be individual predisposition, which create the nature and range of choices (p. 115).

The notion of range of contextual factors alerts us to the basic point that specification of contexts concerns not just criminal adaptations, but also non-criminal choices. Crime choices are made, no matter how constrained these choices may be, in some shared environments with actors making non-crime choices. It becomes difficult to argue that a single factor could be the cause of crime when this same factor applies to the absence of crime. Again, Findlay (1999) provides us with an understanding of this point with reference to examining the relationship between poverty and crime:

For a more sophisticated understanding of the connection between crime and poverty one needs to inquire into who is committing particular types of crime within what context and out of which structures of opportunity. The same needs to be done for those in similar contexts taking non-crime choices. Only then can the particular social context of low-income criminals, and the place of poverty within it, prove instructive (p. 38).

Cloward and Piven (1990) proceed along in a similar manner by arguing that various criminological schools, which are otherwise considered to be opposed, "are in fact each focusing on different aspects of the social context that shape deviant action." (p. 81). For them, the contributions of the various paradigms can be grouped into four categories: social ideas, social resources, social norms, and societal reactions (p. 81). They recommend integrating features of different perspectives to capture these social contexts as deviance is complex behavior not captured with a single factor and/or context. Further, for them, deviant and conforming behavior may have the same roots, requiring the specification of the same factors to explain both types of behavior. Noted criminologist James Short urges us to consider contexts as vital to explanations of crime and deviance:

> Abbott (1997: 1152) argues, is the view that: One cannot understand social life without understanding the arrangements of particular social actors in particular social times and places... No social fact makes any sense abstracted from its context in social (and often geographic) space and social time. Abbott's most barbed criticism of what he calls "variable sociology" is of the assumption that variables have "the same causal meaning" regardless of context. Conflating causal influences with the effects of variables "net of other variables" is, he charges, 'social scientific nonsense'(Short 1998, p. 6).

Meier (2001) also suggests contextual dependence, where social behavior like crime and deviance are constrained by contexts, making it difficult to formulate general propositions and limiting the usefulness of deterministic theorizing.

Contextual approaches at heart involve examining the interactive effects of different factors and help to define situations that reflect these complex interactive factors. One of the key issues then becomes being able to account for these interactive factors and assessing their location across multidimensional and organized spaces. The concept of opportunity structures from a Mertonian perspective is a good candidate to capture such fundamental processes. Contextual analyses help us to recognize that phenomena such as crime and violence are located and that particular conditions are associated with the location of the same phenomena.

A Model For Rates Of Crime and Violence
This study seeks to explain the variation in rates of different types of property and violent crimes across suburban municipalities. In order to accomplish this task, it is necessary to use existing theories that can identify factors that differentiate these places as well as explain the variation in these rates. Criminological theories must be evaluated in terms of various criteria critical to such tasks. As discussed in an earlier

section, we found that the scope and domain of criminological theories differs considerably, with some theories better suited to explain some types of deviant behavior and less able to explain other deviant behavior. Merton's anomie-and-opportunity structures paradigm, for various reasons, emerges as the one of the better theoretical perspectives to explain suburban crime and violence rates. As a preview, it is clear that a good theory must be more limited and specific in scope and domain, probabilistic, sensitive to context and locational differences of various kinds, flexible to accommodate both deviant and non-deviant behavior, allow for identification for multiple factors that influence the variation in rates, and include motivational and opportunity elements (and their interactive effects). This section contains a presentation of various criteria relevant for an evaluation of candidate criminological theories. This section helps to solidify the selection to use the anomie-and-opportunity-structures paradigm as a model to explain variation in suburban crime and violence rates.

Lynch and Groves (1995) discuss the strengths and limitations of a general theory of crime. They argue that a general theory that relies on universal causes of crime is limited as such theories focus on general principles while ignoring conflicting empirical evidence, are highly abstract so poorly represent social life, and tend to be insensitive to contextual differences. Despite these limitations, Lynch and Groves (1995) suggest that theories with greater scope and larger domains are useful if they are able to incorporate necessary elements in any explanation of crime and violence:

> It is now well accepted within criminology that a theory of crime must explain at least three things in order to be complete and efficient: (1) motivation/cause; (2) opportunity structure; and (3) law enforcement activity and the structure of laws to be enforced, or reactive variables (Cohen, Felson, and Land 1980; Cohen and Felson 1979; Gibbs 1987: 831-33). A general theory that relies upon a rational man or pleasure/pain argument may successfully (though we do not believe it does) explain motivation, but it fails to address the other major elements that make up crime (e.g., opportunity structure, enforcement/reactions)"(p. 382).

This list is exhaustive from the perspective of criminology and sociology of crime. Each of these elements have been the focus of criminology theories from its inception. However, there is a tendency for theories to selectively focus on one of these elements to the exclusion of the other two elements. The least frequent type of theory includes all three elements and the most frequent type of theories include just one of these elements. Historically, motivational and reactive theories dominate the field. This is consistent with a divided discipline with different theories, but each selecting to examine different aspects of the phenomena of crime and deviance (Merton 1976). Each has its own problematics, referring to what questions it seeks to answer, that explains their selectivity. Some theories center on explaining the incidence of crime across individuals and groups, a few on opportunities as targets, and others on rates of crime. This compounds problems with these selectivities as theories then control for what others posit are important problematics.

The above list also constructs motivation as a primary causal factor and implies the other two elements are of lesser importance than motivations and consequently, not causal. This is fallacious for two reasons. First, none of these elements are sufficient causes of crime, as they are not by themselves complete as explanations for crime. In addition, all of these are necessary factors in a more complete explanation of crime and reactions to crime. While Lynch and Grove (1995) are mainly arguing against a general theory of crime using a single rationality principle, their insistence on identifying causal explanations of crime is misplaced. Devising theories to develop exacting causes of phenomena such as crime is not possible even for theories of limited scope and/or historically and culturally specific theories.

Using their logic, it is only within contextually grounded approaches, that an appreciation of the interplay of all elements allow contingent explanations (not causes) of crime. The evidence supports the development of theories of limited scope and specific domains, from which the interplay of three elements derive contingent explanations. Building knowledge about crime and violence requires analytical strategies that incrementally contribute to existing theories and empirically assess the utility of these theories in their abilities to explain the multi-faceted aspects of crime and violence.

Given these parameters and others discussed above, the following are offered as criteria to evaluate candidate theories for explaining suburban crime and violence. 1). Problematics on rates of crime and violence; 2). Incorporate at least two of three elements; 3). Contextually applicable; 4). Include structure and agency aspects; 5). Include values and interest; and 6). Explain both criminal and noncriminal behavior.

The emphasis on rates of crime and violence follows directly from Merton. Merton was clear that his approach was helpful in identifying the variation of deviant behavior within different social structures, particularly the different patterns of this deviant behavior in these structures (Merton 1957, p. 123). This is distinct from approaches seeking to explain the incidence of deviance in individuals. Further, Merton sees identifying the location of rates of crime and violence in groups and strata as an important task for a sociologist studying crime:

> If we can locate groups peculiarly subject to such pressures, we should expect to find fairly high rates of deviant behavior in these groups, not because the human beings comprising them are compounded of distinctive biological tendencies but because they are responding normally to the social situation in which they find themselves. Our perspective is sociological. We look at variations in the rates of deviant behavior, not at its incidence (Merton 1957, p. 132).

The nonrandom distribution and patterning of crime and violence also necessitates that the location of crime choices and adaptations be part of an explanation of the variation in rates of crime and violence. The frequency of crime adaptations along with their location varies within society, which is why studying rates rather than incidence is more appropriate. Specifying these social structures in terms of characteristics of its elements, for example status and role, is helpful in understanding why higher (or lower) rates of crime and violence are more likely with particular groups and strata in society. Differences in resources and status approximate the differences in the likelihood of crime and non-crime choices.

Merton's anomie-and-opportunity structure paradigm also directly incorporates two of the three elements (identified above) that researchers use in explaining rates of crime and violence. These are motivations for deviance and opportunities to commit deviant acts. Motivations and opportunities are structured by different conditions and forces, but the interplay of these elements is crucial in locating rates of crime and violence in particular strata. Stinchcombe (1995) makes the basic point of distinguishing between the sources of motivations and opportunities more generally:

> Thus the distinction between the structural sources of motivation and the structuring of alternatives allows us to disentangle the motivational aspect of the structured alternatives from the goals people are trying to reach by choosing those alternatives. The two forces cause variations overt different sets of observations: historical in one case and cross-sectional in the other (p. 84).

The structuring of motivations in this case are due to the general emphasis in American society for material success and achievement of high status for all strata and groups in society. The broader culture motivates societal members to maximize status and not to limit their strivings. However, particular strata are subject to differential pressures or strains to achieve these goals through illegitimate means. Opportunities, on the other hand, are patterned unevenly in social structures. For Merton, action (adaptations) arises from individual choices and "the objective situation, the conditions of action" (Merton 1936, p. 895). Conditions characterizing particular structures, such as the composition of population, determine the opportunities and distribution of these resources across different strata. Individuals occupying different statuses have differential access to these resources and are differentially subject to exclusion to access these resources. Often times, higher rates of crime and violence are accompanied by lower levels of resources, which increase the likelihood of crime choices and/or adaptations. Merton does spend some time in discussing the reaction and response to deviance, however, he suggests that other criminological theories emphasize this element to a greater degree (Merton 1976). The main point is that certain situations having certain accompaniments, motivations and opportunities, increase the probability of higher rates of crime and violence and their concentration in particular groups and strata.

The contextual applicability of Merton's approach is clear. The entire paradigm rests on the nature of a particular social structure (the American case), one where cultural anomie and uneven distribution of means leads to crime adaptations and their higher prevalence in particular groups and strata. It is not just the anomic culture or uneven distribution of resources, but the presence of both in American society that leads to the particular nature of crime and violence in this society:

> However, when we consider the full configuration-poverty, limited opportunity, and the assignment of cultural goals-there appears some basis for explaining the higher correlation between poverty and crime in our society than in others where rigidified class structure is coupled with differential class symbols of success (Merton 1957, p. 137.)

In a stratified, yet more mobile, society such as the United States, the nature and distribution of crime and violence is much different than in a society where mobility is less, opportunities distributed more evenly, and/or a different culture. Further, within American society, the objective conditions and motivations behind individual choices and action are unevenly present and distributed. These provide varied contexts more or less conducive to crime adaptations, which are also differentially located across the social structure.

Discussions of contextual applicability relate to considerations of structure and agency. Both social structures and human behavior are not static and universal in all contexts. Examining the social structures and behaviors of Americans versus Europeans or different strata or class in American society would demonstrate that different structures and actors are present in these different cases, with the contexts quite distinct. While this point is simple and obvious, there is a tendency in social science theory and research to suggest that structures, in comparison to agency, are less static and hence deterministic of agency. Rather, a more balanced view would incorporate the notion that the different contexts of both structure and agency are subject to change; leading to changes in both structure and agency. The anomie-and-opportunity-structures paradigm obviously highlights the importance of both structure (objective conditions beyond the control of individuals) and agency (directly in control of individuals). More to the point, social structures, based on the organization and distribution of statuses, incorporate both structure and agency. Barbano (1968) perceptively makes this point:

> Social structure, however, is not a deterministic factor (as explained more fully below) but a matrix, a source which selects the limits and possibility of social activity, and which in turn, is selectively experienced both by the individual and observer (notice that in discussing the concept of anomie, Merton speaks of structural sources and of socio-cultural sources of anomic behavior. This highlights the particular connection which exist between social structure and human behavior, a connection which is not characterized by determinism nor by contrapositions. Elsewhere, a propos of behavior according to groups of reference, Merton sees in the social structural sources which orientate this behavior) (p. 55).

Agency is critical in this conception of social structures, as are not only individuals the ones acting and behaving in certain ways, but they are also facing and experiencing social and cultural structures. Note that context, structure, and agency are variable and this variability limits the possibilities of deterministic explanations with this paradigm. Rather, these explanations are probabilistic, something that Merton consciously and purposefully noted in his examination of the opportunity structures concept and in his earlier work.

A complete approach to studying crime and violence rates has to examine the influence of both values and interest. As much, if not all, behavior is social (oriented towards others) and takes place in social contexts, simply deriving rates of crime and violence from notions of status positions in social structures would ignore the motivations behind crime and violence. Actors are motivated and make choices in situations where they consider goals, ends, aims, and interest simultaneously. American society possesses a particular culture, albeit this culture influences different strata in varying degrees, that emphasizes individualism, material success, and freedom and independence from governmental authority, especially more centralized governmental entities. These values are an integral part of suburbanization and directly reflect the desire for actors to garner more resources to control their own destinies and maximize status in the metropolitan hierarchy.

Finally, a model for explaining rates of crime and violence must be able to explain both criminal and noncriminal adaptations. This directly reflects in the typology of adaptations developed by Merton in his original paradigm. Both conforming and nonconforming adaptations are included as responses to particular conditions. Many criminological approaches see only the need to explain deviance without seeing the lack or absence of deviance as directly tied to their explanations. Without understanding why rates are lower or higher in particular strata, one may ignore that the same variables may explain both phenomena. The presence of high rates of crime and violence in some suburbs and the absence of others is nonrandom and influenced by larger social and cultural structures. These nonrandom patterns must be explained in a relational sense, whereby the presence and absence of particular conditions are related to each other.

Conclusions

Merton (1995) recently provided an important retrospective piece on the paradigm, an effort that is central to refinement of the paradigm. This chapter reveals that the paradigm holds great promise in future theory and research examining deviant behavior. Unfortunately, the theory of deviant behavior in the paradigm has been subject to criticisms and misinterpretations, but upon careful examination, the paradigm can to hold strong, especially because it incorporates many of the concerns of social scientist to use an integrated cultural-structural model of human behavior and to include both structural and human agency elements in such a model.

Much of the confusion in the secondary literature over the status of Merton's theoretical project in the study of deviance is due to the fact that Merton presented not one, but at least two theories in his 1938 article and his many related publications since (Merton 1938, 1949, 1956, 1964; see Featherstone and Deflem 2003). On the one hand, Merton develops an anomie theory that postulates that an imbalance between cultural goals and socially acceptable means will result in a de-institutionalization of means. On the other hand, Merton presents a strain theory of deviant behavior to suggest that social barriers can restrict people under certain socio-economic conditions from having access to the legitimate means to achieve culturally valid goals, presenting a strain towards the adoption of illegitimate means which Merton classified in a by now widely known five-item typology. Merton's anomie theory has often been mistaken for a criminological theory, but this view neglects that anomie and strain are two distinct concepts and part of two distinct theoretical formulations of two distinct social realities within an over-arching sociological paradigm (Featherstone and Deflem 2003). But Merton's theory of deviant behavior has never been fully developed to any degree of satisfaction, especially for research purposes. Merton has acknowledged as much, particularly when he suggested the incorporation of opportunity structures theory in his criminological perspective, referring to "the theory of anomie-and-opportunity-structures" (Merton 1997, p. 519). This study is one of the first to directly apply Merton's paradigm of anomie-and-opportunity-structures.

CHAPTER 3

Suburban Stratification and Suburban Crime and Violence

Suburban Heterogeneity and Types

Most of urban sociology has taken the homogeneity of suburbs relative to central cities as a given fact. The suburbanization of population and employment largely took place in the 20th century in the United States. Today, suburbs of metropolitan regions (taken as a whole or even in some cases, a few dominant suburbs only) are crucial to the prosperity and vitality of these regions. Ignoring suburban heterogeneity or alternatively focusing only on central cities would result in incomplete models and explanations for many social science phenomena. The term "suburb" refers to settlements of people and employment outside urban areas and/or central places that are usually less dominant in population and employment than the urban core. Viewed as less central and dominant, suburbs were treated singularly, i.e., affluent residential areas. Most descriptions, even until today, have a tendency to discount the diversity of suburban types present now and historically. Many models of urban and metropolitan structures are monocentric. Most comparisons between central cities and their suburbs are made using these unchanging definitions. Within the last two decades, revisions of monocentric models and suburban heterogeneity have led to new approaches to examine suburban diversity and heterogeneity.

The research that does look at the heterogeneity of suburbia has resulted in the development of perspectives that characterize suburbs as providing certain functions for important actors (mainly governments, employers, and residents tied to these geographically specific entities) in their ability to meet basic needs, be competitive in the local and broader metropolitan arena, and to minimize negative externalities. Status considerations are also important in determining suburban character and the desirability and exclusiveness of suburbs. This chapter examines these concepts with the intent to develop a typology on functional and status differences between suburbs and the role of these place level characteristics in the concentration and distribution of crime and violence. We find such concepts and other critical dimensions associated with and explaining suburban variation are ones addressed through the study of race/ethnicity, housing and labor markets, and other demographic and socioeconomic factors.

One of the underlying points to be considered is how existing classification schemes tend to focus on either singular positive or negative aspects of suburban diversity. It is no accident that the distribution of diverse and unequal environments and contexts across new metropolitan forms is a patterned process. This study examines the distribution of crime and violence problems and the function (residential, employment, or mixed) and status of suburbs in the Los Angeles metropolitan region. Specific crime and violence problems, as well as the lack of such problems, relate to the character of suburbs and their location in the metropolitan hierarchy.

The Development and Nature of the Suburban Hierarchy

Two of the most enduring myths of suburbia in the United States are that suburbanization is mostly a post World War II phenomena and suburbs until recently (with the advent of employment suburbanization) were exclusively high-income and upper middle-class residential areas (see R. Harris 1999). Research has documented the existence of suburban diversity in earlier periods with three major types of suburbs: affluent residential suburbs, industrial suburbs, and unincorporated areas approximating as suburbs (and not as formal political jurisdictions). These revisionist arguments have come from historians, sociologists, and geographers. They provide a necessary emphasis on the evolution, character, and distinctiveness of suburban places, aside from suburbs as formal political incorporations. However, these approaches devote little attention to the implications of such diversity in studying current metropolitan regions. The suburban hierarchy links suburbs together in complex ways, which suggest the presence of high levels of interdependence and relationships among these places. A particular suburb develops in a particular way and its unique character partially derives from metropolitan contexts and its place in the suburban hierarchy.

The past metropolitan stratification system was heavily influenced by the dominance of the central city. Central cities tended to house a significant portion of the population and employment of a metropolitan region, although some metropolitan regions had significant concentrations of specific populations and industrial activities in particular suburbs. These never matched the size or scope of the central city. The suburbs that existed at this time were highly specialized with varying levels of overall status.

The dominance of the central city waned, but never disappeared, over the course of the 20th century. Beginning in the 1900s, metropolitan regions saw an increased number of incorporations by suburbs. However, the period after World War II saw the emergence of a wide range of suburbs and the increased diversification of suburbs on function and status. Suburban expansions were the norm and unlikely to reverse or be supplanted by centralizing forces. Unlike earlier periods of the growth of satellite suburbs, whose linkages with the core represented clear and obvious dependence, newer suburbs emerged that exhibited lower levels of dependence and began to locate at further distances from the core. Industry agglomerations and racial residential segregation that distributed population and activity in a selective and limited fashion in earlier metropolitan forms still applied and suggest that centralization of population and employment was still typical. Even though the advent of a service sector based economy and the decline of manufacturing put pressures on this growth, suburbs were more likely to be the areas of largest growth, albeit the growth of suburbs was uneven. For some suburbs, decline was inevitable as restructuring left them with few resources and a large number of problems that lead to decay. Nevertheless, this pattern was selective and not the norm for all suburbs. Suburban expansions distinguish by the types of actors suburbanizing and the resulting metropolitan form. Cervero's (1989) discussion of three waves of suburban expansions, for example, suggests that population suburbanization preceded business-led suburbanization (retail and manufacturing establishments mostly). Chronologically, the next wave of suburban expansion was of workers and businesses in the office and high-technology service sectors. Suburbanization of all three types is now common to many metropolitan regions in the United States. The metropolitan form moved from being monocentric to polycentric in the course of the century.

The first wave began in the early 1900s and continued throughout the century. This was still consistent with a monocentric depiction of metropolitan form. These suburbs corresponded with the depiction of suburban affluence present in urban theories developed to study metropolitan form. The second wave accelerated after World War II with a peak in the late 1960s and early 1970s (coinciding with the decline of the manufacturing sector) and benefited from improvements in transportation and highway infrastructure. In this wave, commercial and industrial businesses in the retail and manufacturing sectors located in suburbs to take advantage of lucrative consumer markets and cheaper land rents. In some cases, manufacturing concentrations led to extreme specialization in function and the creation of exclusively industrial cities. The metropolitan form was clearly changing to a polycentric one, where multiple centers emerged. Nevertheless, the center remained dominant in terms of overall employment and heavily weighed in service sector employment. The last wave of suburbanization brings us to the period from the mid-1970s onwards with the ascendancy of the service sector in the nation's economy. Suburbs became even more urbanized, resembling central cities more so than in past periods of history. Cervero (1989) notes the dramatic change in suburban expansion with this last expansion:

> The third wave of suburban expansion – the arrival of workers
> – particularly those in the office and high-technology sectors –

has brought many American suburbs full circle. With the addition of a day-time workforce population, many suburbs have become virtually indistinguishable from traditional urban centers, featuring a mosaic of places, from office towers and executive parks to fern bars and performing art centers. No longer do Americans vacate suburbs each morning: today's suburbs have become primary destinations themselves (p. 4).

New suburban employment centers or sub-centers in the new metropolis increasingly began to develop their own specific patterns of land uses and became destinations of significance with their own labor sheds (Cervero 1989, p. 73). Commuting patterns emerged where suburb-to-suburb trips exceeded all types of trips in the 1980s and a complex set of interactions characterized the relationships between suburbs themselves (Baldassare 1994, p. 4). Suburbs developing primarily in the third wave of suburban expansion also began to face urban problems similar to central cities including traffic congestion, increased need for services such as road maintenance and fire and policing serving larger daytime populations, and higher jobs-housing imbalances. Cervero (1989) spends a considerable amount of time on the jobs-housing imbalances and finds fiscal zoning weighted toward attraction of high-revenue sources, growth restrictions, worker-earnings/housing cost mismatches, increase in two wage-earner households, and high rates of job turnover contribute to higher ratios of jobs to housing in suburban areas (pp. 49-50). The new metropolitan form is definitely more complex and difficult to characterize than with previous metropolitan forms. The Edge City phenomenon, which consisted of large office space developments mixed with large shopping malls and retail in unincorporated and incorporated portions of the metropolitan area, also blossomed during the latest period.

Despite the maturing of suburbs and increased independence from the center during this last expansion, there remains a strong level of interdependence between suburbs, whereby suburbs depend on each other and the center for economic sustenance and growth. Suburbs are relatively more independent from the core than before, but their fortunes remain tied overall metropolitan vitality and growth. The degree of interdependence, further, varies by the particular function and status of the suburb, with higher-status residential suburbs the least worried about the negative impacts of growing decentralization and economic restructuring. Lower-status, residential suburbs face the greatest difficulties because of deconcentration of population and business, disinvestments, increases in expenditures and needs, and declining fiscal resources. For these suburbs, the degree of dependence on a growing metropolitan economy is precarious. Without healthy growth, suburbs at the lower echelons of the suburban hierarchy are likely to decline during the down swings of the business cycle, show little recovery during upturns, and suffer greatly from secular economic changes. Further, as metropolitan regions vary in their form, interdependence varies across metropolitan regions as well. Some regions have developed in a quintessential suburban fashion with higher rates of minority suburbanization than others. Los Angeles is a leading example of high rates of minority and lower-status group suburbanization historically and more recently as well. However, suburban growth and decline are realities common to many metropolitan regions in the United States and these trends do not seem to be dissipating.

The period of the third wave of suburban expansion has led to increased inequality and polarization between suburbs as well. Lucy and Phillips (2000) characterize this period of suburban expansion as the 'era of suburban decline' (p. 2). For them, more suburban jurisdictions face declining populations, decay, and disinvestments greater than in any past period. Their measures of decline include household income and poverty, which show increased divergence and concentration respectively. The suburbanization of both poverty and wealth is a characteristic of this third wave. In this post-suburban era (with suburban dominance waning), suburban prosperity accompanies suburban decline:

> The most polarizing danger facing metropolitan regions, and many local governments within regions, is imbalance or disequilibrium that leads to polarizing extremes of spatial concentrations of wealth and poverty (Lucy and Phillips 2000, p.43).

The fate of neighborhoods and entire jurisdictions depend upon their ability to retain a healthy base of middle-to-upper status groups and a diversified business base with some high-end service sector employment. Newer housing developments and population growth concentrate in fringe areas and the loss of farmland in ex-urban areas is substantially higher in current metropolitan regions. Housing prices are higher in newer areas and investment to replenish an older housing stock is not available to revitalize suburbs. Smaller size jurisdictions, generally of lower-income, faced the greatest changes in status, but a majority of previously higher-status suburbs lost relative status as well (Lucy and Phillips 2000). In these newer environments, status persistence of suburbs is not a given. The dangers in these new metropolitan forms amplify because of the high rates of residential mobility existing in such forms, with renters moving more often than homeowners. Lucy and Phillips (2000) suggest these rates of mobility, averaging 50 percent over a five-year period, increase competition among suburban jurisdictions in retaining residents with sufficient resources to pay taxes, maintain the housing stock, and ensure stable and safe residential environments (p. 15).

Beginning late in the post-suburban era, an even newer metropolitan form is emerging. Lang (2003) describes the post-polycentric metropolitan form, which involves offices moving to the fringes of metropolitan areas and spread of these offices and housing across a vast land area as compared to higher-density patterns in traditional primary downtowns, secondary suburban downtowns, and Edge Cities. One component of this new form, called 'edgeless cities', involved new settlements far from significant concentrations of retail activity lacking discernible boundaries (Lang 2003; Lang and LeFurgy 2003). Lang and LeFurgy (2003) explain:

> In contrast to Edge Cities, which combine large-scale office development with major retail, Edgeless Cities feature mostly isolated office buildings spread across vast swaths of urban space. These blips of office development lack a discernible boundary and are therefore edgeless (p. 428).

Lang's (2003) study of rental office space in the largest metropolitan regions in the United States found that low-density edgeless cities account for nearly the same amount of leased space as primary downtowns, almost twice that of Edge Cities, and six times that of suburban downtowns (Lang 2003, pp. 54-57). This varied by metropolitan area with some metropolitan regions, such as New York, still having a strong concentration in the primary downtown area and Dallas, which had the highest levels of concentration in Edge Cities (6 percentage points greater of office space in these cities than edgeless cities). These scholars also present an interesting approach to characterizing the debate on new metropolitan forms. Centrists see the emergence of central places in suburbs in metropolitan forms with the same forces of agglomeration previously applicable to dominant cores now relevant to suburban places. Dominant suburbs or suburban central places in multinucleated metropolitan regions provide examples of such centripetal forces (Hughes 1993). Irwin and Hughes (1992) note:

> The metropolitan community is seen to be evolving into a complex system of places, each dominating specific geographic or economic sectors. These smaller systems are incorporated in a multilevel hierarchy. Thus, rather than becoming unidimensional, the metropolitan hierarchy becomes an intricate constellation of differentially dominant places (p. 27).

Lang and LeFurgy (2003) see the decentrist perspective as providing insights into the new forces driving metropolitan form. This newer perspective views the old forces of the separation of land uses (residential, commercial, and industrial) and specialization in function as less applicable. Lang (2003), using the work of Robert Fishman, explains that the decentrist perspective views an individual's use of daily space and personal mobility as key to new metropolitan forms:

> The key element in Fishman's view structural framework is what he refers to as "household networks." Three major household networks exist, based around personal contacts,

consumptive desires, and productive requirements....More important, these networks overlap and in most ways are unrelated to one another; correspondingly, each also possesses its own "spatial logic" (p. 18).

According to this viewpoint, today, household and firm location decisions less obviously link with each other. Decisions on the location of retail activities governed by marketing and physical accessibility considerations differ from locating schools near school-age populations. The absence of suburban retail activities in edgeless cities differs from the development of Edge Cities (Lang 2003). The increased spatial extent of metropolitan regions partly explains these new trends. The result is more spatially delimited activity spaces spread over a large land area (Frey and Speare 1992). With these new forms, we have mini-regions nested within larger metropolitan regions with the size of the suburban core varying significantly or lacking a traditional core.

The spread of activities in suburbs and outlying parts of the metropolitan landscape results in a less centrally patterned mix of land uses, activity spaces, and commuting patterns. An important point derived from this work is that in today's metropolitan environments, more so in the past, suburbs and other metropolitan entities serve dual functions of residence and employment, with a lesser concentration of each functional type. However, in larger and older metropolitan regions, a significant number of suburbs remain primarily residential with little or no employment and industry and a smaller number still serve as employment and industrial centers with very low residential populations. Nevertheless, classification of suburbs into different functional types must recognize this increased decentralizing dual function tendencies in metropolitan regions.

It is clear that Fishman - as do Lucy and Phillips (2000) - focuses on residential and personal mobility as being critical to present metropolitan forms. While residential mobility has increased, one should be careful in assuming that all individuals and groups in metropolitan regions have the same levels of mobility. Further, these approaches reflect a tendency in the literature to examine residential environments independently of employment environments, which misses the inherent diversity of suburban types. Lang (2003) suggests that new metropolitan forms are subject to both centralized and decentralized tendencies and a singular perspective ignores the multiplex realities of metropolitan regions. Ultimately, the debates between centrists and decentrists and questions about the degree of residential mobility reflect the fact that the new metropolitan forms contain elements from the past, but with newer elements interacting to produce different and unique forms and patterns.

This brief review of the phases of suburban expansion suggests that suburbs differentiate along numerous dimensions and have done so throughout their development and ascendancy. A competitive hierarchy of suburbs exists, in which suburbs have distinct land use profiles and different levels of status derived from populations and employment in their boundaries. Suburbs compete to attract suitable land uses and types of population that maximize their composite status. Additionally, people compete to locate in places offering a wide range of amenities (Weiher 1991). To some extent, this competition results in sorting of population and businesses and demonstrates the presence of exclusionary tendencies in metropolitan regions (Cion 1971; Danielson 1976). Adding the fragmentation of local suburban governments that accompany suburban expansions, the importance of these place characteristics substantially increases inequalities and further patterns the suburban hierarchy. These place characteristics and attributes locate in complex and constantly changing ways across the metropolis.

The last waves of suburban expansion have seen relatively higher levels of the suburbanization of poverty and wealth, minority populations, and suburban employment concentrations. Suburban diversity reflects the increased diversity of population and economic activities found generally in metropolitan regions and many other parts of the nation. In large metropolitan regions, we see the growth of affordable housing further away from the core parts of the metropolitan region (Baldassare 1986). Thus, even the housing stock has become diversified and less easily determined by measures of distance to the core and age of housing stock. The ability of suburbs to control such a wide range and diversity of trends lessens as forces derived from various sources result in a large number of unintended and unplanned changes (Lucy and Phillips 2000).

Suburbs do not have complete discretion and control of their own destinies as different types of actors inside and outside their boundaries make decisions more consistent with their self-interests rather than for the collective good of the suburb. This reflects the reality that the operation of housing and labor markets critical to the suburban hierarchy works through the market or private mechanisms. Both populations and employers can move, while local governments must manage and direct growth and decline. The unevenness in the development of suburbs also suggests that suburban diversity and the suburban hierarchy involve both private and public mechanisms. The motives behind incorporation and suburban expansion as well as decline are a product of different actors, individuals and groups, businesses, and local governments, who bring different resources and capabilities to influence these processes and mechanisms. Suburbanization is ultimately a patterned and selective process.

Two major theories informing one of suburban diversity with explicit attention to the selective nature of suburbanization are: i). spatial assimilation and ii). place stratification or consolidated advantages. The former examines group level differences in suburbanization as the product of different abilities of individuals and/or groups to convert socio-economic achievements into residential returns (suburban residence). Some racial/ethnic groups tend to have different experiences in assimilation and acculturation to suburban life (African Americans are considered to be the least assimilated with the socio-economic institutions of broader American society).

In general in these models, suburban life provides considerable advantages for its residents through homeownership and stable property values to high quality schools to increased status and desirability. The majority of empirical testing in spatial assimilation models is at the individual/group levels and structural and organizational factors are used as controls in multivariate regression models. As residence in suburbia is the primary outcome being measured, spatial assimilation theory suffers from neglect of suburban diversity occurring through changes in function (i.e., employment centered suburbs) and increased diversity in suburban socioeconomic status. Nevertheless, these models are consistent with findings from the place stratification model with regard to the racial/ethnic differences in minority suburbanization (D. Harris 1999). The place stratification model incorporates both racial and place stratification mechanisms in differentiating suburbs. The stratification of places occurs through social status mechanisms, whereby more advantaged groups differentiate themselves from more resource deprived and lower status groups by living in higher-status areas. These advantaged groups with higher levels of a diverse range of resources and power, including business elites (industrialists and real estate developers), high-status individuals and groups, and select local government leaders, promote growth as inherently good for the collective population of the entire metropolitan region. The existence of suburban stratification and hierarchy of places is at the heart of the place stratification approach:

> Similarly, place inequality is both cause and consequence of differences among places. Those in control of the top places use place status to maintain privileges for their locations, often at the expense of the lesser locales. Often with the help of place-based organizations, they manipulate transportation routes, secure desired zoning, and keep out unwanted social groups (Logan and Molotch 1987, p. 49).

Competition is inherent in the suburban system. Places compete for certain types of residents and businesses. Further, suburban places compete not only for high-status groups but also for investments and capital (Logan and Molotch 1987, p. 42).

Racial stratification mechanisms involve limiting the movement of particular racial/ethnic groups and their channeling into lower-status areas. Racial discrimination in housing and the lack of affordable housing in higher-status suburbs contribute to the selective nature of minority suburbanization. The distribution of locational amenities across suburbs and locational attainment into particular suburbs are crucial manifestations of place stratification. The richer suburbs provide for a wide range of amenities for their residents including good schools, shopping, and crime-free environments, all of these are lacking in lower-status and minority dominated suburbs.

There are numerous advantages to the place stratification approach. First, it recognizes that minority suburbanization is selective and certain racial/ethnic groups have lower rates of suburbanization than other groups. Fong and Shibuya (2000) found that place stratification effects where strongest for African-Americans with low rates of suburban home ownership for these groups. These populations also had disproportionately higher rates of suburban renting; Whites and Asians have the highest rates of home ownership. The approach also helps to understand that the racial/ethnic composition of the area correlates strongly with amenities, quality of life, and life-chances (Hwang and Murdock 1998a). Race and class directly link with larger numbers of lower-status minority groups living in a selective number of suburbs. Alba et al. (1999) make an important point that the impact of suburbanization is group and context specific and suburbanization does not involve a uniform process in all situations (pp. 131-132).

Second, the place stratification approach directly addresses differences in status and political power between suburbs and the organized competition for power and status in metropolitan areas. Other approaches ignore competition by places and collectively organized actors and focus on competition between disconnected actors (e.g., individual land users). It is not simply an aggregation of individual decisions that result in suburban inequalities and diversity, but the purposeful and organized actions of particular powerful groups to increase the status of their places and control the movement of populations, housing, and employment into their jurisdictions. A related third advantage of the place stratification approach is that it recognizes the inherent interdependence underlying patterns in the suburban hierarchy. This involves functional interdependence (as well as status interdependence):

> The types of suburbs which evolve are functionally interdependent-the growth of employing suburbs depends upon the availability of new housing in residential suburbs, while many of the residents of exclusive residential suburbs work elsewhere in the region (Logan 1976, p. 340).

With the place stratification model, suburban status inequalities are excepted outcomes, which reflects and results in further increased inequalities in suburban status. Logan (1978) explains:

> I argue that the differentiation of places implies sets of advantages and disadvantages for persons who are tied to each place and this affects the chances for individual upward or downward mobility...I hypothesize that spatial differentiation tends to be transformed over time into an increasingly rigid stratification of places (p. 404).

Place stratification theorists purposefully contrasted their approach against other approaches that ignored the underlying stratification of places and people. Places and actors have different levels of resources and autonomy (power), which is suggestive that place abilities to benefit from the current metropolitan hierarchy differ as well. Other approaches minimize the underlying stratification of places and people in terms of status and resources. The other approaches specifically contrasted include the ecological, economic, and public choice perspectives. Logan and Molotch (1987) write about the public choice model for example:

> Some places do indeed end up with nicer packages than others, but these are for the most part nicer for anybody. The real differences between jurisdictions-between good schools and lousy ones, smooth streets and rutted ones, well-connected neighbors or powerless ones-are intercorrelated and determined primarily by social class. The public choice model trivializes the inequalities that develop among places by treating these inequalities as differences in taste (p. 42).

Similarly, ecological models tend to suggest that differences in status and resources are natural processes and result from the aggregation and interaction of individual actors. The stratification of actors is mostly ignored.

The limitations of the place stratification approach relate to its advantages. The approach emphasizes the residential characteristics (versus the employment characteristics) of places, treats outcomes for actors rather than places as the focus of examination, and fails to use place characteristics as influential in shaping place outcomes. Hwang and Murdock (1998a) suggest that empirical testing of place stratification models has not adequately incorporated place characteristics:

> Place characteristics which, according to the place stratification model, differentiate suburbs in terms of their exclusiveness and desirability (Berry et. al. 1976), are often not used as independent variables in those analyses. Instead, suburban characteristics (e.g., the proportion of population which is Anglo, opportunities of minority-Anglo contact, and median household income) are often used as outcome variables, with their variation among different minority groups being explained by individual and group characteristics. Although metropolitan characteristics have been included in several analyses (e.g., Alba and Logan 1991; Massey and Denton 1987, 1988) as controls for structural context, few empirical examinations of the place stratification model (e.g., Alba and Logan 1991; Logan, Alba, and Leung 1996) have focused on measures specific for suburbs (p. 116).

Rather, similar to spatial assimilation models of suburbia, testing has considered suburban characteristics as the outcomes of different racial/ethnic group actors. Treating place characteristics as independent, rather than dependent or outcome variables, also necessitates the examination of the full composite of place characteristics, which relate to both functions and the status of suburbs. With regard to function, past research applying the place stratification model has emphasized residential functions over employment ones. The place stratification approach acknowledges the diversity of functions. Logan and Molotch (1987) discuss three major types of suburbs, affluent employing suburbs, working class residential suburbs, and exclusive residential towns (pp. 187-192). However, the diversity of suburbs on function and status are not fully specified and a majority of the testing of this approach examines residential functions almost exclusively.

Suburbs are obviously both places of residence and of work, ignoring these multiple functions may lead to incomplete analyses and inferences. Even if a suburb is primarily residential, for example, the absence of employment in this type of suburb must be established and not assumed. Further, classifying residential suburbs along status dimensions is a useful step in distinguishing between these types of suburbs. Place characteristics specific to differentiating suburbs are assessed by examining the function (as a place of work and place of residence) and status (ranking of desirability and exclusiveness of suburbs) of each jurisdiction.

Hwang and Murdock (1998b) test the place stratification model by defining the ideal suburban life as a cultural goal promoted by broader American society. Using a version of the anomie-and-the opportunity structures paradigm to explain suburbanization by different racial/ethnic groups, they argue that the means available for different groups to achieve a positive suburban image are distributed unevenly through socio-economic structures and that higher-status suburbs use explicit policies to limit access of lower-status and particular racial/ethnic groups to these areas. They criticize economic and ecological approaches for ignoring differences in means between individuals and groups located in different suburbs. The authors (Hwang and Murdock 1998b) state their position on this issue:

> The rationale for the synthesis is that, although the ecological and economic perspectives are necessary for understanding why suburbanization is occurring, they are insufficient to explain the selective nature of the suburbanization process. Both the ecological and economic explanations of suburbanization are color- and class-blind, and as such, they are not be able to explain why certain groups in this society are more likely to be involved in suburbanization than other groups. We believe that suburbanization can be better understood by combining ecological and economic explanations with a sociological perspective that views social

behaviors as normatively guided yet structurally constrained by the man-made environment (Merton 1968) (p. 271).

Their model predicts the movement of different groups into different types of suburbs through incorporation of the level of attractiveness between suburbs and concerns of affordability motivating and structuring such movements. While their model moves toward direct testing of the place stratification model through characterization of places, it tends to focus more on the residential functions and statuses of suburbs and ignores the interdependency of residential and employment functions leading to particular spatial patterns of suburbanization. The largest problem with this and other approaches applying the place stratification approach has to do with studying suburbs from multiple metropolitan regions together. Intra-metropolitan variation on function and status and the different and unique contexts of metropolitan regions must be incorporated in future applications. Hwang and Murdock (1998a) understand and control for contextual effects using the central city as the basis for comparison:

> The sharing of a common metropolitan identity by several suburbs is likely to create unique contextual effects. For example, while suburbanites in Boston may consider a 40-mile commuting trip to be too far, the same distance is likely to be viewed differently by Los Angeles' commuters...Besides the explicit benefits of controlling for contextual effects, the relative measures used allow us to incorporate into our measures the conventional wisdom that mobility decisions are often made by evaluating the relative utility of the place of origin and destination (Lee 1966) (p.128).

In fact, the operationalization of dependent (rates of suburbanization for different racial/ethnic groups) and independent (image, structural, and other control indicators) variables in their model uses the central city as the relevant base of comparison (Hwang and Murdock 1998a, 1998b). This method of comparison is useful, but still focuses on old metropolitan forms.

Metropolitan regions are spreading and growing outward so that the dominance of the core and other secondary centers is declining. While the central city may be a valid comparison for inner-ring and more closely located suburbs, suburbs located in the fringes of metropolitan regions (at considerable distances from the core) cannot be expected to have similar residential functions with their closer employment sub centers as with the central city. In fact, they may serve as bedroom communities for employment sub-centers in close proximity. Further, individual suburbs and/or surrounding suburbs may have significant concentrations of employment and business activity in particular economic and industrial sectors. Functionally, suburbs are less specialized than in the past, housing some economic sector activities. Retail establishments tend to spread across the metropolitan region. The likelihood of being exclusively residential in function is less than in the past.

In addition, measuring differences in status across suburbs requires closer attention to the relevant comparison base. Although central cities and employment sub-centers tend to have both residential and employment functions, the crucial relationships with surrounding residential suburbs have to do with the employment function. Higher-status suburban employment suburbs more likely are surrounded by or in close proximity to higher-status residential suburbs. The same would be likely with low-status employment and residential suburbs. Similarly for retail oriented suburbs, the nature of the surrounding suburbs and the interactions between the retail suburb and these contiguous suburbs are of primary importance in defining its function and status. Past approaches have standardized both dependent and independent variables using metropolitan statistical areas as the appropriate base of comparison; however, the more appropriate base should be the county a place is located in or for further located suburbs, the nearest county in addition to county location.

Function, Status, and Suburban Types

A recent national report on U.S. metropolitan regions reviewed and evaluated numerous research studies on metropolitan specific problems (Altshuler et al. 1999). While focused on the existence of inequalities of opportunities and outcomes and the role of metropolitan governance in ameliorating these disparities, the National Research Council (NRC) sponsored report clearly pointed to the major challenges facing urban studies and policy researchers and practitioners. One of the major challenges given a higher priority was the need for researchers to move beyond crude central city-suburban distinctions in order to understand the nature and extent of metropolitan disparities. The report recommends the following:

> Efforts are urgently needed to classify jurisdictions within metropolitan areas on more sensitive dimensions, such as condition or function, and to use these classifications both for descriptive and for research purposes. We need to move beyond simple comparisons of central city and suburb so as to compare jurisdictions by income (poor, middle-income, wealthy), by fiscal capacity (high, medium, low), and by function (residential, commercial, industrial, mixed). This will require not only research on how to classify jurisdictions within metropolitan areas, but also a reaggregation of data into the relevant classification categories (Altshuler et al. 1999, p.119).

Irwin and Hughes (1992) raise the same challenge to researchers and practitioners:

> These results also call into question the ability of broad spatial constructs, such as "metropolitan areas," "center city," and "suburb" to capture meaningful sociopatial units. Within the Anaheim/Santa Ana/Garden Grove SMSA (Figure 4A) for instance, Fullerton and Yorba Linda are very clearly different types of suburbs; yet they are typically classified together when dichotomies such as "center city/suburb" are used. Changes affecting the "suburbs" may not affect Fullerton and Yorba Linda equivalently. Thus, a sociological interpretation of social phenomena, such as the suburbanization of crime and poverty, may be clouded by disparate trends among communities (p. 45).

A significant amount of research on suburbs recognizes the need for refined and accurate dimensions in differentiating suburbs. Additionally, past research on explaining suburbanization and differences between suburbs in the United States has acknowledged the need for classification of suburbs (Friedman, 1994; Hughes, 1993; Logan and Semyonov 1980; Logan and Golden, 1986; Stahura, 1987). Schnore developed the most popularly used typology with three categories of suburbs: residential, intermediate, and employing. The employment to resident workers in specific sectors (trade and manufacturing) differentiated residential from employment suburbs with residential suburbs having a ratio of one half jobs to every worker and employing suburbs more jobs than workers. The types of suburbs evenly divided among the three types, which surprised many viewing suburbs as mainly residential.

Orfield (2002), building on past research, has developed a newer classification scheme of suburbs centering on fiscal capacity. Suburbs have been classified based on a variety of indicators including tax revenues and spending on services, distance to central city, age of suburbs and housing, jobs-housing ratio, employees to residents ratio, population growth, network position, industry specialization, and property tax base per capita (Logan and Schneider, 1981; Logan and Molotch, 1987). Some examples of classified suburbs include working class residential suburbs, high-income exclusive residential suburbs, single-use versus mixed-use suburbs, suburban employment centers, and suburban satellites (Cervero, 1989; Logan and Molotch, 1987).

Others have recommended classification schemes based on employment concentrations, population size, and population density. Under the auspices of the Office of Management and Budget (OMB) Metropolitan Area Standards Review Committee, proposals to change the OMB's metropolitan area (MA) standards focused on the identification of significant centers of employment, trade, entertainment, and other social and economic activities. OMB (2000) recommended the dropping of central cities in identifying areas arguing that their dominance has decreased in metropolitan settings. Instead, the committee recommended the use of principal cities. These include a). the largest incorporated place or census designated place (CDP) of a core based statistical area along with b).additional incorporated places or CDPs with population of 250,000 or in which 100,000 persons work and c). additional incorporated places or CDPs with a minimum population of 10,000, one-third the size of the largest place, and in which employment meets or exceeds the number of employed residents (OMB 2000). The third type of principal city, while smaller in population than a traditional central city, emerges as a significant settlement pattern in modern metropolitan regions as a localized employment center.

Frey and Speare (1992) in a study for the committee recommended use of the employment to working residential-population ratio to characterize suburban and other non-core employment centers. That work identified three major types of settlement patterns: a). Urban Centers – municipalities or county subdivision areas with high employment/population ratios that satisfy minimum population and density requirements; b). Primary Residential Areas – places or county subdivision areas with low employment/population ratios and residential in character; and c). Primary Employment Areas – places or subcounty areas that are urban, but do not meet population size and density requirements to be classified as urban and have high employment/population ratios (Frey and Speare 1992). Frey and Speare (1992) explain the logic of this classification scheme:

> This proposal advocates defining settlement areas on a purely functional basis in light of the decoupling of resident-workers' activity spaces and local labor market areas from older physical configurations. These activity spaces can now occur totally within the "suburbs" or "nomteropolitan territory" as they are classed under the present system... They are based simply on the assumption that community and local labor market activities cluster within spatially delimited areas (p. 31).

In a different study extending the original work, Frey and Geverdt (1998) develop a more detailed and specific typology to analyze metropolitan regions. This typology has five categories, two employment centers (inner and outer), two residential suburbs (inner and outer), and a low density one. The inner and outer distinction uses distance to the center of the major city as the measure of differentiation with inner places being 10 miles or less from the major city. The employment/residence (E/R) ratio and a measure of the extent that resident workers work in their place of residence differentiate employment centers from residential suburbs. The authors place great significance on the E/R ratio, but recognize that classifying suburbs as employment centers requires additional criteria. These include a substantial amount (40 percent) of the residential working population working in their place of residence and places with populations of at least 10,000. Population size and density are the criteria that differentiate residential suburbs from low-density areas (low-density areas can include entire counties in this typology) (p. 12). Residential suburbs must have populations of at least 10,000 and a population density of 1000 persons per square mile. Applying this typology to study race-ethnicity and demographic patterns in the Los Angeles, Atlanta, and Detroit metropolitan areas, Frey and Geverdt (1998) find that the number of each type of suburbs varies across these three metropolitan regions. Los Angeles had the largest numbers of outer centers and suburbs with Detroit having the largest numbers of inner centers and suburbs. A majority of the growth of population is taking place in outer centers and suburbs and low-density areas (pp. 12-13).

These typologies represent new approaches to study changing metropolitan forms and settlement patterns in highly suburbanized regions. They combine traditional measures of employment concentration, population size and density, fiscal capacity, and distance to cores to distinguish suburbs. However, most notably, these typologies focus on identifying functional differences and do not examine existing status differences across suburban places as criteria of suburban differentiation (Ashton 1984). Rather, these studies ascertain status differences only after using functional criteria to distinguish suburbs. This is a dramatically different focus than that of the place stratification approach, which focuses almost exclusively on status. More importantly, the place stratification approach suggests that status differences themselves lead to the functional and status stratification of suburbs.

A number of reasons could explain the neglect of status and the emphasis on function in newer typologies. For one, functional attributes of suburbs such as their housing stock, manufacturing plants, and office buildings within their boundaries are more enduring and fixed. Functional attributes concern the physical or built environment characteristics of suburbs. The type and quantity of land use in an area changes, but physical environmental constraints, among other constraints, limit the possibility of increasing land uses indefinitely or even having particular land uses. Status attributes, as they involve populations of persons, families, and households, are subject to greater change as population units move more frequently and the characteristics of the resident populations may not correspond to the enduring characteristics of suburbs. Additionally, the daytime populations of visitors and workers contribute to the overall status of a suburban jurisdiction, but their characteristics are not easily measured. Statuses are the building blocks of social structures, which make up the social, cultural, and economic environments of suburban areas and their residential and less-permanent populations. These social and economic environments are located in physical as well as social and economic space applying to individual and group actors. In other words, social and economic structures, unlike physical environments, lack fixed physical location and/or clear boundaries.

Secondly, related to the first point, status is much more difficult to measure than function. The number of statuses of population groups is usually greater than the limited number of land uses in a given area. Individuals and groups occupy statuses, but the number and types of statuses is determined through the actions and interactions between these actors. That is, the number of status positions and the organization and distribution of statuses is beyond the control of a single individual or group. A status system or social structure reflects an arrangement of elements (positions in a hierarchy for example) that may be specific to a small subset of a population or involve entire nations. Status heterogeneity within ecological and social structures is much more likely to be greater than heterogeneity of land uses or other functional attributes. Status is a multi-dimensional construct embodying elements of power and resources of individuals and groups who have multiple statuses. The accepted concepts of achieved and ascribed status in sociology alert us to the countless combinations of status and actors in multiple social structures that one can examine.

Further, status embodies norms and values through the performance of roles - these cultural elements are intangible and not easy to measure. Finally, status is a more controversial and sensitive issue than function. Altshuler et al. (1999) alluded to the controversy in the use of income and fiscal measures in the quote above, which involve labeling of entire suburban places on status bases. One possibility relating to the controversy behind status differences is that these dimensions capture the competitive and divisive nature of the suburban hierarchy:

> This is because, in general, problems perceived to involve the redistribution of important resources-income, employment, tax base, social status and values, access to valued locations-are more intrinsically divisive, since they are seen to be "zero-sum" in nature, that is, creating winners and losers...In general, it is the system maintenance and common-purpose problems that are the easiest to solve. Problems involving the redistribution of resources but not necessarily involving changes in social access and interaction are considerably more difficult to address. Problems whose solutions require redistribution of resources and redistribution in terms of life-style and access have proven the most intractable (Altshuler et al. 1999, p. 14).

Local government officials, businesses, and populations living and working in suburbs of lower-status suburbs are reluctant to publicize these disparities in fear of losing valuable resources (Chapman 1981). Status more directly captures the hierarchical differences between the residential populations of suburbs. Marcuse (2001) argues that among the three dimensions dividing cities and metropolitan regions, culture/ethnicity, function, and status, status is the most problematic. His logic is that cultural and functional differences taken by themselves are non-hierarchical, result from voluntary actions of individual and group actors, and are generally tolerated and accepted. On the other hand, status and power differences and clustering of populations with differential levels of status and power are hierarchical and non-voluntary, imposed on groups by others (Marcuse 1997).

Marcuse (2001) further points out that status divisions are not to be tolerated and the state (local government mainly) reinforces these status distinctions by failing to regulate populations and businesses seeking to maximize their own status and power and not the overall status and power of their collectivities and the broader metropolitan region. As such, status differences are rooted in differences in a multitude of types of power. This is why Marcuse (2001) puts blame on the state, who having a monopoly of legal, military, and political power in metropolitan areas, fails to use its powers to eliminate segregation by race/ethnicity, status and related divisions. Marcuse (2001) recognizes that status differences can derive from functional divisions (e.g., separation of land uses) and both culture and functional divisions combined with status differences can lead to the formation of segregated enclaves and ghettos. These enclaves and ghettos may be exclusionary in some cases so that only certain populations and land uses locate within their boundaries. Other areas will have only single land uses or combine populations and establishments of a particular status. As a result, differences in power and status maintain the hierarchies of cities and metropolitan regions and the different types of settlement patterns.

This reluctance to study status differences between suburbs is real. However, developing approaches incorporating both functional and status divisions between suburbs is possible (Ashton 1977; Hoch 1984, 1985). To help examine and explain property and violent crimes across suburban Los Angeles, we develop a two-part typology centered on the functional and status characteristics of suburban jurisdictions below. It is critical to point out the differences between the proposed typology and existing typologies. The proposed typology centers on function and status as place characteristics (rather than characteristics of individuals and groups) and the spatial and locational distribution of these characteristics across suburbs. As a whole, place characteristics represent the physical, social, and economic environmental conditions existing in each suburb. The distribution of these conditions into particular suburban environments are influenced by a variety of status-driven processes such as zoning in the case of land uses and housing stock and the requirement of a certain level of education for jobs and the concentration of particular occupational groups in suburban residences. Note that status differences are less physically bounded and/or specific to jurisdictions - as the locations of social and economic space do not correspond directly with jurisdictional space. Functional characteristics strongly correspond to the conditions of the physical environments in places, although differentiating on status elements as well. This includes the value of the housing stock in a suburb, which differs across places. Functional characteristics partly distinguish the quantity and quality of different types of property in suburbs. From the routine activities perspective, where opportunities are viewed as attractive and suitable targets, the functional characteristics of a place strongly associates with different types of property crimes in a suburban jurisdiction. To clarify, these associations between functional place characteristics and property crime rates are probabilistic and not deterministic. Further, we attempt to explain if these characteristics of suburban environments relate to their crime problems (or lack of them), not to identify the causes of functional and status attributes. Instead, we are interested in how function and status distribute (locate) across the metropolitan region and its suburbs.

Following Merton, the prevailing conditions (physical and non-physical) in a jurisdiction determine the composite resource profile of an area. Resources can only be accessed and used by actors and thus, higher levels of high-value property are not equated with higher levels of resources for actors living and working in these suburban jurisdictions. Rather, access to resources relates to positioning in social and economic structures. It is in these structures, where the ultimate values to different types of property and targets are given. Resource abundance in an area refers to the higher-value and status of property characteristics located in a suburb. The determinants of resource abundance partly fall outside of the inherent characteristics of properties themselves, but result from the operations of different social structures and actors. Property markets for office buildings, for example, involve actors of various types seeking to maximize their statuses in these markets. In fact, the general rule assumed in this typology and the following analysis is that population units and actors want to maximize statuses of all types.

Status characteristics specific to places reference conditions having to do with the social and economic environments in suburbs. This includes the unemployment rate, for example, which measures the percentage of the residential working population without employment. Although this can be a short-lived condition in a suburb influenced by various macro and micro forces, this condition represents an objective situation for the residential population attempting to maximize their employment status. It certainly reflects more directly the environments of this suburban place in that suitable jobs for the residential working population are not available, but cannot tell us about job availability in other suburbs in the metropolitan region. Some functional measures such as the employment/residence ratio do tell us if a suburb has a high concentration of jobs in an area, but the unemployment rate in this jurisdiction does not necessarily relate to the working population in a suburb. Population units including individual persons, households, and families, as well as subsets of these population units, measure status conditions. These are place characteristics about the types of populations residing in a suburb. Determining suburban or place status is a relative exercise since complete status homogeneity of residential populations is unlikely. Place status approximates the types of conditions that residential populations in a jurisdiction are likely facing.

Status clustering of all types reveals the presence of some enduring conditions specific to jurisdictions. These conditions, if truly enduring, help us to determine the resource profile of a jurisdiction. Favorable conditions allow for easier access to resources by particular status groups (usually having high levels of resources and higher status). These groups are able to accumulate more resources under these conditions. Generally, the types of conditions and the resources derived from them allowing for accumulation of resources associate with high-status places with favorable physical and non-physical environments. The reverse is true for low-resource groups.

Resource deprivation of all types that place limits on maximizing status (again, of different types) will increase the likelihood of violent crimes in suburbs as actors compete among themselves for the remaining scare resources. The effects of status-motivated resource deprivation are more likely to be indirect with other intervening factors determining violent outcomes. Research has linked resource deprivation and high rates of violent crimes in many types of environments including suburbs (Land et al. 1990; Vold et al. 2002). Disputes and conflicts are more likely to end in lethal violence in these environments through various unspecified reasons. Using the anomie-and-opportunity structures paradigm, resource deprivation links with higher violent crime rates because it increases the likelihood of structural strain and limited resources combining to increase the likelihood of criminal (innovation) adaptations. Motivational and resource elements interact to produce concentrations of violent criminal choices or adaptations. This perspective is inherently structural, in which objective situations or conditions, rather than situations subjectively experienced by actors, influence the location of structural strain, limited resources, and crime choices in social space. This may coincide with physical space, as status measures reference residential population units more directly relevant for violent crimes. Before detailing and operationalizing the suburban typology, a final note of caution is required.

Analyses of any typology examining characteristics of places and populations are subject to faulty inferences and fallacies. These include the widely known ecological fallacy, whereby generalizations about individuals and populations derive directly from the characteristics of ecological units. These fallacies are reflective of a problem of using data at one level of analysis (residents of the city of Los Angeles and metropolitan Los Angeles for example) for particular units of analysis (individual residents and suburban places) to test individual criminal behavior and suburban crime and violence rates. Testing of hypotheses about crime and violence rates must use data on suburban places and data collected on individuals and their characteristics is not appropriate for testing these relationships. An example of this relevant for our purposes is generalizations about African Americans and high violent crime rates based on the quite common finding of higher violent crime rates and the percentage of the population that is African American in a substantial amount of research. The inference of the violent nature of African Americans from this finding remains poorly specified and is not obvious. Generalizing to all African Americans based on this finding demonstrates faulty reasoning and incorrect inferences. A variety of interpretations and inferences are possible, including the lack of social control and social capital in African American neighborhoods or the lower-status of African American dominated areas. Each interpretation is subject to empirical testing if applied to the African American population or individuals and groups not places. Structurally-based explanations for rates of crime and violence, on the other hand, require data on extra-individual and group units. Further, this fallacy reminds us that characteristics of structural entities do not tell us about the degree of homogeneity of extra-individual units with regard to particular characteristics such as the statuses of the residential African American population. Multiple place indicators capture the composite character of a place in more meaningful ways than single indicator based models.

These place characteristics derive from data on housing, employment, and demographics available through the Economic Censuses (EC) and the Censuses of Population and Housing (CPH). The former surveys establishments and the later dataset surveys households and persons. For disclosure and confidentiality reasons, both the EC and CPH do not contain data on the specific characteristics of establishments and households. The Economic Censuses provide data on employment, total number of establishments, and total sales in major economic sectors (retail, wholesale, services, manufacturing) for each suburban location. Employment data helps to establish whether a suburb is an employing center with larger daytime working populations and smaller residential populations. These are place of work data and no information on the characteristics of the working population and/or the physical structures is available. If a suburb provides employment functions by hosting businesses and employers, one would anticipate that a particular mix of land uses and physical structures (property) locate in this suburb. Establishment and sales data provide no clear indication of the composite status of a suburban jurisdiction or the mix of properties and their values by location. These data are conceptually similar to employment in that they provide information on the concentration or lack of concentration of economic activity in suburban locations.

Function, as employed here, is a term referring to the nature and extent of identifiable and patterned activities providing structured access and use to a significant number of groups and individuals. An employment function signifies the presence of businesses employing individuals and producing goods and providing services within the boundaries of a suburb. Residential functions refer to the types of housing available (or lack of) for residence.

Economic censuses are available every five years since 1967 for some economic sectors for places greater than 2500 in population. Data are also available for a select number of jurisdictions with a large number of establishments and employment. The economic base and the sectoral composition of jurisdictions can be determined from these censuses. Status data of the residential populations derive from the CPH. These are place of residence data on the characteristics of different population units, households, families, and persons as well as a few measures on area (total population and land area) and housing stock (type, age, and value) of suburbs. These population data include labor force, industry and occupational, racial/ethnic, demographic, and household (based on housing units) characteristics. The residential function of an area derives from the types of housing structures (e.g., single-unit) existing in a suburb. Data on population units help determine the composite profile of a suburb on many types of status. For example, we can speak about tenure status, employment status, or educational status. As with EC data, these are place summary level data and the CPH provides only overall characteristics of places, but no data is available on specific characteristics of population units. That is, information on the overall number of population units in a particular category is available, but no data is available specific to population units.

Demographic and socioeconomic characteristics represent status dimensions in this typology. These dimensions reflect characteristics of population units associated with different types of status including employment, income, poverty, and ethnic status as well as the different types of household status. Using the definition of status as a social position in a social structure, one uses information on the status characteristics of a place to approximate the particular social and economic conditions and potential access to resources associated with these conditions. Labor characteristics apply to the residential working population helping us to determine the employment and education status of this population. A suburb with a high unemployment rate suggests that population units in this place face unfavorable conditions providing low levels of resources and will be of lower-status. Finally, housing status characteristics of households in these suburbs help to assess the tenure status and other relevant household attributes.

Demographic/socioeconomic, housing, and labor status characteristics of population units relate to each other in particular ways through common population units. Some demographic, socioeconomic, and household characteristics are collected for households. Data derived from these two categories taken together provide information on the types of households within a jurisdiction. One expects that different indicators correlate with each other so that particular types of households define a place. This explains why place characteristics of median household income correlate with homeownership; a particular level of median household income associates with a particular tenure status. Demographic, socioeconomic, and labor status characteristics link through a particular sub-set of persons, the residential working population. Again, particular labor force characteristics of this population (e.g., employment status) unit may correlate with the demographic and socioeconomic characteristics (e.g., ethnic status) across jurisdictions. Using information on multiple characteristics is more useful to understand the particular nature of suburban jurisdictions. Assessment of the location of conditions and status groups of different types in places is more easily accomplished through use of multiple indicators.

Two primary reasons influenced the selection of these elements in the typology: i). past research has found that differentiating suburbs requires separating outcomes of individuals and groups from characteristics of places and ii). function and status have distinct spatial and locational patterning across suburbs. The first reason to capture suburban diversity concerns avoiding descriptions of places solely based on the demographic and socio-economic profiles of residents and employers in each suburb. Consistent with the place stratification model, it is better to characterize places with regard to the resources they provide for residents and employers rather than to consider places as the end result of individual and group processes only. If it was only a matter of individual and group choice in locational attainment, then the characteristics of a place would matter very little in terms of the functions it provided and the status it embodied.

Table 2 - Typology of Suburban Status and Function

CHARACTERISTICS CATEGORIES	ATTRIBUTE DIMENSION	MEASURING UNIT/CATEGORIES OF INDICATORS	DATA SOURCE	SAMPLE INDICATOR
Demographic and Socio-Economic/Population	Status	Residential Population (Households, Families, and Persons) - Income; Poverty Rate; Household Types; Race/Ethnicity; Nativity Status	Census of Population and Housing (CPH)	Median Household Income
Housing/Property	Function	Housing Stock–Type of Housing; Rent and Value of Housing; Age of Housing	CPH	Housing Property Values
Housing/Population	Status	Residential Population (Households)– Tenure; Persons in Household	CPH	Homeownership
Labor/Population	Status	Residential Working Population – Employment Status; Occupational Status; Industry of Work; Class of Worker; Educational Attainment	CPH	Unemployment Rate
Employment/Functional	Function	Employment in Specific Industries and Sectors	Economic Censuses (EC)	Employment to Residential Working Population (in Specific Economic Sectors) Ratio

Rather, the 'character' of a place is determined through the configuration of conditions located within it and the activity patterns occurring there. From a sociological perspective, the character of a place in terms of the scale, density, and cohesiveness of activities and resources within a definable area needs to be determined to posit structural and contextual conditions as influencing individual and group behavior and adaptations. Further, one cannot explain rates of crime and violence using individual-level data. Rather, independent variables representing place characteristics and conditions are appropriate.

The second issue concerns the distribution of functional and status conditions by spatial location. The basic logic of emphasizing location and patterning is that the distribution of place-specific employment and population characteristics across suburban places expect to exhibit clustering and concentration across suburbs. Places specialize on function and house particular status groups. More specifically, the interaction of function and status leads to concentration of particular types of populations, housing, and employment across suburban places.

While we do not focus on the determinants of function and status, it is clear that the location of housing and jobs results from the operation of housing and labor markets. These markets themselves are segmented so that there are a plurality of submarkets applying to specific types of populations and businesses. Each place tends to differentiate itself from other places by catering to particular groups and actors for particular types of markets. Significant clustering by housing stock, households and populations, and employment defines the unique functional and status attributes of suburbs. For our purposes, the location of particular conditions in the physical and nonphysical environments in suburbs link with the crime (or lack of) mix of these jurisdictions.

By no means are these dimensions and data sources exhaustive or comprehensive; however, they serve as surrogate measures given the lack of data availability and coverage for metropolitan regions. For determination of functional attributes of places, the most direct and telling method would be to use land-use data for each suburb. Banerjee and Verma (2001) examine the land use portfolios of municipalities in Los Angeles County to differentiate places. They use nine different categories of land uses from vacant to low density residential to commercial to industrial. Suburban places differentiate into six different clusters of land uses. The largest cluster includes almost half of the cities with land uses concentrated in low density (mean of 46 percent), medium to high density (12 percent), commercial (11 percent), and the rest spread over a wide range of land uses. The next two largest clusters, which make up seventeen percent of the total municipalities, had concentrations of land use in low density and the other in vacant land and low-density use. Six of the eighty-eight municipalities had high concentrations in industrial land uses with small low-density uses – clearly, these are industrial suburbs. Four cities had a mix of extraction, industrial, transportation, and low-density residential land uses. The remaining cities (four also) had significant use in medium to high density residential land uses. This exercise demonstrates the utility of land use data to differentiate suburbs on function.

Others have suggested using population size or density data and commuting data to assess the functions of suburbs. Larger cities and more dense cities usually have a mix of land uses and provide dual functions. Population size and density are useful to differentiate residential suburbs as seen in Frey and Geverdt's (1998) typology above. However, land areas of municipalities, which are the denominators for population density measures, vary significantly within metropolitan areas and leads to unclear differentiation. Size measures do not specify the functions of suburbs, but indicate the likelihood of mixed functions rather than single functions. Journey to work data is valuable to determine employment and residential functions of suburbs, but place-specific information is not available on these measures.

For status determinations, data based on surveys of residents and employers within each suburb on exclusiveness, desirability, issues of concern, and satisfaction with services would be more appropriate. Survey data capture the view of residents and employers on the quality and quantity of resources in each place. These include the physical and nonphysical environments and their conditions in each suburb. These tell us if a suburb is a destination of choice for a significant number of metropolitan residents and employers. Unfortunately, such data is not readily available, especially for coverage across the metropolitan region.

The Nature and Distribution of Suburban Crime and Violence

A diverse range of research focuses on patterns of suburban crime and violence and explanations for these patterns (Dunn 1980a,1980b; Evans 1995; Harries 1997). The scope and domain of this research varies considerably. Some focus on specific types of crime and deviance including delinquency, property and violent crimes, and in limited cases, single crimes such as arson or burglary. Scope conditions remain poorly specified in these studies as they generally ignore the changed nature of metropolitan environments, where assertions are made of general phenomena like social control, social organization, and affluence to characterize the majority of suburbs. The evidence of high levels of social control in suburbia is lacking and the limited research suggests that suburbs do not exhibit high levels of community organization and bonding between suburban residents (Baumgartner 1988; Palen 1995).

The literature minimally addresses suburban diversity and differentiation, with the exception of a few studies, particularly in terms of place characteristics and their differences. This also reflects a tendency to use and apply theoretical approaches more consistent with old metropolitan forms, earlier periods of history, and dramatically different environments. Additionally, research focuses on different aspects of crime and violence in suburbs, including the consequences of living in high-crime suburbs on mobility of populations and differential exposure of groups to different suburban crime and violence environments. Consequently, the focus of these later approaches differs from one seeking to explain the variation in suburban crime and violence in metropolitan region(s).

The largest (and related) problems with research on suburban crime and violence are the lack of a systematic approach to study both the presence and absence of high crime and violence rates and to examine different types of property and violent crimes. Much of the emphasis is on suburbs with high rates of crime and violence and how these suburbs either attract crime or generate crime. For example, property crimes are higher in suburbs with attractive targets because the presence of attractive targets and violent crimes are higher in suburban areas with the presence of crime-prone populations. The assumption is that areas with low or intermediate rates of property crime and violence lack attractive targets and/or motivated offenders. However, one questions such essentialist thinking that dichotomizes explanatory variables as the variation in both crime and place characteristics differs considerably suburbs. Suburbs have different levels (no matter how low) of property and violent crimes, which differ, but few suburbs lack any attractive targets and/or motivated offenders. Rather, the interactive effects of multiple place characteristics combine to provide the crime profile of jurisdictions. The particular crime problem or lack of any crime problem also present useful information to explain crime and violence patterns within metropolitan regions. The particular patterning of crime and violence rates in specific metropolitan regions are poorly accounted by the literature and the same general factors differentially operate in different metropolitan regions. This is because most of the research analyzes suburbs from multiple metropolitan regions, ignoring contextual aspects of suburban crime and violence.

Research poorly differentiates between categories of property and violent crimes that are more or less prevalent and the extent of association with targets and motivated offenders. Some research recognizes that robberies differ from other violent crimes, especially aggravated assaults (Logan and Messner 1987), residential and non-residential burglaries are subject to different dynamics (Conklin and Bittner 1973), and the most common suburban property crimes are shoplifting, larcenies from motor vehicles, and motor vehicle thefts (Gross and Hakim 1982). However, use of data on separate offenses and the crime mix in suburbs are largely missing and poorly applied. Crime prevention in suburbs will be limited with current approaches.

The literature consistently finds that property and violent crimes have different etiologies and potentially different explanatory factors explain the variation of these different types of crimes. However, these approaches for the most part provide little theoretically based explanations for the differences in variation between property and violent crimes. Hakim et al. (1978) suggest crime attraction differs from crime generation. The targets of property crimes differ from violent crimes requiring different standardization, types of property for property crimes and populations for violent crimes (Deutsch et al. 1984). From their perspective, property crimes result from the level and characteristics of targeted properties available in suburban jurisdictions with these targets attracting crime. High-value and attractive targets locate in suburbs and offer many rewards for offenders (Brown 1982). Further, the targets of these crimes are particular types of property and not individuals (Hakim 1980, p 266).

The major problem with this approach is that the empirical testing of this research examines particular types of suburbs (residential and commercial suburbs that are more affluent) and does not account for the simultaneous variation in suburban types. The majority of the testing these kinds of models is with monocentric metropolitan regions (Buck and Hakim 1981). The argument is that central cities export motivated offenders and suburban environments are not influential in the local generation of property crimes. For example, Gross and Hakim (1982) recognize that their "study area does not include any slums or poverty pockets." (p. 51). Such assumptions about suburbs clearly ignore the changed nature of suburbs and metropolitan forms. One of the important findings from this research, however, is the importance of wealth on property crimes. Hakim et al. (1978) find that wealth consistently is associated with higher rates of property crimes. This is suggestive of the importance of higher-status places as areas of resource abundance, which partly contributes to higher property crime rates, at least for primarily residential and/or mixed suburbs.

Crime generation, on the other hand, applies to violent crimes. According to this logic, violent crimes are not economically motivated, occur between individuals and groups, and take place mostly within the residences of both offenders and victims. The journey to crime for violent crimes is much smaller than property crimes. The generation of violent crimes involves different motivations than property crimes and the characteristics and composition of populations and their residential environments more closely associate with these types of crimes (Brown 1982). Offenders concentrate in areas of low status, high unemployment, and physical deterioration (Brown 1982). Brown (1982) labels these concentrations of offenders as crime-prone populations. This approach is limited as it discounts the importance of physical environments and targets specific to locales that may attract and generate property crimes locally (Deutsch et al. 1984). Further, with the suburbanization of poverty and the tendency for places to have dual functions, the spread of crime-prone populations into many suburban parts of metropolitan regions and the contribution of non-resident populations on violent crime rates are greater (Massey 2001; McNulty 1999). To fully account for the variations in suburban violent crime rates, other factors differentiating suburbs besides motivated offenders are required. Again, it is the combination of place attributes that will better explain a suburb's crime rate and using a single construct of motivated offender misses the different motivations behind even the same type of crime as well as the different contexts in which these motivations influence crime. The presence of motivated offenders and/or targets increases the probability and risk of property and violent crimes in a jurisdiction, but the full characteristics of a place better specify the types of motivated offenders and targets leading to higher or even lower crime rates. Intra-metropolitan analyses capture metropolitan and place-specific characteristics and allow for contextual analyses.

Brown (1982) examines the spatial distribution of property and violent crime rates in suburban Chicago. Using spatial autocorrelation techniques combined with regression analyses, she finds that little interjurisdictional spillover of violent crimes exists across suburbs. In this study, property crimes do not spatially cluster or have a specific distribution with distance to the central city. Violent crimes exhibit clustering but are unrelated to accessibility to downtown Chicago. Brown (1982) summarizes:

> Property crime is not distributed in a clustered fashion (Table 2), in large part because the distribution of retail employment is not (Table 5) and RETAIL is highly correlated with property crime (r=0,53). Violent crime is distributed in a clustered fashion (Table 2) because two of its close correlates (BLACK and VALUEHSE) have significant positive spatial autocorrelation. Once the influence of these two variables is removed through regression analysis, no spatial patterning remains (p. 260).

Importantly, Brown (1982) also suggests that property crimes are mostly intrajurisdictional, which is similar to violent crimes, because of significant effects of crime-prone populations (minority, young adult, and poverty populations). However, some interjurisdictional effects of retail and manufacturing activities on property crimes are present. These results suggest that both crime generation and attraction apply for suburban property crimes and mostly crime generation applies for suburban violent crimes. However, theoretical rationales for both the distribution of motivational and target elements are not provided.

The literature provides little guidance on which theoretical approaches best explain these patterns. Most of the research has tended to extend existing criminological explanations of crime and violence, mainly social disorganization and social control theories, or to focus on particular forms of crime, violent and property. To be sure, none of them consider the locational aspects of the distribution of crime and violent rates as being directly important to its observed patterning or how this distribution directly links to the organization and distribution of socio-economic conditions, functions, and status across suburbs.

One of the main problems remains the use of suburbs from multiple metropolitan regions. These do not allow for the proper assessment of functional and status attributes of suburbs, as the role and position of these suburbs in metropolitan regions is not determined. Stahura and Huff (1986) find that zones of transition are decentralizating to suburbs further away from traditional cores and these spread of these zones in suburban areas relate to increases in suburban crime from 1960 to 1980 (see also Stahura and Huff 1979, 1981). All zones saw increases in property and violent crime rates. Transitional zones moved further away from the core over time for both property and violent crimes. By 1980, the lowest rates of property and violent crimes were for suburbs closest to the central city (distance of 0-10 miles). Nationally, this research found the highest property crime in the second to furthest zone (20-30 miles) and the highest violent crime rates were highest in the twenty to thirty mile zone. Stahura and Huff (1986) note that their analysis does not include new suburbs and smaller suburbs (less than 25,000 in population), but argue that these do not change the trend of decentralization of crime rates (p. 58). Property crime rates persist over time, but the persistence is less than that of violent crimes across suburbs. Stahura and Huff (1986) argue that persistence is explained by the persistence of functional and population characteristics:

> A suburbs' housing stock and employment specialization determines to a large extent what types of people are attracted to it. For example, if a suburbs develops in response to an industry employing a substantial number of blue collar workers, it will develop housing in accordance with blue collar demand (p. 66).

Further, this and related research does find that suburban property crimes are higher for suburban employment centers and increase significantly over time for suburbs transitioning into employment functions (Stahura and Huff 1979; Stahura and Huff 1986). Suburban violent crimes more closely associated with suburban income as well as a limited extent to functional specialization (Stahura and Huff 1986). However, the percentage of African American population in a suburb is the strongest determinant of violent crime rates. Even though, this research studies violent and property crimes for suburban Chicago and Los Angeles, no separate analyses for explanatory factors accounting for these changes for both crime rates exist.

The large majority of the work of Stahura and his colleagues invoke social control (mostly informal social control) type explanations in accounting for concentration of suburban crime and violence (Stahura, Huff, and Smith 1980; Stahura and Huff 1979, 1981, 1986). For example, Stahura and Huff (1986) state:

> Suburbs that are denser and more employment-oriented tend to attract people who are less concerned with the social control behavior within the community; this lack of social control is, in turn, associated with higher rates of crime. If the people who are attracted to denser, employing suburbs are also black, even higher crime rates may be expected. This is not to say (nor could it reasonably argued) that black population composition is a direct cause of higher crime rates; rather, the presence of a large black population in a racially mixed community creates a situation of subcultural conflict wherein

community social control mechanisms are further broken down because of the racial boundaries and conflicts that exist in our society (p. 67).

These types of inferences do not follow from their research and remain speculative. Measuring social control differences across suburbs is difficult and much of such research is at the neighborhood level and for central cities. The application to suburban environments is hardly straightforward, as suburban diversity limits making such generalizations. Additionally, some research suggests that even suburban middle-class areas have low levels of bonding and ineffective crime-preventive social controls:

A factor that seems more clearly to influence the predominance of nonconfrontation in the normative life of the suburban middle class is the morphology of their social relationships. As noted earlier, these people tend to be socially anchored only loosely into atomized and shifting networks of weak ties. Their high rates of mobility means that bonds between persons are frequently ruptured and replaced with new and equally temporary ones, so that relationships often have short pasts and futures...If the preceding analysis has merit, it implies that a nonconfrontial style of social control- including such tactics as tolerance, avoidance, and conciliatory approaches- will be found wherever social life is characterized by transiency, atomization, and the fragmentation of social ties (Baumgartner 1984, p. 95).

Conflict avoidance and weak ties characterize many suburban places so that making statements about social control and social organization in suburban residential life remains incomplete without further empirical analyses (Palen 1995, p. 97). A survey of residents in the Los Angeles metro region finds that "people living in the suburbs do not express a stronger sense of attachment to their communities or neighbors, a stronger sense of mastery over their lives, or better life satisfaction than do Los Angeles residents, controlling for reported crime and other social factors" (Adams and Serpe 2000, p. 621).

To their credit, Stahura and collaborators do acknowledge the growth in suburban crime across all types of suburbs; the disappearing inverse relationship between distance from central city and suburban crime and violence rates; the linkages between racial and socioeconomic factors and crime and violence; and the stability of violent crime patterns across suburbs in comparison to property crimes. Further, this research incorporates functional and status variables in models and provide rationales for their inclusion. However, model specifications ignore the interactive effects of function and status specific to suburban places and group suburbs from metropolitan regions together in empirical analyses. Most importantly and correctly, Stahura and company are careful to point out that the relationships found between explanatory factors and suburban crime and violence are both direct and indirect. The vast majority of relationships between independent indicators themselves and between independent and dependent variables were indirect and many variables mutually correlated with each other. Thus, any findings, by their acknowledgement, remain underspecified unless better fit between theories and empirical testing is advanced.

For our purposes, these issues give stronger credence to taking an integrated approach between theory development, classification of suburbs, and examining crime and violence patterns and trends across suburbs. It is clear also that using multivariate regression and other techniques for classification of suburbs by function and status and studying property and violent crime patterns and rates separately and for each offense making up these broad categories is necessary for better theory development and testing. In essence, specification of existing models of suburban crime and violence requires additional enhancements.

While existing models and interpretations have considerable merit, they remain incomplete and lacking with regard to specification of the particular location of socially disorganized suburbs and/or areas within the metropolitan hierarchy; identifying the factors responsible for such concentrations; and describing the relationships between organizational arrangements and distribution of crime and violence rates. Newer routine activities theories of crime and violence are closely related theoretically and empirically with social control and social disorganization theories. In particular, the shared assumption of widely distributed motivated offenders is suspect. Their application in examining suburban crime and violence has been more limited, but the findings and explanations derived from them are similar to social control and related theories and models.

In a study applying routine activities theory to examine suburban crime and violence rates, Stahura and Sloan (1988) find that routine activities' and their differential distribution across suburbs explains the variation in property crime rates, but not violent crime rates. The study uses the three elements, motivations, opportunities, and guardianship, identified in routine activities and examines their distribution across suburbs. The mechanisms that distribute these three elements derive from the place stratification approach, where advantaged higher-status groups are able to deflect the preconditions for crime and violence from their residential environments. The authors find support for the consolidated advantages or place stratification model in terms of the abilities of affluent suburbs to reduce crime rates by restricting the number of motivated offenders and how suburbs becoming more employment oriented tend to experience higher crime rates (property rates especially) than similar status, residential suburbs. Motivational elements explain violent crimes and changes in opportunities explain property crimes. This article remains one of the few attempts to integrate and test different theories and to find strong compatibility between them.

In turn, this attempt also confirms and supports research on the effects of racial residential segregation on explaining suburban violence patterns and the reciprocal positive relationships between these two sets of factors and conditions (Logan and Messner 1987). Violent crime rates can also increase racial residential segregation, which is consistent with notions that suburbs with fewer resources (status attributes) and specialized functions (residential minority) are concentrated and differentially distributed. Logan and colleagues have been the most prominent in developing and testing exposure models of crime and violence related to community properties and their contextual influences on crime and violence rates (Alba et al. 1994; Logan and Stults 1999). The focus is different from ones seeking to explain variations in suburban crime and violence. Logan and Stults (1999) explain:

This is the phenomenon that we study here—not what characteristics of neighborhoods might be seen as the causes of crime, but what kinds of people are most exposed to it by virtue of where they live. We treat victimization or, conversely, security as a characteristic of an urban environment, comparable to other place resources, like quality of schools and public services, the social class of neighbors, or environmental amenities (p. 251).

Their perspective is informative and considers a crime-free environment as a locational amenity in itself, a resource appropriated by individuals and groups to achieve common goals in metropolitan contexts such as living in high-status residential environments and being able to find high-paying jobs. Their research finds support for the effects of contextual variables such as the extent of poverty, racial composition, and population size on both property and violence rates' exposure by different racial/ethnic groups and the effects of individual status variables and attainment in explaining the crime level in individuals' residential environments. Notably, Logan and Stults (1999) find that exposure to property crimes differed very little, while the exposure to violent crimes differed significantly by race and ethnicity. The authors explain this finding:

Thus, whites who move to the suburbs will experience low levels of crime regardless of socioeconomic characteristics, while the suburban experience of blacks is highly dependent on social class...Indeed, poor suburban blacks live in places whose violent crime rates are not far below those of the central city, and even affluent blacks live in places with more than double the violent crime rate to which poor whites are exposed (p. 269).

The limitations of their models include lack of separation of different offense categories within property and violent crime rates and their relationships, if any, with contextual racial/ethnic groups and individual residence exposure variables. Further, they ignore the particular configuration of functional and status characteristics differentiating suburban places that may have stronger influences on differential exposure on different categories of property and violent crimes and fail to consider that locational amenities are distributed by extra-individual forces. The stratification of places underlying this patterning of locational amenities suggests that place characteristics are multi-faceted and analytically distinct from characterization of places as just crime-saturated or crime-free environments. This set of research also tends to focus on residential environments and populations.

The influence of nonresident populations also requires consideration in analyzing suburban crime and violence. Research recognizes that crime rates may be inflated or deflated and poorly represent the nature of the crime problem. Property crimes are higher in suburbs with low residential and high non-residential populations. The reverse is true for suburban violent crimes – low residential populations do not account for the contributions of nonresident populations on a suburb's rate. As a result, property crimes require deflation and violent crimes require inflation (Lewis and Louch 2000; Stahura and Huff 1981). As mentioned earlier, one standardization approach for property crimes involves using a measure of the targets available in a jurisdiction. Hakim et al. (1978) propose standardized property crimes by using the size of the developed area. More developed suburbs offer more attractive targets for potential offenders. Others have suggested the use of explanatory factors that capture the extent of commercial and other activities as well as the presence of non-residential populations. Some research includes the employment to residential workers ratio as a measure of functional specialization (Stahura et al. 1980; Stahura and Hollinger 1988). The contribution of nonresidential populations on property crime rates seems greater than for rates of violent crimes. Lewis and Louch (2000) suggest that this "surge problem" is not easily measured:

> Difficulty emerges because measures one might use to characterize nonresident surge (for example, a city's position in the retail hierarchy) represent not only elements that may

bias the denominator of crime rates, but also elements that may attract criminal activity-by bringing potential offenders and targets closer together in space and potentially reducing guardianship behavior. One can actually distinguish two, somewhat distinct, possible effects of population surge on crime rates: 1. Greater opportunity for criminal gains and potential targets for crimes and 2. Greater social contact between potential perpetrators and victims (p. 7).

Their study of California municipalities finds that a measure of retail sales per capita strongly predicts property crimes and better predicts violent crimes (robberies and assaults) than the job-population ratio. The inference that follows from their analysis is that retail activities more directly relate to crime rates than other employment-generating activities. Surge measures are contextual variables that capture the extent of non-residential activities in different areas. Measures of nonresidential activities and populations necessitate inclusion as their exclusion may give greater explanatory weight to other variables (e.g., alcohol establishments) when the relationships with crimes is weaker after controlling for these surge measures. Wang and Minor (2002) find that a job accessibility measure (which they argue is superior to the job-to-resident workers ratio) explains the concentration of property crimes as well as violent crimes although to a significantly lesser magnitude. Non-residential populations and activities more directly explain the variation in property crime rates.

Another promising approach to account for the target-specific nature of area crime variation examines the mediating effects of targets (opportunities) on property crimes (Kleck and Chiricos 2002). This research examines specific crimes (various types of robberies, shoplifting, residential burglaries, and thefts of types of vehicles) and their relationships with target-specific measures (e.g., convenience stores per capita) for Florida Counties. The findings do not support the effects of target availability and specific types of targets on specific types of crime. Kleck and Chiricos (2002) argue that targets are widely available and saturated "so that the variation in the level of opportunities has little relevance for the frequency of criminal behavior" (p. 670). While these findings caution against using target-specific measures, an examination of intra-county and municipal variation in specific crimes may be a better application of these measures.

Conclusions

The review of the suburban hierarchy, differentiation, and suburban crime and violence demonstrates the need for newer approaches to study suburban stratification and suburban crime and violence. Suburban stratification and the distribution of crime and violence across suburbs are linked processes so that suburbs have unique crime and violence problems that derive from their position and role in the suburban hierarchy.

A typology is proposed that categorizes suburbs on functional and status elements. These elements are place level characteristics that define the unique characteristics of suburbs and their populations and residential and employment functions. This typology uses measures from the Census of Population and Housing and Economic Censuses to distinguish suburbs. Building on existing research on the suburban hierarchy, it provides academics and policymakers with the theoretical and methodological background necessary to develop tools to understand metropolitan phenomena and problems.

The next chapter applies this typology to various model specifications aiming to explain how crime and violence rates are distributed and located in different kinds of suburbs.

CHAPTER 4

An Examination of Suburban Los Angeles

Introduction

This chapter applies the theoretically based conceptions of opportunities (targets and resources) and function and status developed in earlier chapters. This chapter then moves to describing the unique data set on crime and violence used in this study. This data set contains supplemental offense data on property and violent crimes and provides the dependent variables for the development of various models. Empirical analyses in this chapter are crime-specific, target specific, and status specific. The chapter also includes a description of the independent variables in these models measuring functional and status characteristics of suburbs.

Generally, functional place characteristics offer environments more closely linked with different types of property crimes and relate to the distribution of targets in different economic sectors (retail, wholesale, services, and manufacturing). These functional attributes approximate the physical or built environments characterizing suburban places. The major data sets used are Economic Censuses from various years. Municipalities with a concentration of employment activities in different sectors usually contain a larger number of attractive targets and non-residential populations contributing to increased rates of property crimes. Place status characteristics and variables related to built environments also contribute to suburban property crimes. Housing stock variables, derived from the Census of Population and Housing (CPH), provide information on the residential functional characteristics of suburbs. These variables also represent the level of resources accessible by status-specific population units. Larger levels of employment activities imply higher levels of resources in suburban jurisdictions. As many suburban municipalities have dual functions of resident and employment, higher rates of specific types of property and violent crimes are expected.

Status characteristics of suburban places offer environments more closely associated with different types of violent crimes and relate to the distribution of the composite place status and resource levels of population units across suburban places. These status measures approximate the social and economic environments characterizing suburban places. The sources of these data are decennial Censuses of Population and Housing. Suburbs with concentration of lower-status groups face environmental conditions that offer fewer accessible resources. A concentration of resource- deprived actors in a suburb should associate with higher levels of violent crimes.

All data and models are collected and applied to municipalities in the Los Angeles Consolidated Metropolitan Statistical Area (CMSA) for three periods of time, 1980, 1990, and 2000. Intra-metropolitan models offer meaningful analyses and findings to explain the nature of suburban crime and violence in metropolitan regions.

Data Sources

The notion of crime mix is not new, but limited debate and discussion of its utility for academic and practical applications exist. Instead, most of its applications in criminology and applied criminal justice remain implicit. Crime pattern analyses and geographic analyses of crime and violence are leading examples of applications incorporating the notion of crime mix. Generally, any analysis of crime and violence patterns and distributions of these patterns disaggregate offense data into meaningful categories. These categorical distinctions are necessary to ascertain the crime mix characterizing particular spatial and temporal patterns. The same applies to analysis of offender and victim patterns. Crime mix refers to the particular offense categories of property and violent crimes characterizing various spatial (political entities such as municipalities and counties and policing organizations such as local police departments) units. The type of crime problem(s) facing these organizational units differs considerably due to the different types of environments and populations present in their boundaries. Lynch (2002) formulates the importance of analyzing the crime mix for cross-national analyses, but the same points are applicable for local analyses:

The importance of crime classification for cross-national comparisons cannot be overstated. As we will see in a later section, the differences in the mix of crime across nations is much greater than the differences in the level of criminal activity. Crime-specific comparisons across nations will tell us much more than comparisons of total crime (p. 15).

As such, each spatial unit has greater levels of particular offenses more consistent with their physical and nonphysical environments. For example, shoplifting rates tend to be higher in suburbs with concentration of retail activities. The greater prevalence of lethal violence (homicide, robberies with use of firearms, and armed aggravated assaults) in poorer areas directly supports the assertion that higher rates of violence correspond with the overall status of suburban jurisdictions (Ackerman 1997). Higher rates of larcenies in the higher dollar value categories characterize higher-status suburban jurisdictions. Each of these examples suggests the use of crime-specific, target-specific, and status-specific models to explain suburban crime and violence. Suburban crime and violence problems, in the plural, are of a diverse range of types and levels of severity.

Crime-specific analyses require disaggregated offense data. An original data set of supplemental property and violent offenses is used to develop crime-specific measures and for model specifications. The source for these offense data is the California Department of Justice. These include crimes reported to municipal police departments and County Sheriff Offices. These offense data are available at the municipality level. The data set contains all major index offenses, larceny/thefts, burglaries, motor vehicle thefts, arsons, homicides, rapes, robberies, and aggravated assaults. However, each offense with the exception of homicide has various subcategories, which represent different supplemental offense data. Appendix A contains the definitions and classification of the supplemental offense categories as the well as the temporal coverage available for the offense data.

It is useful to review the supplemental offense data and classifications behind each category of offense for various reasons. The different status motivations behind crime (pecuniary, non-pecuniary, or a combination) may be specific to particular types of supplemental offenses. Additionally, specific offenses may be target-specific (property crimes) or involve the escalation of disputes and conflicts between persons (violent crimes). Most property crimes as well as robberies are target-specific involving some degree of pecuniary motivations. Violent crimes are less target-specific, with the exception of robbery, and involve status-specific motivational elements including the competition for resources. Supplemental offense data link to the particular environmental contexts within which these different offenses take place.

The standard distinction between property and violent crimes is by the target of the offense for these crimes. In the case of property crimes, the targets are various types of property and the victims can be individuals or businesses. For violent crimes, both targets (directly) and victims are individuals, although the ultimate victims can be property owners as in the case of robberies occurring in commercial establishments, banks, and gas/service stations. One can consider robbery as a property crime as it involves using force and/or threat of violence to obtain property. Generally, crimes against persons are violent crimes and crimes against property are property crimes. Almost universally, every jurisdiction has higher rates of property crimes than violent crimes, but certain jurisdictions may have higher rates of particular categories of violent crimes. Further, the ratio of property crimes to violent crimes varies and is not equivalent across jurisdictions. Suburban employment centers have significantly higher rates of property crimes than violent crimes. Some primarily residential suburbs have higher violent crime rates than rates of property crimes.

For property crimes, data on larceny-theft offenses breaks down into two major types: larceny types and larceny value. There are eight different categories of larceny types with the highest rates being shoplifting, theft from motor vehicles, and theft of motor vehicle parts and accessories. Larceny types classify by the type of property stolen and location of theft. Pocket-picking and purse-snatching require some offender contact with individual persons, but involve no force. Rates of pocket-picking, theft from coin operated devices, and purse snatching are significantly lower than for other types of larcenies. Larcenies from buildings and larcenies from other miscellaneous structures fall into the intermediate categories for many jurisdictions, but generally thefts from buildings are higher for commercial areas and thefts in the miscellaneous category are higher for residential areas. Larceny value data fall into four categories by the value of stolen property for each incident – value under $50, $50-199, $200-499, and over $400. The range of rates for the dollar value of stolen property in these categories is evenly spread for many jurisdictions with higher-status suburbs having higher larceny rates in the over $400 category and lower-status areas having higher rates in the lower values categories. These amounts are somewhat arbitrarily determined, but the fact that a significant number of larcenies fall into the lower categories for many jurisdictions suggests that larcenies are the least serious of all index offenses. Larcenies are the most frequent type of property crime and the largest proportions of all index crimes.

The next largest property crime offenses are burglaries. Burglaries have two major classifications, burglary types and burglary location and time. Burglary types capture the commonly held definition of burglaries as breaking and entering with three categories, forcible entry, no forcible entry, and attempted forcible entry. Forcible entry burglaries are usually larger than the two other categories. The burglary location data differentiates the types of structures, residential and nonresidential, that are subject to unlawful entry with the intent to commit a felony or theft. Generally, residential burglaries tend to be higher than nonresidential burglaries for many places, but certain locations have higher or more even levels of nonresidential burglaries. This depends on the specific characteristics of the place, especially the types and quantity of physical structures located there. For both nonresidential and residential burglaries, three times-of-day classifications (day, night, and unknown) are available. While generalizing is difficult for the relative frequency of each type of time of burglary, a higher number of nonresidential burglaries tend to occur at night and daytime residential burglaries are more frequent than nighttime ones.

The third category of property crimes is motor vehicle thefts. Three major offenses are provided by the type of vehicle stolen - automobiles, trucks/buses, and other vehicles. Most often, auto thefts are larger than thefts of trucks/buses and smaller vehicles. Many consider motor vehicle thefts to be the most accurately reported crimes (along with homicide) because of higher rates of reporting by victims to police departments in order to collect insurance.

The least frequent type of property crime is arson. Arson was included as an index crime only in the early 1980s. Arson incidents include three major types – structural, mobile, and other. The classification distinguishes between all three subtypes by the type of property targeted; nonresidential and residential structures for structural arsons, motor vehicles for mobile arson, and open property for the other arson category. As arsons are relatively rare, any generalizations about the frequency and distribution of the different types of arsons are extremely difficult to make.

Violent crimes generally involve individuals as victims and occur in the presence of individuals. Most consider these types of crimes as the most serious of all offenses because of the use of force and/or weapons and the potential for bodily injury and death. For violent crimes, supplemental offense data are not available for homicide in this data set. The classifications and definitions differentiate homicides from aggravated assaults by the outcome, death in the case of homicide and bodily injury for aggravated assaults. Additionally, attempted murder and assaults resulting in murder are included in the aggravated assaults category. This determination is legal as the intent to kill (nonegelient) is critical for classifications of homicide. Homicides are the least frequent type of violent crime, but the most accurately reported.

The next least frequent violent crime is forcible rape. Many consider the reporting of rapes to be the most problematic because victims for numerous reasons are reluctant to involve the police and the law into their private lives. In other cases, rape victims are subject to violent threats and continued victimization by their attackers and reporting to the authorities is often difficult and can be dangerous. Rapes fall into two types in this dataset, forcible rapes and attempted forcible rapes. Little research exists on the expected prevalence of these two classifications of rapes in different places.

Robberies are the second most prevalent type of violent crimes. As mentioned above, one may consider robberies as property crimes as they frequently involve pecuniary motives. Further, the Uniform Crime Reporting (UCR) definition and classification of this violent crime notes that robbery involves a larceny or theft, but requires a different classification because of the presence of a victim and the use of or threat to use force. Definitions of property crimes do not include these elements of force and presence of victims. The possibility of a robbery involving non-pecuniary motives (such as status or respect) also prevents one from classifying this crime exclusively as a property crime.

The supplemental offense dataset contains data for two major categories of robberies, robbery types by weapons used and robbery location. There are four major subcategories of robbery types distinguished by the weapons used (this same sub-classification is also available for aggravated assaults): firearm, knife, other dangerous weapon, and strong arm. The classification considers robberies involving weapons as armed robberies and this does not include strong-arm robbery. In most cases, higher levels of firearm and strong-arm robberies than the other two robbery types exist in many jurisdictions. However, the differences in rates of firearm and strong-arm robberies vary across jurisdictions. Firearm robberies are more lethal, with a larger potential to result in death, and strong-arm robberies the least lethal.

Robbery location supplemental offense data have seven different categories. As robberies involve the taking or attempting to take property from individuals, the sub-classification by location refers to where the robbery occurred and the type of stolen property. The highway and miscellaneous categories generally occur in public spaces or structures more accessible to the public. The label of highway robberies can be misleading as the definition states that these offenses locate in streets and other visible locations and not just highways. Highway robberies occur exclusively outside of physical structures. Miscellaneous robberies locate in public buildings, public and private transportation, churches, and public open spaces. Commercial, gas/service, convenience store, and bank robberies occur in private property structures owned by individuals and corporations for purposes of business and commerce. The remaining category of residential robbery occurs in private residential spaces.

Highway, commercial, convenience, and gas/service station robberies are more frequent than the other types. Prior to 1982, gas/service station and convenience store robberies grouped with commercial robberies. For many jurisdictions, commercial robberies of all types especially convenience store robberies are more frequent than highway robberies. However, for some residential areas, rates of highway robberies are usually higher. Contrary to expectations, bank robberies tend to be the least frequent type with residential and miscellaneous robberies about equal in frequency and higher than bank robberies. Robbery location offense data can be useful in determining if the ultimate targets of these crimes and the different motivations behind these types of offenses. One expects commercial and bank robberies to be target-specific with highway, residential, and miscellaneous robberies as less target-specific directed partially against individuals and groups. However, these assertions are speculative and not based on empirical evidence and research.

The most frequent violent crimes are aggravated assaults, making up a significant proportion of the total number of violent crimes. In some cases, robbery rates are higher or equal to aggravated assault rates. This is particularly true for commercial areas and for a fewer number of residential areas. Under the UCR guidelines, aggravated assaults fall into a separate category than simple assaults on two criteria, the use of weapon and/or the seriousness of the injuries to victims. Although no offense data are available for simple assaults, only arrest statistics, these types of assault are more frequent than aggravated assaults. Some research suggests that mandatory arrest policies for domestic violence incidents in the state of California and other states led to a significant (but temporary) surge in aggravated assaults rates in the mid-1980s (Petersilia 1992). There is only a single category of aggravated assaults available from the supplemental offense data set, assault types. This is composed of four subcategories, the same as for robbery type, of weapons used in assault incidents. Lethality of aggravated assaults expects to vary by the potential for severe bodily harm or death with strong-arm assaults being the least lethal and firearm-assaults potentially the most lethal. There is a less clear distribution of assault types across jurisdictions, which limits any other assertions about the variation of assault types and environmental contexts.

This review of the classification and definitions of various supplemental offenses in the property and violent crimes clearly demonstrates the need for specific model specifications for particular types of offenses. The next section outlines the methodological plan and model specifications following this primary logic. For all offenses, the absolute numbers convert into rates of crime and violence by dividing by the residential population and multiplying by 100,000. This is standard practice in the crime-focused academic and practitioner fields. Even though population standardization does not capture the contribution of non-residential populations and the overall risk from crime profile of jurisdictions, the lack of data on targets and specific information on offenses limits use of other standardization techniques. Standardization by land area is inappropriate as jurisdictions differ considerably on this measure. Supplemental offense data for some jurisdictions in Riverside and San Bernardino Counties is unavailable for 1980 and model specifications do not include these cities. These include five cities in Riverside County and five cities in San Bernardino County.

Functional and status measures derive from the Economic Censuses and Censuses of Population and Housing. Table lists the specific measures and operationalization of these measures used for model specifications. Most notably, we use multiple measures of functional place characteristics based on employment in four major sectors, retail, services, wholesale, and manufacturing. The employment to residential workers in these sectors is calculated for each of these four sectors. The denominator used is residential working population in each industrial sector rather than the total residential population as the later would be unable to capture the concentration of employment for larger suburbs and the functional specialization by sector for suburbs. The Economic Censuses cover only these four sectors at the municipality level. Appendix B lists the kinds of businesses included in the retail, service, and wholesale sectors and available for municipalities. The coverage of retail and wholesale is much more complete than service sector. These include a variety of businesses offering final demand services for the retail sector and distributive services in the case of the wholesale sector. For the service sector category, businesses in the final demand services category are mostly included with some coverage of lower-end business services. Producer services employment such as finance, real estate, banking, legal, and professional services is unavailable in the Economic Censuses before 1997. There is no coverage for other intermediate types of service industries such as the transportation, communications, and utilities sector. From these data sources, adequate representation of the retail and wholesale sectors is apparent, while the service sector remains underrepresented. Employment data in the Economic Censuses is unavailable for municipalities with populations less than 2500. Consequently, the cities of Bradbury, Hidden Hills, Irwindale, and Rolling Hills are missing in the model specifications. For both the EC and CPH, data is only available for municipalities incorporated at the time of data collection.

The status variables used for empirical analyses group into four major dimensions: housing, labor, demographic and socioeconomic, and area. Based on the typology developed in Chapter 3, each of these status variables represent place level characteristics not the characteristics of individuals. Rather, the assumption is that place characteristics are analytically distinct from individual characteristics. Population units are convenient measuring units to develop place-level functional and status characteristics. For each of the status variables, Appendix C provides the universe or population for calculation of variables and to what population units these variables apply. The datasets include multiple variables derived from the CPH, but the final set of variables were selected by theoretical importance in explaining the dependent variables, supplemental offense crime rates, as well as after multiple regression analyses not shown below. The explanatory power of a large number of variables derived from the CPH is poor and these variables are not included in the final model specifications.

Methodological Plan and Model Specifications

The primary purpose of the empirical analyses in this study is to explain the variation in suburban crime and violence rates in metropolitan Los Angeles. This objective is more appropriately and efficiently reached using multiple model specifications with multiple sets of independent variables. The application of single models with the same set of explanatory variables is theoretically and empirically suspect. Given the diverse nature of suburban places and the differences in suburban crime mix, single model specifications are clearly not appropriate. For suburban jurisdictions, the overall levels of property and violent crime rates may be similar, but the varied levels of different supplemental offenses contribute to these overall rates. Using place level offense-specific rates is a methodologically sound strategy to address the components of the crime mix across and within suburban jurisdictions. The location and distribution of these offense rates varies across suburbs as well. Further, the same set of explanatory factors for each offense rate is not expected. Places have differing physical and nonphysical environments that relate to the concentration of different functional and status attributes within their boundaries. These attributes are consequential to the rates of crime and violence in a suburban jurisdiction as well as across suburban jurisdictions.

Our review of supplemental offenses above showed that property crimes are target and function specific and violent crimes with the exception of robberies are situation and status specific. A useful categorization of supplemental offenses may include interrelated elements of the motivations behind the crimes and the location and types of environments these crimes take place. These distinctions are not exhaustive and complete, but offer useful ways to explain variation in offense rates. While the development of a complete typology of offense types on function and status is difficult to formalize (and is not available), offense patterns do differ on their relationships with functional and status attributes. Of the supplemental offenses, shoplifting, thefts from buildings, thefts from motor vehicles, nonresidential burglaries, commercial robberies are target-specific and expect to be more prevalent in nonresidential environments. Other property crimes, such as pocket-picking, purse snatching, bicycle thefts, and coin-operated machines thefts are relatively rare and less location-specific. This is the case with thefts of motor vehicle accessories, which although quite common, occur in both residential and nonresidential environments. Arsons are more difficult to characterize and probably involve both status-specific and target-specific elements. Violent crimes with the exception of target-motivated robberies are less target-specific and more situation-specific. Violent crime offenses more commonly occur in situations of direct contact between victims and offenders and their residential environments. Status motivations for these types of crime are less pecuniary in orientation and more situation-specific. Homicides, rapes of all types, strong-arm robberies and assaults, and residential robberies are examples of situation-specific crimes. Considerations of offense types by function and status suggest the use of cross-sectional empirical analyses that capture contextual aspects of the variation in suburban crime and violence.

The research designs used for empirical analyses are mostly cross-sectional, but comparisons of these models for three different time periods captures the temporal stability of the estimated model parameters (independently and as a group). Two major criteria drive the development of the research designs for the empirical analyses. First, multiple model specifications of different types of supplemental offenses are used. Each model specification for the different offenses undergoes a process of refinement. In each case, multiple variables are included and tested in model specifications. The elimination of variables uses criteria of significance and explanatory power of the overall model. Municipality level function and status variables that are insignificant and/or do not provide explanatory power to the overall model are eliminated. These considerations apply to the independent variables in model specifications.

The second criterion in the research design involves selecting offenses for model specifications. The choice of offenses used as dependent variables in the models requires consideration of offenses that adequately represent the suburban crime and violence mix and variation of these offenses across suburbs as important objectives. Six supplemental offenses (three each from property and violent crimes) represent the diversity aspects of the suburban crime mix. The six include shoplifting, commercial robberies, non-residential burglaries, highway robberies, firearm assaults, and strong-arm assaults. Shoplifting, commercial robberies, and non-residential burglaries are more target-specific property offenses. The rates and distribution of these offenses varies across suburbs mainly due to the variation in suburban functional attributes. Shoplifting is a prototypical example of a target-specific and location-dependent offense. Commercial robberies similarly cluster by location and distribute on functional characteristics.

The selection of non-residential burglaries is due to the greater proportional contribution of burglaries to overall property crime rates for many jurisdictions and the need to include a type of burglary offense. The selected property crimes exclude arson and motor vehicle thefts because the classifications underlying the supplemental offense data for these crimes do not easily distinguish these offenses as target-specific and location-dependent. Highway robberies, firearm assaults, and strong-arm assaults are more situation-specific and status characteristics of places more directly influence the variation in the rates of these offenses. Homicide types are unavailable and rape types are limited to only two major types. The exclusion of a robbery weapon type is mainly due to the selection of commercial robberies as a target-specific offense. As mentioned earlier, the classification of robberies as violent crimes is not straightforward and firearm-robberies may be both target-motivated and situation-specific.

Highway robberies provide a direct example of the contribution of residential environments to violent crimes. The reasons for selection of two types of assaults include the large proportional contribution of these offenses to the overall violent crime rates of suburbs and to understand the distribution of lethal and non-lethal violence across suburbs. Firearm-assaults are more lethal and expect to concentrate in specific suburbs, while strong-arm assaults evenly distribute across jurisdictions with relatively smaller variation in rates of these offenses. Model specifications for each of the selected offenses are developed and analyzed for a three- decade period from 1980 to 2000. EC and supplemental offense data are available for 1982, 1992, and 1997. CPH data are available every ten years starting in 1980. Due to the inconsistencies of coverage of municipalities with these datasets, the final data set used for empirical analyses excludes municipalities where no data is available in any one of these datasets. The research design covers changes over time through development of model specifications for each offense over the three decades. Two separate sets of models using the same predictors for each offense are developed and analyzed - one for all jurisdictions appearing in all three decades and the second for all jurisdictions in a given year. The total number of municipalities with available data in 1980 is 132 and these municipalities comprise the baseline model for comparisons for the first set of models. The number of municipalities with data available was 162 and 171 respectively for 1992 and 2000. The second set of temporal model comparisons uses these municipalities for model specifications.

To assess the stability of the parameters over time, the same model specifications used in the first decade are applied to the subsequent two decades. In particular, comparisons of the direction, magnitude, and significance of the same predictors used in the first decade for the other two decades help to assess the explanatory power of individual predictors. The coefficient of multiple determination (R^2) of each model is used to overall contribution of significant predictors on explaining the variation in offense rates across municipalities. In each decade and for all model specifications, the possibilities of multicollinearity between independent variables can potentially bias estimations and model specifications. In particular, estimating the true independent effects of explanatory variables becomes difficult with multicollinearity between explanatory variables. The examination of the tolerance and variance inflation factors helps to identify highly collinear variables. Each model specification provides these diagnostics for each independent variable.

Further, in each model due to issues of the bias in estimation from the presence of outliers, a few models excluding these outliers are developed. Two cities are significant outliers having extreme values (high or low) on the dependent variables in metropolitan Los Angeles. These are the cities of Industry and Vernon. This is primarily due to their low number of residential populations and high concentration of commercial and industrial activities in these cities. As the offense rates of these cities are extremely high and for these reasons are significant outliers skewing any results, all model specifications exclude these municipalities. Other municipalities may be less extreme outliers and examining these municipalities has some heuristic value. Substantively, these outliers are of interest in by themselves as they may be unique places with substantially different characteristics and/or have different values (higher or lower) of the same significant predictor variables. Model outliers are determined on the standard criterion of values of three standard deviations from the mean. All model specifications use multivariate regression techniques.

An important additional issue relevant to examining a study explaining variation in suburban crime and violence rates concerns the special geographic and spatial nature of the data. The spatial location of municipalities in reference to each other and the arrangement of these spatial units can lead to unique independent effects on estimations of the parameters and overall model fit and prediction. Continuous jurisdictions can have similar or different offense rates across the metropolitan space. Spatial associations or effects are common for many social science data and phenomena. Difficulties arise in separating effects due to the arrangement of spatial units from the effects of independent explanatory variables. For the dependent variables, offense rates, the clustering of these rates in neighboring municipalities and across space does not necessarily result from the clustering of significant predictors. However, clustering of offense rates is substantively important as it suggests similar crime or lack of crime problems between adjoining or closely located municipalities. Spatial effects are of two major types: spatial dependence and spatial heterogeneity. Anselin and Getis (1992) define these types:

> Spatial dependence refers to the relationship between spatially referenced data due to the nature of the variable(s) under study and the size, shape, and configuration of the spatial units..Spatial heterogeneity occurs when there is lack of spatial uniformity of the effects of spatial dependence and/or of the relationships between the variables under study (p. 24).

As these problems of spatial dependence (spatial heterogeneity is a special case of spatial dependence) impact estimation and model specifications, diagnostic measures to test for autocorrelation across space are available. The most widely used measure of spatial contiguity effects or spatial autocorrelation is the Moran's I. This statistic defines as follows:

$$I = \frac{N}{S_0} \sum_i \sum_j w_{ij}(x_i - \mu).(x_j - \mu) / \sum_i (x_i - \mu)^2$$

where, N is the number of observations; w is the element in the spatial weights matrix corresponding to the observation pair I,j; x_i and x_j are observations for location I and j (with mean μ); and S is the scaling constant (i.e., the sum of all spatial weights). The Moran's I ranges from values of +1 to –1. Positive spatial autocorrelation (approaching a value of 1) indicates that similar values of a variable cluster in space, while negative spatial autocorrelation (approaching a value of – 1) indicates that similar values on a variable are dispersed across space. Strictly speaking, this Moran's I coefficient is for the entire population of spatial units examined and holds under assumptions of spatial homogeneity or stationarity. This statistic is termed as the Global Moran's I. With large metropolitan regions such as the Los Angeles metropolitan region, one would anticipate that localized (rather than global for the entire region) clusters of offense rates would exist. Local Moran's I coefficients have been developed to detect non-stationarity in the data. There are also cases of spatial outliers as opposed to clusters or random dispersion of similar values of a variable. Spatial outliers are municipalities, in the case of this study, with high or low offense rates and with neighbors (sharing boundaries) with dissimilar offense rates. For these municipalities, the Local Moran's I coefficients are insignificant and do not approach values of positive 1 or negative –1 (no local spatial autocorrelation is detected). Examining spatial outliers is instructive as it helps to understand the uniqueness of municipalities from their contiguous neighbors. Global Moran's I for the six supplemental offenses are reported for 1990 and 2000 (as 1980 boundary files are unavailable) and determined using the interface of ArcView, a geographical information systems (GIS) tool, and SpaceStat, a spatial statistical package. Moran's I scatter plots are also provided through these tools, which help in identifying local clusters of offense rates and spatial outliers in the Los Angeles metropolitan region.

An additional issue with model specifications related to spatial data also requires examination. As the Los Angeles metropolitan region includes over 175 municipalities in five counties, differences between places in one county and another county should be significant (Allen & Turner 1996, 1997). These county level differences on functional and status attributes undoubtedly contribute to county-specific offense patterns. Further, the geographic spread of the land area and distribution of municipalities of this five-county region is extremely high. The Inland Empire counties of San Bernardino and Riverside contain vast amounts of federal government owned and/or undevelopable land. The distance between municipal jurisdictions in these counties is quite high in comparison to municipalities in Los Angeles and Orange counties that are physically closer. Additionally, despite widespread notions of the sprawling nature of metropolitan Los Angeles, the region shows considerably diversity in land use and population densities. A study by Fulton et al. (2001) found metropolitan Los Angeles to be second to the New York region using various density measures. The lack of urbanized land for development for any land use is a major constraint for the Los Angeles region (Hale 2003). Population densities are significantly lower for municipalities in the Inland Empire counties and Ventura County. This contrasts to high densities in Los Angeles and Orange counties. Topographically diverse, the whole region and various counties and municipalities locate adjacent to an array of mountain ranges, valleys, desert, and the ocean.

For these and related reasons, each model specification contains dummy variables for the county the municipality is located in. The reference region is Los Angeles County. Using dummy variables partly accounts for physical and nonphysical differences between municipalities in different counties and for the presence of local clustering of offense rates and functional and status characteristics of places.

Figure 1. The Los Angeles Metropolitan Region in 2000

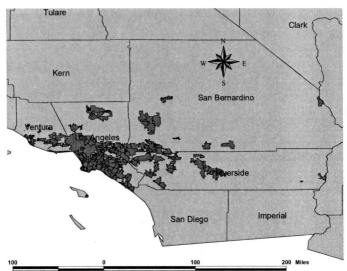

Explaining Metropolitan Crime and Violence in Los Angeles

This section contains model specifications for each of the six supplemental offenses selected for empirical analyses. The 1980 models come first to provide the baseline for comparison to subsequent decades. The 1990 and 2000 model specifications follow. The section after the examination of the two later decades contains comparison models over time for each offense.

<u>1980 Shoplifting</u>
Shoplifting, which is a prototypical property crime, tends to be dependent on the availability and concentration of targets. For shoplifting and each offense to follow, the best fitting model specification in terms of significant predictors is used. The 1980 model baseline specification, for all available jurisdictions (number = 132), includes two major functional variables, retail employment and

wholesale employment concentration. Both functional variables positively related to shoplifting offense rates. This confirms the importance of functional specialization leading to higher rates of shoplifting.

Existing literature confirms the importance of concentration of retail activities and significant relationship with property crime rates, but this model specification confirms this for shoplifting rates (Lewis and Louch 2000; Brown 1982). Lewis and Barbour (1999) in a study focused on the generation of local sale taxes in California municipalities suggest that retailing centers locate close to highways and auto-oriented retail is the most popular form of retail. One example in the Los Angeles metropolitan region of an auto-oriented retail center is the city of Montclair in San Bernardino County. Interstate Route 10 passes through both the north and south sides of Montclair. Montclair has a significant number of retail establishments especially a major shopping mall and auto dealerships located along this major interstate highway. Montclair's shoplifting rate in 1980 was 1162 per 100,000 persons, ranking ninth out of 132 municipalities. This increased significantly in 1990 and 2000. However, many other cities with higher rankings also locate near or around highways, supporting the relationship between retail centers, highway location, and higher shoplifting rates. Nevertheless, this assertion remains untested and it is unlikely that all retail centers are located near highways or include large shopping malls. The positive and significant coefficient for wholesale employment concentration in the shoplifting model is not easy to understand, but can be explained partly explained by the relationship between retail employment with wholesale employment concentration. That is, retail centers tend also to have significant concentrations of wholesale activities and employment.

The unemployment rate also positively relates to shoplifting rates. This variable is a measure of the status of the residential working population. Since jurisdictions with higher shoplifting rates are retail and wholesale centers as well, the residential populations of these centers probably face social and economic conditions providing lower status and resources. The unemployment rate in this model specification and with other model specifications shown below has significant and positive correlations with many status measures including lower-paying occupations, lower household income, lower educational attainment levels, and the percentage of the housing units for rent in a jurisdiction. Measures of these later variables, when included in model specifications with the unemployment rate, reduce the magnitude of the unemployment rate coefficient as well as increasing tolerance and reducing variance inflation factor levels. These variables and the unemployment rate are highly collinear with each other and present multicollinearity concerns. However, all of these variables together provide support for an inverse relationship between place status and shoplifting rates.

The model specification is robust with a R-square of .579. There are no significant issues with multicollinearity between predictor variables as seen by the values for tolerance and the variance inflation factor of each predictor variable. With regard to county differences, the dummy variable for Riverside County is significant and positive, while other county dummies are insignificant. An analysis of significant outliers for the 1980 shoplifting model specification helps to explain why the Riverside dummy coefficient is positive and significant. Blythe and Perris emerge as significant outliers in this model with shoplifting rates of 2871 and 2371 per 100,000 persons. Blythe has significant concentration of retail and wholesale employment and a relatively high unemployment rate. Perris, on the other hand, is not a wholesale center and does not show high levels of retail activities. Perris is more residential than Blythe. Other cities in Riverside County having relatively high rates of shoplifting include Coachella, Indio, and Beaumont. These cities are also residential with low employment to residential workers ratios. Perhaps, a separate model specification for Riverside County is required, but the total number of municipalities is quite small and model specifications exclude five cities from this county because of missing shoplifting offense data. Another strategy is to exclude these outliers (Blythe and Perris) in a model with the same predictors.

With this revised model specification (not shown), we find the same significant predictors as in the overall model except the coefficient for the Riverside dummy is now insignificant. Clearly, as outliers skew coefficient estimations, model specifications improve after the exclusion of these outliers.

Table 3 - Shoplifting Model Specification (1980)

Variable	Unstandardized Coefficients (B)	Standardized Coefficients (Beta)	t	Significance Level	Collinearity Statistics	
					Tolerance	Variance Inflation Factor
(Constant)	-170.7 (112.03)		-1.5	.13		
Orange	59.2 (79.06)	.048	.75	.455	.826	1.211
San Bernardino	162.26 (109.45)	.092	1.5	.141	.891	1.122
Riverside	468.33 (110.19)	.276	4.3	.000	.813	1.23
Ventura	-76.29 (116.15)	-.039	-.66	.513	.952	1.051
Retail E/R	261.23 (53.92)	.313	4.9	.000	.826	1.211
Wholesale E/R	46.22 (6.97)	.422	6.6	.000	.846	1.182
Unemployment Rate	53.85 (15.07)	.244	3.6	.001	.737	1.357
R^2	.579					

Overall, shoplifting rates are higher in retail and wholesale centers and with cities with higher unemployment rates. An analysis of the dynamics of shoplifting requires inclusion of both functional and status elements.

1990 Shoplifting
For model specifications for 1990 and 2000, measures of spatial association of offense rates are included. Along with visual examinations of local Moran's scatter plots, spatial outliers and local clusters of high or low offense rates are determined.

The Global Moran's I for shoplifting rates in the Los Angeles region with a value of -.0557 indicates no spatial autocorrelation or clustering of similar or dissimilar shoplifting rates across geographic space. This confirms expectations of little spatial clustering as shoplifting has a random distribution across suburban jurisdictions from a spatial perspective and consistent with the view that shoplifting occurs in many jurisdictions. Some spatial outliers are identified for shoplifting rates in 1990.

Figure 2 – Moran Scatter plot and Global Moran's I Value for Shoplifting Rates (1990)

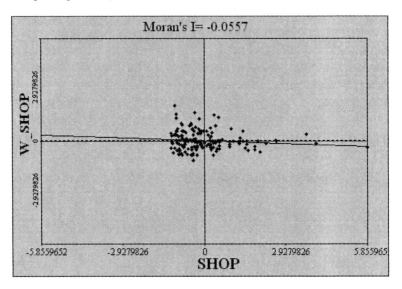

These outliers have higher shoplifting rates, but their neighbors have either significantly lower or relatively lower rates. Using the Local Moran's I scatter plot tool in Arc view, one can visually examine and identify spatial outliers. These spatial outliers include the cities of Montclair, Perris, Commerce, Coachella, Santa Fe Springs, Redondo Beach, and Victorville. Using the same local Moran's I scatter plots, a cluster of similar moderately high shoplifting rates is identified. These are a block of cities in Orange County including the cities of Anaheim and Santa Ana. Local clustering is more common for more densely clustered cities than for less dense cities and/or cities at further distances from each other. These later two conditions are more common to cities in the outlying Inland areas and along the coast.

Using the same predictors as in the 1980 model specification, two different models are developed for 1990. One includes the original jurisdictions in 1980 and the other model includes all jurisdictions for which data is available. Similar to the 1980 model, the same predictors (retail and wholesale employment concentration and unemployment rate) are significant for the 1990 shoplifting model specification for the original cities. Unlike the 1980 model, however, we find the dummy for San Bernardino County is now significant along with the dummy for Riverside County (which was the same as in 1980).

Two outliers for the 1990 shoplifting with original jurisdictions are identified, the cities of Montclair and Redondo Beach. As shown above, these are spatial outliers as well. Montclair is in San Bernardino County and Redondo Beach is in Los Angeles County. Montclair in this 1990 model with the original jurisdictions has the highest shoplifting rate of all 132 municipalities. Redondo Beach ranks sixth in the same comparison. Like Redondo Beach, Montclair does not have significant wholesale employment concentration, specializing in retail primarily. Both cities have relatively low unemployment rates, perhaps indicating that these cities have higher relative place status than other cities. However, Montclair does have relatively higher rates of violent crimes, which limits this interpretation for this case.

A shoplifting model in 1990 for the original jurisdictions (not shown) excluding these two cities finds the same significant predictors as in the main 1990 model, but the dummy for San Bernardino County is now insignificant. A model was specified for 1990 that includes all jurisdictions with available data (a total of 162 municipalities).

The same set of predictors (retail concentration, wholesale concentration, the unemployment rate, and dummies for Riverside and San Bernardino Counties) for the 1990 original jurisdictions specification and the 1980 shoplifting model specification are significant.

The outliers in this model include the cities of Coachella, Montclair, Redondo Beach, and Rancho Mirage. The first three identify as spatial outliers and outliers from model specifications. Rancho Mirage, located in Riverside County, is a different outlier from these three with low shoplifting rates, a high retail employment to residential worker ratio, a low wholesale employment to residential worker ratio, and a low unemployment rate. This municipality has retail concentrations of significance, but significantly higher status that protects it from high shoplifting rates.

Table 4 - Shoplifting Model Specification for Original Jurisdictions (1990)

Variable	Unstandardized Coefficients (B)	Standardized Coefficients (Beta)	t	Significance Level	Collinearity Statistics	
					Tolerance	Variance Inflation Factor
(Constant)	-94.86 (124.31)		-.763	.447		
Orange	95.37 (92.29)	.076	1.033	.303	.828	1.207
San Bernardino	386.29 (125.72)	.215	3.073	.003	.924	1.082
Riverside	440.22 (126.07)	.255	3.492	.001	.850	1.177
Ventura	3.76 (137.22)	.002	.027	.978	.933	1.072
Retail E/R	320.77 (64.02)	.404	5.010	.000	.697	1.435
Wholesale E/R	29.14 (10.84)	.211	2.688	.008	.736	1.358
Unemployment Rate	59.64 (22.55)	.209	2.645	.009	.727	1.375
R²	.439					

2000 Shoplifting

The same analyses above for 1990 were performed for 2000 shoplifting rates. The Global Moran's I value for the 2000 shoplifting model reveals no spatial autocorrelation similar to the 1990 shoplifting model. Many of the same spatial outliers identified in 1990 are outliers in 2000. However, two cities, the cities of Signal Hill and Laguna Hills, are also spatial outliers with relatively higher shoplifting rates than their neighbors. Both are retail centers, but Signal Hill is also a significant wholesale center.

Table 5 - Shoplifting Model Specifications for All Jurisdictions (1990)

Variable	Unstandardized Coefficients (B)	Standardized Coefficients (Beta)	t	Significance Level	Collinearity Statistics	
					Tolerance	Variance Inflation Factor
(Constant)	-131.76 (102.94)		-1.28	.202		
Orange	102.23 (86.02)	.081	1.189	.236	.820	1.220
San Bernardino	248.74 (93.14)	.176	2.671	.008	.876	1.142
Riverside	348.04 (95.92)	.241	3.628	.000	.859	1.165
Ventura	.80 (128.78)	.000	.006	.995	.928	1.078
Retail E/R	323.81 (53.19)	.435	6.087	.000	.742	1.348
Wholesale E/R	28.32 (10.38)	.191	2.729	.007	.771	1.297
Unemployment Rate	68.32 (19.45)	.242	3.513	.001	.797	1.254
R^2	.417					

The 2000 shoplifting with original jurisdictions shows only retail concentrations and the unemployment rate as significant predictors. The wholesale employment to resident workers ratio and the Riverside County dummy are no longer significant. Apparently, the original jurisdictions changed with regard to the composition of their functional characteristics and unidentified characteristics for cities in Riverside County. Montclair and Rolling Hills Estate identify as outliers in the 2000 model. Rolling Hills Estate has significant retail activities, but is primarily a high-status residential suburb in Los Angeles County.

For 2000, a model specification including all jurisdictions for which data is available reveals the same significant predictors and outliers as the model including only the original jurisdictions. It seems that wholesale concentrations are now less able to predict shoplifting rates than in earlier decades. One reason, explored in the next section, concerns the decentralization of wholesaling from traditional centers to more inland areas. Other possible reasons include the inclusion of

newer cities with less wholesale employment concentration and/or
newer cities that are primarily residential.

Figure 3 - Moran Scatter plot for Shoplifting (2000)

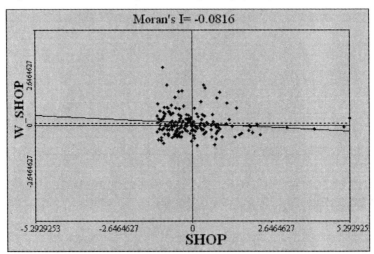

Shoplifting Comparisons
Model specifications explaining the variation in shoplifting rates for
three decades have been developed. It is useful to compare changes in
the sign, magnitude, and significance of explanatory variables and the
overall model explanatory power.

Comparing predictors across models requires using the
standardized coefficients of these predictors. For shoplifting rates,
Table 8 shows that the retail employment to residential workers ratio
and the unemployment rates consistently have a positive and significant
coefficient for all decades as well for all model specifications. The
magnitude of the retail E/R coefficient is much larger than the
unemployment rate and has increased in magnitude for the original
jurisdiction and all jurisdictions models for 2000.

Models developed to explain shoplifting rates must include retail
activities as an explanatory factor. The wholesale E/R ratio coefficient
was significantly and relatively high in 1980, declined in significance
and magnitude in 1990, and was insignificant and extremely low

magnitude for 2000. The earlier relationship between wholesale and retail employment concentration has weakened with many more retail centers that have little wholesale activities. Another factor has been the movement of wholesale activities from Los Angeles County to other counties in the region. The city of Ontario and other municipalities in the Inland Empire are emerging as wholesale centers. The decentralization of wholesaling distribution centers away from the port areas and traditional centers in Los Angeles County is a trend that can explain the reduced explanatory power of wholesale concentrations in explaining shoplifting rates.

Table 6 - Shoplifting Model Specification for Original Jurisdictions (2000)

Variable	Unstandardized Coefficients (B)	Standardized Coefficients (Beta)	t	Significance Level	Collinearity Statistics	
					Tolerance	Variance Inflation Factor
(Constant)	-108.52 (58.24)		-1.86	.065		
Orange	35.64 (43.85)	.054	.813	.418	.800	1.250
San Bernardino	139.58 (59.50)	.146	2.346	.021	.900	1.111
Riverside	-30.98 (57.76)	-0.34	-.536	.593	.883	1.133
Ventura	5.35 (64.30)	.005	.083	.934	.926	1.079
Retail E/R	239.53 (24.61)	.667	9.733	.000	.746	1.340
Wholesale E/R	3.77 (3.88)	.067	.971	.333	.745	1.343
Unemployment Rate	21.90 (6.42)	.235	3.412	.001	.738	1.356
R²	.565					

The coefficients for county dummies changed as well with Riverside County showing significance in earlier decades and the dummy for San Bernardino County increasing in significance in 1990 and 2000. Newly incorporated residential suburbs with little retail or other employment concentrations in Riverside County could partly explain the decline of this county's dummy coefficient. The city of Ontario is located in San Bernardino County and the increased significance of the dummy for this county could be capturing the impact of that and other cities in the county on shoplifting rates.

Table 7 - Shoplifting Model Specifications for All Jurisdictions (2000)

Variable	Unstandardized Coefficients (B)	Standardized Coefficients (Beta)	t	Significance Level	Collinearity Statistics	
					Tolerance	VIF
(Constant)	-144.71 (47.94)		-3.018	.003		
Orange	64.76 (39.13)	.096	1.655	.100	.795	1.258
San Bernardino	144.26 (41.68)	.194	3.461	.001	.862	1.160
Riverside	-10.69 (41.42)	-.014	-.258	.797	.873	1.146
Ventura	18.68 (59.65)	.017	.313	.755	.922	1.084
Retail E/R	249.19 (21.74)	.673	11.465	.000	.781	1.281
Wholesale E/R	2.47 (3.71)	.040	.666	.506	.760	1.317
Unemployment Rate	24.85 (5.37)	.267	4.626	.000	.811	1.233
R²	.561					

The overall explanatory power of the models over the three decades has remained around a moderately tight range. Both 1990 models have lower values for R-square as well as higher significant coefficients for the dummies for the two Inland Empire counties. Perhaps, these model specifications require inclusion of other variables not considered in these analyses. Overall, model specifications for shoplifting support that retail functional specialization and the lower status of suburbs contributes to higher shoplifting rates.

Table 8 - Shoplifting Model Comparisons for Three Decades (1980-2000)

Variables	1980 Baseline	1990 Original Jurisdictions	1990 All Jurisdictions	2000 Original Jurisdictions	2000 All Jurisdictions
		Standardized Coefficients			
Orange	.048	.076	.081	.054	.096
San Bernardino	.092	**.215**	**.176**	**.146**	**.194**
Riverside	**.276**	**.255**	**.241**	-0.34	-.014
Ventura	-.039	.002	.000	.005	.017
Retail E/R	**.313**	**.404**	**.435**	**.667**	**.673**
Wholesale E/R	**.422**	**.211**	**.191**	.067	.040
Unemployment Rate	**.244**	**.209**	**.242**	**.235**	**.267**
R²	.579	.439	.417	.565	.561

Bold – significant at p < .01 level

1980 Nonresidential Burglaries
The next supplemental offense examined is nonresidential burglaries. Much like shoplifting, the availability and concentration of commercial targets contribute to higher rates of these offenses. The model specifications for nonresidential burglaries share many similarities with model specifications for shoplifting rates. The best fitting model specification for this offense in 1980 includes the retail employment to residential workers ratio, the wholesale employment to residential workers ratio, and the unemployment rate as significant and positive predictors of nonresidential burglary rates. These are the same as for shoplifting. In this case, the coefficient for retail E/R is larger than the one for the 1980 shoplifting model specification and larger than the coefficient measuring wholesale employment concentration. Retail centers tend to offer more attractive and higher-value targets than wholesale targets as well as retail targets are more widely available than wholesale targets. However, municipalities that are significant retail centers also are significant wholesale centers. This phenomenon overrides status differences so even some higher status suburbs are retail and wholesale centers.

A new predictor emerges for nonresidential burglary rates, travel time to work under 30 minutes. This predictor is significant at the 5% level. This predictor measures the commuting time of residential workers in municipalities and a higher value on this variable indicates that the workplaces of workers are fairly close to their residences. It is difficult to fully explain why this predictor explains nonresidential burglaries, but one possibility is that more dense suburbs and/or lower-status cities tend to have residential working populations that choose to live close to work or face mobility constraints in residential location. Higher-status individuals and groups with greater amount of resources are able to afford housing further away from work. Nevertheless, this predictor loses its explanatory power in subsequent decades as seen below.

Another difference with the shoplifting model is the lack of significance of the county dummies for 1980. However, the county dummies, especially the dummy for Riverside County, increases significantly in the next two decades. Model outliers include the cities of Blythe and Santa Fe Springs. Both cities have relatively high unemployment rates and are retail centers. However, Santa Fe Springs is a significant wholesale center with a ratio of 17 wholesale sector workers per one residential worker in the wholesale sector. Ratios with values above one generally signify the presence of a wholesale center. Thus, for both cities, other predictors not included in the model, explain high rates of nonresidential burglaries. A model excluding these two outlier cities (not shown) finds that the same predictors except travel time under 30 minutes are significant and the coefficient for the wholesale E/R ratio is greater in magnitude than the retail E/R coefficient. In this model, the city of Commerce, with a wholesale E/R ratio of 47 (the highest in the sample), may be skewing the results. Like the cities of Industries and Vernon, which are excluded from all empirical analyses, Commerce is a significant employment hub in many economic sectors and is unique in comparison to almost all municipalities in the Los Angeles metro region. However, the municipality has a substantial residential population of about 10,000 persons, which does not merit its exclusion from empirical analyses. All of the model specifications developed to explain offense ratios are subject to the effects of these significant unique cases as multivariate regression techniques identify predictors on ability to explain variation in the dependent variables. Overall, the model specification for 1980 has high explanatory power with a R-square value of .554. This is comparable to the 1980 model for shoplifting and with most of the same significant predictors.

Table 9 - Nonresidential Burglaries Model Specification (1980)

Variable	Unstandardized Coefficients (B)	Standardized Coefficients (Beta)	T	Significance Level	Collinearity Statistics	
					Tolerance	Variance Inflation Factor
(Constant)	-421.70 (244.03)		-1.73	.087		
Orange	2.11 (76.34)	.002	.028	.978	.821	1.218
San Bernardino	71.44 (113.11)	.043	.632	.529	.773	1.293
Riverside	62.18 (112.91)	.039	.551	.583	.717	1.394
Ventura	-216.60 (113.34)	-.120	-1.91	.058	.926	1.080
%30min	7.10 (3.58)	.141	1.979	.050	.715	1.399
Retail E/R	314.15 (52.77)	.403	5.953	.000	.796	1.257
Wholesale E/R	32.65 (6.73)	.320	4.853	.000	.841	1.190
Unemployment Rate	54.39 (14.52)	.264	3.745	.000	.735	1.360
R²	.554					

1990 Nonresidential Burglaries

The Global Moran's I value for nonresidential burglaries in 1990 is .0326. As with shoplifting, there is little spatial autocorrelation or clustering of similar or dissimilar nonresidential burglary rates at the municipality level in the five-county Los Angeles metro region. Unlike with shoplifting, there is a different set of spatial outliers having high levels of nonresidential burglaries surrounded by neighbors with significantly lower rates. The cities of Santa Fe Springs, Commerce, Lake Elsinore, Signal Hill, Needles, and Desert Hot Springs are these spatial outliers with high rates of nonresidential burglaries. The first two cities have already been identified as model outliers for the 1980 model specification. The later four cities are interesting examples of cities that do not share any borders with incorporated jurisdictions, locate a significant distance from urban settlements, and/or are surrounded by another city.

Figure 4 - Moran Scatter plot for Nonresidential Burglaries (1990)

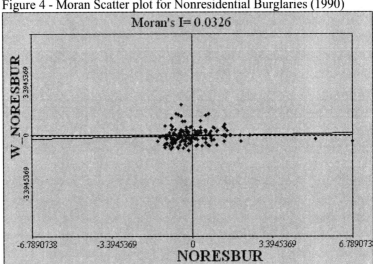

Signal Hill is an example of a city with its total land area engulfed by the city of Long Beach and shares only one border. This city is also an example of a jurisdiction with high concentrations of wholesale and retail activities, but physically isolated from other jurisdictions. Other cities in Los Angeles County almost similar examples of physical isolation include the cities of Beverly Hills, Santa Monica, Culver City, and West Hollywood, which are engulfed by the City of Los Angeles. These cities do border at least one other jurisdiction besides the city of Los Angeles. All the other spatial outliers in terms of rates of nonresidential burglaries are located in the Inland Empire counties and do not share any land borders with other jurisdictions. In the case of Needles, which is located in the desert, physical isolation includes being located a considerable distance from other incorporated jurisdictions.

The 1990 model specification with the original 1980 jurisdictions changes considerably with wholesale E/R ratio being the most significant predictor of nonresidential burglaries.

Table 10 - Nonresidential Burglaries Model Specification for Original Jurisdictions (1990)

Variable	Unstandardized Coefficients (B)	Standardized Coefficients (Beta)	t	Significance Level	Collinearity Statistics	
					Tolerance	VIF
(Constant)	126.65 (198.95)		.637	.526		
Orange	39.39 (52.86)	.043	.745	.458	.805	1.242
San Bernardino	186.76 (71.06)	.141	2.628	.010	.922	1.084
Riverside	217.49 (71.63)	.171	3.036	.003	.839	1.192
Ventura	-20.75 (79.09)	-.014	-.262	.793	.895	1.117
%35min	.38 (2.85)	.008	.133	.894	.799	1.252
Retail E/R	95.45 (36.98)	.163	2.581	.011	.666	1.502
Wholesale E/R	65.25 (6.16)	.642	10.596	.000	.727	1.375
Unemployment Rate	55.35 (13.64)	.263	4.142	.000	.660	1.515
R^2	.672					

Again, the spatial outlier cities of Commerce and Santa Fe Springs have significantly high wholesale employment concentrations as well as high rates of nonresidential burglaries. The later is also a model outlier. Dropping these two cities from the same specified model reduces the magnitude and significance of the wholesale concentration predictor, but also reduces the overall explanatory power of the model with R-square dropping to a value of .432 from the R-square.672 in the full model. Further, the unemployment rate and the Riverside County dummy become the strongest predictors. All this suggests that different types of factors may be driving the rates of nonresidential burglaries in different parts of the region and for different types of suburbs.

Table 11 - Nonresidential Burglaries Model Specification for All Jurisdictions (1990)

Variable	Unstandardized Coefficients (B)	Standardized Coefficients (Beta)	t	Significance Level	Collinearity Statistics	
					Tolerance	Variance Inflation Factor
(Constant)	72.85 (156.41)		.466	.642		
Orange	38.00 (51.40)	.041	.739	.461	.812	1.231
San Bernardino	160.38 (55.49)	.154	2.891	.004	.873	1.145
Riverside	212.13 (57.29)	.200	3.703	.000	.852	1.174
Ventura	-31.98 (77.44)	-.022	-.413	.680	.908	1.101
%35min	.87 (2.21)	.021	.393	.695	.859	1.164
Retail E/R	116.35 (32.17)	.213	3.617	.000	.718	1.393
Wholesale E/R	62.26 (6.20)	.573	10.042	.000	.765	1.308
Unemployment Rate	56.45 (12.00)	.273	4.705	.000	.741	1.349
R^2	.619					

The 1990 model with all jurisdictions shows the similar strength of the wholesale concentration measure as the strongest predictor. A new outlier is identified, the city of Lake Elsinore. This city was also a spatial outlier, but was not included in the 1980 models for all offenses because of missing offense data. This city does not have significant wholesale concentration, a small amount of retail, and is primarily residential. Other reasons for its relatively high rates of nonresidential burglaries not identified in these model specifications are required. The county dummies for Riverside and San Bernardino Counties are significant, which suggests some other factors specific to these county's municipalities drive the higher rates in these counties.

2000 Nonresidential Burglaries

The global measure of spatial association for 2000 rates of nonresidential burglaries shows no spatial autocorrelation with a Moran's I value of .1518. Spatial outliers include the cities of Signal Hill, Santa Fe Springs, and Desert Hot Springs. These cities continue to have relatively high rates of burglaries in comparison to their neighbors. However, the rates of nonresidential burglaries are much lower than in earlier decades and the gap between the high rate cities and other cities has significantly reduced. In fact, the cities of Perris, Lake Elsinore, Santa Paula, Brea, Needles, and Temecula qualify as spatial outliers, but do not have significantly high rates of nonresidential burglaries.

Figure 5 - Moran Scatter plot for Nonresidential Burglaries (2000)

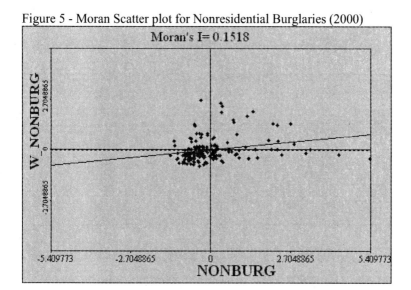

Only in comparison to their neighbors (or lacking boundaries with other jurisdictions) do these cities qualify as spatial outliers. Local clustering of low rates of these types of burglaries is evident from visual examination of maps and shows that many residential suburbs tend to obviously have low rates of nonresidential burglaries.

Nevertheless, non-residential burglary rates are significantly lower for most jurisdictions in 2000.

A 2000 model with the original 1980 jurisdictions is shown in Table 12. Retail and wholesale employment concentration and higher unemployment rates still positively and significantly relate to nonresidential burglary rates. The magnitude and significance of the wholesale concentration measure has dropped from the 1990 period. This is true for the unemployment rate as well. The retail E/R coefficient and the dummy coefficient for Riverside County are the strongest predictors in this model. As seen in 1990, the travel time measure no longer is a significant predictor and the sign of that coefficient is now negative instead of the positive coefficients found in earlier models.

Table 12 - Nonresidential Burglaries Model Specification for Original Jurisdictions (2000)

Variable	Unstandardized Coefficients (B)	Standardized Coefficients (Beta)	t	Significance Level	Collinearity Statistics	
					Tolerance	VIF
(Constant)	41.67 (124.10)		.336	.738		
Orange	28.03 (35.50)	.055	.790	.431	.744	1.343
San Bernardino	66.18 (46.47)	.090	1.424	.157	.900	1.112
Riverside	301.35 (45.49)	.427	6.624	.000	.868	1.152
Ventura	77.87 (51.75)	.097	1.505	.135	.872	1.147
%35min	-.50 (1.86)	-.018	-.267	.790	.814	1.228
Retail E/R	104.18 (19.52)	.377	5.338	.000	.724	1.382
Wholesale E/R	14.83 (3.04)	.341	4.884	.000	.742	1.348
Unemployment Rate	13.56 (5.26)	.189	2.577	.011	.670	1.493
R^2	.556					

There are three outliers in this model, the cities of Desert Hot Springs, Signal Hill, and Santa Paula. The first two are both model and spatial outliers in earlier models and with the spatial analyses. The third is identified as a spatial outlier in 2000. This city has a higher nonresidential burglary rate than its neighbors. The regression model predicted a burglary rate of 250 burglaries per 100000 in population and the actual rate for Santa Paula was 690 per 100000 in population. Located in Ventura County, on the northwestern edge of the region, this city is primarily residential with low retail and wholesale E/R ratios, but a relative high unemployment rate of close to 8 percent in 2000.

The 2000 model for nonresidential burglaries for all available jurisdictions confirms the importance of retail and wholesale employment concentrations, the unemployment rate, and the dummies for Riverside and San Bernardino Counties on nonresidential burglary rates in the region. These predictors consistently relate to burglary rates in the positive direction and explain both the functional and status aspects of suburbs. The unemployment rate is highly collinear with other status measures not included in final model specifications and together these capture the low-status residential environments of high nonresidential burglary rate cities. The retail and wholesale E/R ratios capture the employment functions provided by suburbs, representing the physical and built environmental characteristics of suburbs.

Differences in both function and status as well as interactive aspects across suburbs strongly relates to the variation in nonresidential burglary rates in these suburbs. The model has an additional outlier, the city of Blythe, to the three identified in the 2000 original jurisdictions model. In this case, unlike for other outliers, the model predicted an offense rate much higher than the actual rate of nonresidential burglaries. The prediction was for a rate of 640 per 100000 persons based on Blythe's values on the predictors, but Blythe's rate in 2000 was 185 per 100000 persons. Blythe's rate of nonresidential burglaries has come down significantly over the period from rates of over 800 in the early 1990s. Other factors obviously played a role in reducing this city's nonresidential burglary rate.

Nonresidential Burglaries Comparisons
A comparison of models for nonresidential burglary rates over three decades demonstrates that predictors vary in strength and significance over time. The coefficient for the unemployment rate decreased significantly from the earlier decades and the magnitude of the coefficient declined from a high of .273 in 1990 to .137 in 2000.

Unemployment in the Los Angeles region declined significantly after 1992, tracking the business cycle trough. Most jurisdictions in the area saw decreased rates of unemployment during the 1990s. As this measure derives from the Census of Population and Housing, one should point out that all CPH data for the last four decades were collected during the peak years of the business cycle. These measures cannot capture business cycle changes, but rather represent secular or long-term changes. However, these measures do accurately capture differences in place characteristics.

Table 13 - Nonresidential Burglaries Model Specification for All Jurisdictions (2000)

Variable	Unstandardized Coefficients (B)	Standardized Coefficients (Beta)	t	Significance Level	Collinearity Statistics	
					Tolerance	Variance Inflation Factor
(Constant)	-40.77 (84.79)		-.481	.631		
Orange	3.36 (30.92)	.006	.109	.914	.758	1.320
San Bernardino	79.91 (32.16)	.137	2.485	.014	.862	1.160
Riverside	307.57 (32.03)	.528	9.603	.000	.869	1.151
Ventura	60.78 (46.81)	.071	1.298	.196	.891	1.122
%35min	1.00 (1.25)	.044	.801	.425	.870	1.150
Retail E/R	112.19 (17.04)	.388	6.585	.000	.757	1.322
Wholesale E/R	13.71 (2.87)	.281	4.781	.000	.759	1.318
Unemployment Rate	10.01 (4.29)	.137	2.332	.021	.756	1.322
R^2	.574					

The coefficients for retail and wholesale employment concentration are more volatile over this period. As indicated earlier, the impact of wholesale concentration was the greatest in the 1990 period, but had declined in strength by 2000, especially with the all jurisdictions model. The retail coefficient showed some decrease in strength in 1990 (wholesale coefficients were relatively much larger), but was the strongest predictor by 2000. The largest gain in coefficient magnitude was with the dummy coefficient for Riverside County. All these coefficients were positive and significant. This suggests that something specific about the county and its jurisdictions explain its higher rates of nonresidential burglaries.

Table 14 - Nonresidential Burglary Model Comparisons for Three Decades (1980-2000)

	1980 Baseline	1990 Original Jurisdictions	1990 All Jurisdictions	2000 Original Jurisdictions	2000 All Jurisdictions
Variables	**Standardized Coefficients**				
Orange	.002	.043	.041	.055	.006
San Bernardino	**.043**	**.141**	**.154**	.090	**.137**
Riverside	.039	**.171**	**.200**	**.427**	**.528**
Ventura	-.120	**-.014**	-.022	.097	.071
%35min	*.141*	.008	.021	-.018	.044
Retail E/R	**.403**	**.163**	**.213**	**.377**	**.388**
Wholesale E/R	**.320**	**.642**	**.573**	**.341**	**.281**
Unemployment Rate	**.264**	**.263**	**.273**	**.189**	**.137**
R²	.554	.672	.619	.556	.574

Bold – significant at p < .01 level, Bold/Italics – significant at the p < .05 level

The analyses identifying spatial outliers identify many jurisdictions in this County that have high rates of nonresidential burglaries, but whose neighbors have relatively lower rates. These spatial outliers reveal a patchwork distribution of offense rates with some unique effects for this county. By 2000, many jurisdictions throughout the region had significantly lower offense rates. Some changes during the 1990s probably explain this reduction in rates.

The overall R-square changed little over the three decades except for the same increase in the strength of the wholesale measure, which is responsible for the large spike in the 1990 models. Overall, nonresidential burglaries are strongly influenced by differences in functional and status characteristics between places. Employment centers have higher rates of these offenses and offer targets that increase the likelihood of increased prevalence in these types of suburbs.

Status measures, such as the unemployment rate, capture the residential place status of jurisdictions and these are important in the levels of rates of nonresidential burglaries. Places of varying status levels suffer from nonresidential burglary rates, but lower-status jurisdictions have higher rates of these crimes.

1980 Commercial Robberies
Commercial robberies are difficult offenses to classify. Since the location of these crimes is in commercial establishments, the target of these crimes usually relate to some sort of property available in these establishments. However, these offenses involve direct contact between individuals and some degree of force and potential for serious injuries. The location of the offense could be either incidental or have lower significance than features of commercial establishments and other factors underlying these crimes. In our case, commercial robberies are considered as property crimes offering available high-value targets for potential offenders. The physical and nonphysical features of the environments in which these offenses occur are pertinent in explaining the frequency and prevalence of these offenses across suburban jurisdictions.

The relative rates of commercial robberies are lower than for other comparable offenses. For example, the highest rate of commercial robberies in the 1980 sample was for the city of Inglewood, with a rate of 300 commercial robbery incidents per every 100,000 persons. For the same period, Inglewood's overall robbery rate was 1475, its assault rate was 576, and its overall violent crime rate was 2218. The percentage of commercial robberies in overall rates of different robbery types was only 20 percent. In comparison, highway robberies accounted for close to sixty seven percent of all robberies. Inglewood may be unique in having such a high proportion of highway robbery incidents, but the overall rates of commercial robberies are significantly lower than for property crimes in many jurisdictions.

The best fitting model specification for 1980 is presented in Table 15. The best predictors in this model specification are dramatically different than for shoplifting and nonresidential burglaries. In this model, a service employment concentration measure has a positive and significant with rates of commercial robberies. This is not surprising as the kinds of businesses included in this measure include services for consumers and lower-end business services. However, the coefficient for service employment concentration is smaller and less significant versus the two major predictors in the model. These are the percentage of the population that is African-American and percentage of housing units that have more than five units (multiple housing units). From the extant literature, the significance of the Black population measure is expected. Many variables measuring concentrations of African American populations in many different environmental units positively relate with higher violent crime rates. However, this model confirms this is true for commercial robberies as well.

The other major predictor with relatively high magnitude and significance of its coefficient is a measure of the multiple housing units. Being positively and significantly related to higher commercial robberies, one interpretation of this measure relates to the types of targets in suburbs offering high-rises and apartments. Cities with higher levels of rental than single-family homes may provide commercial targets that are more accessible and visible to potential offenders.

Additionally, commercial targets in these types of residential environments are denser and nonresidential populations and businesses are more likely to locate in these environments than exclusively single-family and owner-occupied residential environments (Baumer et al. 1998). This last point also helps to understand why the measure of the median household income negatively relates to commercial robberies. Even though the measure for median household income and multiple housing units are collinear with each other, the models for later decades show that multiple housing units is less significant and of smaller magnitude.

Table 15 - Model Specification for Commercial Robberies (1980)

Variable	Unstandardized Coefficients (B)	Standardized Coefficients (Beta)	t	Significance Level	Collinearity Statistics	
					Tolerance	Variance Inflation Factor
(Constant)	23.39 (16.36)		1.43	.155		
Orange	8.34 (8.01)	.074	1.04	.300	.857	1.168
San Bernardino	10.79 (11.57)	.066	.93	.353	.849	1.178
Riverside	-11.23 (11.79)	-.072	-.95	.343	.755	1.324
Ventura	2.16 (12.26)	.012	.176	.860	.908	1.102
Service E/R	9.46 (4.24)	.151	2.23	.027	.935	1.070
Multi-Housing Units	1.38 (.30)	.365	4.55	.000	.665	1.504
Median Household Income	-.00 (.00)	-.165	-2.0	.046	.636	1.571
African-American Population	1.99 (.32)	.421	6.18	.000	.920	1.087
R²	.479					

The 1980 model specification confirms that some functional and status attributes interact and jointly contribute to the rates of commercial robberies for suburban jurisdictions. Taking all the predictors together, one interpretation is that higher rates of commercial robberies are more common for larger cities or cities located close to the urban core (the city of Los Angeles and Los Angeles county in this case). These cities tend to offer a mix of high-density employment and residential functions and the environments in these cities is favorable for higher commercial robbery rates. At this point, these models suggest that commercial robberies are an urban phenomenon.

None of the dummy coefficients for the four counties are significant, however, the reference region of Los Angeles County has more cities with higher rates of commercial robberies. Three major model outliers for 1980 are the cities of Inglewood, Culver City, and Ojai. The first two are in Los Angeles County. Inglewood has a heavy concentration of black populations and a low median household income, but its levels of service employment concentration and multiple housing units probably led to the lower predicted rate by the model. Culver City is a service center with low level of African American population, which may have led to underprediction of its commercial robbery rate in the model. Ojai is in Ventura County having a low African American population and does not provide many multiple housing units. The overall R-square of the 1980 model is .479, which is comparable to shoplifting and nonresidential models.

1990 Commercial Robberies
The Global Moran's I for commercial robberies in 1990 is higher than the values of this statistic for shoplifting and nonresidential burglaries. The value of .3258 still does not qualify as indicating significant spatial concentration of these rates. Values of .5 and above generally indicate some significant level of spatial association for any spatial data. There are some local clusters of jurisdictions with moderately high and high rates of commercial robberies, mostly in Los Angeles County, parts of Orange County, and three cities in the Inland Empire counties. All these clusters of municipalities are either more centrally located, with high levels of Black populations, and/or offer some attractive (high value) and accessible targets. The later cities include the cities of Beverly Hills and Santa Monica. Many of these same cities are also spatial outliers in the sense that at least one of its neighbors has lower rates, but they are part of local clusters because at least one significant neighbor has similarly high rates. Pure spatial outliers for commercial robbery rates in 1990 do not seem to exist. As mentioned above, the range of commercial robbery rates is smaller than for other offenses, so the differences in rates between these cluster cities and other jurisdictions are not relatively large.

The 1990 model with the original 1980 jurisdictions shows that the coefficients for African American populations and median household income continue to remain significant and in the expected direction. The next largest predictor, service employment concentration, remains positively related to commercial robbery rates as in the earlier model.

Figure 6 - Moran Scatter plot for Commercial Robberies (1990)

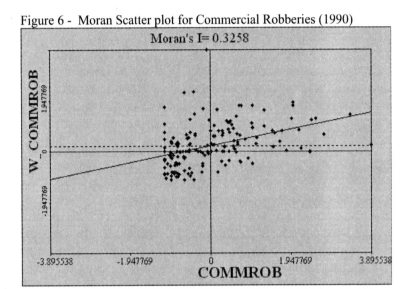

Multiple housing units drops out of the model as a significant predictor of commercial robbery rates. The largest changes with coefficients concern the significance of the county dummy coefficients for Orange, Ventura, and Riverside Counties. All of these coefficients are negative suggesting that rates of commercial robberies in these counties tend to be lower on average and especially in comparison to Los Angeles County. The city of Pomona, in Los Angeles County, is the model outlier. Pomona has a very high commercial robbery rate, but does not have service employment concentration.

In the 1990 model with all jurisdictions with available data, the ordering of the strength and significance of the predictors is mostly consistent with the more limited 1990 model. One change is the dummy coefficient for San Bernardino County is now significant and negatively associated with commercial robbery rates. This is similar with other counties. The two model outliers in the 1990 model are

Montclair and Pomona. These two cities are outliers in other models shown above.

Table 16 - Model Specification for Commercial Robberies for Original Jurisdictions (1990)

Variable	Unstandardized Coefficients (B)	Standardized Coefficients (Beta)	t	Significance Level	Collinearity Statistics	
					Tolerance	Variance Inflation Factor
(Constant)	113.64 (17.70)		6.42	.000		
Orange	-25.01 (9.38)	-.189	-2.7	.009	.847	1.180
San Bernardino	-2.27 (13.22)	-.012	-.17	.864	.884	1.132
Riverside	-51.91 (13.44)	-.283	-3.9	.000	.790	1.266
Ventura	-44.07 (14.35)	-.211	-3.1	.003	.902	1.108
Service E/R	7.16 (3.03)	.160	2.37	.020	.930	1.076
Multi-Housing Units	-.10 (.34)	-.022	-.29	.773	.721	1.386
Median Household Income	-.00 (.00)	-.364	-4.5	.000	.646	1.548
African-American Population	2.28 (.46)	.353	5.02	.000	.860	1.163
R^2	.477					

2000 Commercial Robberies

The Global Moran's I for 2000 is lower in value than for 1990 and reveals no spatial autocorrelation for commercial burglary rates. This result is explained by noting the reduction in commercial burglary rates throughout the region, especially for higher rate jurisdictions. For these reasons, there are a number of pure spatial outliers including the cities of Santa Fe Springs, Gardena, and Commerce all located in Los

Angeles County. These cities have much higher rates of commercial robberies than their neighbors.

Table 17 - Model Specification for Commercial Robberies for All Jurisdictions (1990)

Variable	Unstandardized Coefficients (B)	Standardized Coefficients (Beta)	t	Significance Level	Collinearity Statistics	
					Tolerance	Variance Inflation Factor
(Constant)	95.74 (15.51)		6.18	.000		
Orange	-24.62 (8.93)	-.180	-2.8	.007	.828	1.208
San Bernardino	-37.52 (10.30)	-.246	-3.6	.000	.780	1.282
Riverside	-45.12 (10.40)	-.290	-4.3	.000	.796	1.257
Ventura	-38.34 (13.65)	-.176	-2.8	.006	.900	1.111
Service E/R	6.67 (2.67)	.152	2.49	.014	.948	1.055
Multi-Housing Units	.31 (.30)	.075	1.05	.295	.703	1.422
Median Household Income	-.00 (.00)	-.324	-4.5	.000	.674	1.483
African-American Population	2.43 (.44)	.351	5.49	.000	.866	1.154
R^2	.458					

Primarily residential suburbs tend to have lower commercial robbery rates as anticipated, but these low rate cities locally cluster in space mostly in southeastern Orange County and parts of Ventura County. These jurisdictions offer few attractive targets that would lead to higher commercial robberies.

The 2000 model for the original jurisdictions is little different than earlier year models except the county dummies for Orange and San

Bernardino Counties are no longer significant. Part of this could be the related to the inclusion of newly incorporated jurisdictions in these counties that are more residential and less likely to have high commercial robbery rates.

Figure 7 - Moran Scatter plot for Commercial Robberies (1990)

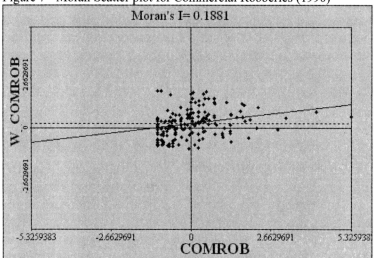

The other fact is the general decline of robbery rates is more applicable to many of the jurisdictions in these two counties. These are speculative assertions.

The second model for 2000 commercial robbery rates is essentially the same as the first. Median household income and African American population concentrations continue to be significantly related to higher commercial robbery rates. Commercial robberies are more frequent in nonresidential environments with significant African American population concentrations. These tend to larger cities and/or urban areas.

Higher-status residential suburbs have the lowest rates of commercial robberies and lower-status urbanized suburbs tend to have the highest rates of these offenses. For both 2000 models, Commerce and Gardena are outliers. These cities are also spatial outliers, suggesting some unique characteristics of these places explain their higher rates of commercial robberies.

Table 18 - Model Specifications for Commercial Robberies for Original Jurisdictions (2000)

Variable	Unstandardized Coefficients (B)	Standardized Coefficients (Beta)	t	Significance Level	Collinearity Statistics	
					Tolerance	Variance Inflation Factor
(Constant)	67.13 (9.39)		7.15	.000		
Orange	-9.35 (5.08)	-.136	-1.8	.068	.848	1.179
San Bernardino	-8.50 (7.23)	-.086	-1.2	.242	.868	1.152
Riverside	-18.97 (7.23)	-.200	-2.6	.010	.803	1.245
Ventura	-24.16 (7.74)	-.223	-3.1	.002	.913	1.096
Service E/R	8.78 (3.06)	.208	2.87	.005	.882	1.134
Multi-Housing Units	-.29 (.20)	-.124	-1.5	.147	.651	1.536
Median Household Income	-.00 (.00)	-.447	-5.2	.000	.643	1.556
African-American Population	1.12 (.28)	.303	4.02	.000	.821	1.218
R^2	.426					

Commercial Robberies Comparisons

Commercial robberies are more frequent in urbanized areas, but these are not necessarily areas with significant employment concentrations. A comparison of models over three decades reveal the strength of residential factors such as the socioeconomic and demographic composition of the population also play a role in increasing commercial robbery rates. African American dominated areas and suburbs with higher minority populations that are poorer tend to have higher commercial robbery rates consistently over time.

Table 19 -Model Specification for Commercial Robberies for All Jurisdictions (2000)

Variable	Unstandardized Coefficients (B)	Standardized Coefficients (Beta)	t	Significance Level	Collinearity Statistics	
					Tolerance	Variance Inflation Factor
(Constant)	59.87 (7.96)		7.52	.000		
Orange	-9.87 (4.53)	-.144	-2.1	.031	.825	1.213
San Bernardino	-23.30 (5.27)	-.306	-4.4	.000	.751	1.332
Riverside	-18.52 (5.28)	-.243	-3.5	.001	.747	1.338
Ventura	-20.62 (7.10)	-.183	-2.9	.004	.906	1.104
Service E/R	7.42 (2.75)	.172	2.7	.008	.882	1.133
Multi-Housing Units	-.11 (.16)	-.052	-.69	.494	.634	1.577
Median Household Income	-.00 (.00)	-.418	-5.7	.000	.675	1.481
African-American Population	1.20 (.26)	.308	4.66	.000	.822	1.217
R^2	.418					

The overall significance and magnitude of important predictors is very consistent over time. This is also true for the overall explanatory power of the models. Status plays a more important role than function in the determination of commercial robbery rates. In general, suburbs with particular types of residential populations varying by status are more or less prone to high or low commercial robbery rates. Poorer suburbs offering fewer resources and lower overall status have the highest rates of commercial robberies in the Los Angeles region.

Table 20 - Commercial Robbery Model Comparisons for Three Decades (1980-2000)

Variables	1980 Baseline	1990 Original Jurisdictions	1990 All Jurisdictions	2000 Original Jurisdictions	2000 All Jurisdictions
		Standardized Coefficients			
Orange	.074	-.189	-.180	-.136	*-.144*
San Bernardino	.066	-.012	-.246	-.086	-.306
Riverside	-.072	-.283	-.290	-.200	-.243
Ventura	.012	-.211	-.176	-.223	-.183
Service E/R	*.151*	.160	.152	.208	.172
Multiple Housing Units	.365	-.022	.075	-.124	-.052
Median Household Income	*-.165*	-.364	-.324	-.447	-.418
African American Populations	.421	.353	.351	.303	.308
R^2	.479	.477	.458	.426	.418

Bold – significant at p < .01 level, Bold/Italics – significant at the p < .05 level

<u>1980 Highway Robberies</u>
Highway robberies are more directly classified as violent crimes. Even though the ultimate target may be the property of individuals, the element of force and serious injuries suggests that these targets are not uniquely available in particular areas of employment concentrations. Functional characteristics of place have little to do with highway robberies. Involving direct confrontation between individuals and occurring in public settings, these offenses usually involve personal conflicts and disputes that are publicly visible. The visibility of disputes and conflicts partly relates to the involvement of formal third

party mediators to resolve these disputes. More often than not, this is the police, especially in poorer environments. These disputes and conflicts have escalated into potentially serious crimes that could result in life-threatening and lethal outcomes.

Table 21 - Model Specification for Highway Robberies (1980)

Variable	Unstandardized Coefficients (B)	Standardized Coefficients (Beta)	t	Significance Level	Collinearity Statistics	
					Tolerance	Variance Inflation Factor
(Constant)	-63.25 (21.75)		-2.91	.004		
Orange	-62.62 (19.57)	-.146	-3.20	.002	.817	1.224
San Bernardino	-64.48 (27.00)	-.104	-2.39	.018	.889	1.125
Riverside	-84.67 (26.27)	-.143	-3.22	.002	.867	1.154
Ventura	-45.72 (29.07)	-.068	-1.57	.118	.921	1.086
Service E/R	51.80 (10.11)	.218	5.12	.000	.936	1.069
Multi-Housing Units	2.87 (.66)	.201	4.38	.000	.803	1.245
Poverty Rate	6.84 (1.51)	.218	4.52	.000	.732	1.366
African-American Population	11.39 (.79)	.636	14.35	.000	.863	1.159
R^2	.793					

Violent crimes tend to status-specific in the sense that the socioeconomic environments of suburbs have greater influence on the location and distribution of these rates. Poorer and lower-status suburbs tend to have higher rates of highway robberies and violent crimes. These may be due to the competition for scare resources in these low-resource environments. Conversely, richer and residential suburban environments see lower rates of highway robberies. This is true for most violent crimes as well, but strong-arm assaults and aggravated assaults in general are more common in many more types of environmental conditions than highway robberies.

The 1980 model specification for highway robberies confirms our expectations. The coefficient for the poverty rate is among the highest of all significant predictors. Poverty is a stronger predictor than median household income (which is negatively related with highway robberies) for this model. As with the 1980 commercial robberies model, the model for commercial robberies has the same set of significant predictors, multiple housing units, service employment concentrations, and percent of the population that is African American. These predictors have the same direction of association as with the commercial robbery model. This suggests this offense, at least in 1980, is also an urban phenomenon.

Multiple housing units are significant in this model and retain their significance over time. This predictor more closely links with the residential functions of suburbs, especially residential areas in Los Angeles County. This variable captures the specific characteristics of Los Angeles County's jurisdictions, which tend to have higher numbers of apartments and rental units than owner-occupied single-family homes more common to the other counties in the region. Further, unlike that of the case of commercial robberies, service employment concentrations lose their significance in later decades. For these reasons, highway robberies are more likely tied to residential environments than the degree of urbanization. Moreover, the poverty coefficient becomes the strongest predictor in the later highway robbery models as seen below.

The county dummy coefficients except Ventura County's coefficient are all significant and negative supporting the notion that high rates of highway robberies are uncommon for many of these counties' cities. The model outlier in this case is the city of Beverly Hills. Well known as a wealthy enclave with significant retail activities, this jurisdiction has higher actual rates of highway robberies than predicted by the model because of its higher place status and low concentration of Black populations. The overall explanatory power of the 1980 highway robbery model is significantly high with a R-square of .793. This remains high until 2000 when it drops significantly. This is again due to the reduction in violent and property crimes seen after 1990. The Los Angeles region is not unique in seeing dramatic reductions in overall crime rates.

1990 Highway Robberies

Highway robberies show some spatial autocorrelation across the metropolitan region in 1990. The Global Moran's I value is .4973, which shows some moderate positive spatial autocorrelation. In general, violent crimes cluster across space much more so than property crimes. This is the case for highway robberies as well. The city of Compton has the highest highway robbery rate in the region with a rate of 991 incidents per 100,000 persons. Another Los Angeles County jurisdiction, Inglewood, has the second highest rate in the sample and is located close to Compton. Both cities have significant concentrations of African American and poor populations as well. The city of Lynwood, adjacent to Compton, faces higher rates of highway robberies as well. Los Angeles County municipalities dominate as high rate highway robbery jurisdictions with the two exceptions outside of this County being the cities of San Bernardino and Palm Springs. Palm Springs and San Bernardino are spatial outliers with higher rates than their neighbors.

The status characteristics of these cities' residential populations distinguish them from their neighbors. West Hollywood, Gardena, Huntington Park, and Santa Monica, all located in Los Angeles County, have high rates of highway robbery rates. The one exception of a low rate city that is a spatial outlier seen earlier is the city of Signal Hill. Signal Hill is a spatial outlier with a low rate landlocked by the city of Long Beach, which has a higher rate.

The 1990 model with the original 1980 jurisdictions finds the same significant predictors as in 1980. The poverty rate coefficient is a stronger predictor with the standardized coefficient being higher than in 1980 and larger in magnitude than the coefficients for multiple housing units and service employment concentrations.

The dummy coefficients for the same four counties in the 1980 model are negatively related to highway robberies and significant. Notably, there are no model outliers here. Larger cities elsewhere in the region and poorer jurisdictions in Los Angeles County tend to have higher rates of highway robberies. The 1990 model for all jurisdictions is much the same as with these other models. The dummy coefficients for all the counties have greater significance reinforcing the importance of Los Angeles County as an older and more urbanized part of the region with higher highway robbery rates.

West Hollywood is a model outlier aside from being a spatial outlier. This city, which incorporated in 1984, has a significant mix of employment activities and rental housing and diversity in population composition and status. This city's high rate of highway robbery offenses is due to status and functional diversity. The major reason the city is an outlier for the model is due to the lower value on the African American populations coefficient.

Figure 8 - Moran Scatter plot for Highway Robberies (1990)

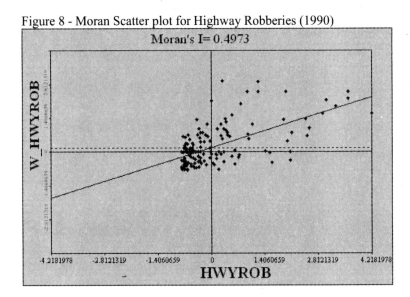

Table 22 - Model Specification for Highway Robberies for Original
Jurisdictions (1990)

Variable	Unstandardized Coefficients (B)	Standardized Coefficients (Beta)	t	Significance Level	Collinearity Statistics	
					Tolerance	Variance Inflation Factor
(Constant)	-84.73 (27.32)		-3.1	.002		
Orange	-53.39 (25.64)	-.107	-2.1	.039	.827	1.209
San Bernardino	-117.57 (35.06)	-.164	-3.4	.001	.916	1.091
Riverside	-186.95 (35.22)	-.272	-5.3	.000	.839	1.191
Ventura	-63.36 (38.66)	-.081	-1.6	.104	.906	1.104
Service E/R	27.99 (8.17)	.167	3.43	.001	.930	1.076
Multi-Housing Units	2.91 (.85)	.173	3.42	.001	.857	1.166
Poverty Rate	13.46 (1.68)	.436	8.00	.000	.740	1.351
African-American Population	11.88 (1.24)	.489	9.57	.000	.844	1.185
R^2	.729					

<u>2000 Highway Robberies</u>
The 2000 measure of spatial association finds a reduction in overall
clustering throughout the region. The Global Moran's I value is .4252.
This is mainly due to the much lower overall rates of highway
robberies for most jurisdictions. In 2000, Huntington Park has now the
highest rate of 459 per 100,000 persons with Compton and Inglewood
second and third with significantly reduced rates of highway robbery
rates than in 1990. The rates of highway robberies are 331 and 274
incidents per 100,000 persons respectively for Compton and
Inglewood. The spatial distribution of these rates across jurisdictions is
similar to the 1990 case despite such dramatic reductions in these
offense rates. Local clusters exist for higher-status and primarily
residential places. Pockets of higher-status suburbs having low rates are

visible through visual examination especially in the southeastern portions of Orange County and Ventura County. Lower highway robbery rate cities with significant numbers of poor populations are in outlying areas of Los Angeles County and San Bernardino Counties. Other low-rate cities are not spatially adjacent - this is the case for a few lower-status municipalities in Riverside and San Bernardino Counties. This suggests that the reduction in highway robbery rates is not necessarily true for only higher-status suburbs.

Table 23 - Model Specification for Highway Robberies for All Jurisdictions (1990)

Variable	Unstandardized Coefficients (B)	Standardized Coefficients (Beta)	t	Significance Level	Collinearity Statistics	
					Tolerance	Variance Inflation Factor
(Constant)	-75.34 (24.68)		-3.1	.003		
Orange	-62.51 (24.66)	-.124	-2.5	.012	.812	1.231
San Bernardino	-130.12 (27.04)	-.230	-4.81	.000	.846	1.182
Riverside	-137.05 (27.64)	-.238	-4.9	.000	.842	1.188
Ventura	-61.89 (37.33)	-.077	-1.7	.099	.899	1.112
Service E/R	23.97 (7.31)	.148	3.28	.001	.948	1.055
Multi-Housing Units	4.17 (.75)	.269	5.57	.000	.827	1.210
Poverty Rate	10.77 (1.54)	.350	7.02	.000	.775	1.290
African-American Population	11.54 (1.23)	.450	9.40	.000	.842	1.188
R^2	.704					

The 2000 highway robberies model for 1980 jurisdictions is dramatically different than earlier models as the service employment concentration coefficient is now insignificant and the magnitude of the African American populations and multiple housing units coefficients have been significantly reduced.

Figure 9 - Moran Scatter plot for Highway Robberies (2000)

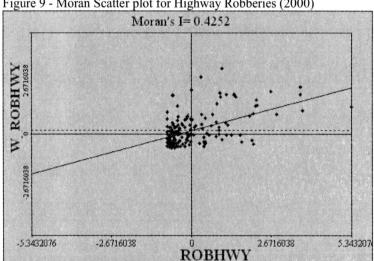

The poverty rate coefficient, in contrast, remains significant and becomes larger in magnitude. The reduction in overall rates of highway robberies could explain why some of these predictors are no longer as significant. Smaller differences between the highest and medium to low rate cities means smaller variation in the dependent variable, rates of highway robberies. The variation in the explanatory factors may not correspond as closely to the variation in offense rates as in earlier periods. The model outlier is the city of Huntington Park, which is a residential suburb but which has the highest highway robbery rates in the region in 2000.

This city has a significant Hispanic population and mostly single-family homes, which partly explain the low predicted value from the model. Huntington Park is also an outlier for the fuller 2000 model discussed next.

The final model for highway robberies is the 2000 model with all available jurisdictions. This model is largely consistent with the earlier 2000 model with the poverty rate, African American populations, and multiple housing units as significant predictors.

Table 24 - Model Specification for Highway Robberies for Original Jurisdictions (2000)

Variable	Unstandardized Coefficients (B)	Standardized Coefficients (Beta)	t	Significance Level	Collinearity Statistics	
					Tolerance	Variance Inflation Factor
(Constant)	-30.95 (13.83)		-2.2	.027		
Orange	-19.22 (12.80)	-.098	-1.5	.136	.822	1.217
San Bernardino	-46.99 (17.71)	-.166	-2.7	.009	.889	1.125
Riverside	-60.55 (17.59)	-.223	-3.4	.001	.833	1.200
Ventura	-28.46 (19.17)	-.092	-1.5	.140	.912	1.096
Service E/R	4.82 (7.67)	.040	.629	.531	.864	1.157
Multi-Housing Units	1.00 (.45)	.150	2.21	.029	.762	1.312
Poverty Rate	5.64 (.79)	.507	7.16	.000	.695	1.438
African-American Population	3.40 (.70)	.320	4.86	.000	.805	1.242
R²	.571					

The model outliers in this case are the cities of Huntington Park and Signal Hill. In this model, a higher value for Signal Hill was projected based on its characteristics of the explanatory variables. The model over predicted this city's highway robbery rate by a significant amount, forecasting a rate of 153 per 100,000 persons. Clearly, something unique about this place had to do with this unexpected outcome.

Comparisons for Highway Robberies

Comparing models for highway robberies suggests that the poverty rate has emerged as the most significant predictor, while the coefficient for African American, although significant, has decreased in magnitude. Two reasons for the reduction for the later coefficient include the movement of significant numbers of African Americans to the Inland Empire Counties and the movement of Hispanics into traditionally Black areas (such as Compton and Pomona). Both these trends could have led to the suburbanization of the African American population into outlying counties and the distribution of the Black population across municipalities in the region changed significantly. Many more cities, especially in the Inland Empire Counties, have sizeable Black populations than in earlier decades.

The coefficient for multiple housing units has also shown some consistency over time, demonstrating that suburbs with a significant amount of apartment rental housing tend to suffer from higher highway robbery rates. Even with a reduction in overall rates of highway robberies across the region, particular municipalities in Los Angeles County, continue to suffer from relatively higher rates of these offenses.

The overall explanatory power of the models have decreased over time, but the three strongest predictors continue to explain more than the half of the variation in highway robbery rates of municipalities across the Los Angeles region. Lower-status suburbs with poorer populations tend to suffer from highway robbery rates relative to middle and higher-status municipalities. As a violent crime, highway robberies are more status-specific.

Table 25 – Model Specification for Highway Robberies for All
Jurisdictions (2000)

Variable	Unstandardized Coefficients (B)	Standardized Coefficients (Beta)	t	Significance Level	Collinearity Statistics	
					Tolerance	Variance Inflation Factor
(Constant)	-25.51 (11.02)		-2.3	.022		
Orange	-21.58 (10.82)	-.113	-2.0	.048	.805	1.243
San Bernardino	-53.62 (12.02)	-.253	-4.5	.000	.802	1.247
Riverside	-41.48 (12.02)	-.195	-3.5	.001	.801	1.248
Ventura	-28.61 (16.72)	-.091	-1.7	.089	.908	1.101
Service E/R	4.95 (6.55)	.041	.756	.451	.867	1.154
Multi-Housing Units	1.32 (.36)	.222	3.72	.000	.720	1.390
Poverty Rate	4.77 (.64)	.447	7.51	.000	.727	1.375
African-American Population	3.20 (.62)	.295	5.18	.000	.793	1.260
R^2	.584					

Table 26 - Highway Robbery Model Comparisons for Three Decades (1980-2000)

	1980 Baseline	1990 Original Jurisdictions	1990 All Jurisdictions	2000 Original Jurisdictions	2000 All Jurisdictions
Variables	Standardized Coefficients				
Orange	-.146	-.107	-.124	-.098	-.113
San Bernardino	-.104	-.164	-.230	-.166	-.253
Riverside	-.143	-.272	-.238	-.223	-.195
Ventura	-.068	-.081	-.077	-.092	-.091
Service E/R	.218	.167	.148	.040	.041
Multiple Housing Units	.201	.173	.269	.150	.222
Poverty Rate	.218	.436	.350	.507	.447
African American Population	.636	.489	.450	.320	.295
R²	.793	.729	.704	.571	.584

Bold – significant at p < .01 level, Bold/Italics – significant at the p < .05 level

1980 Firearm Assaults

Aggravated assaults are violent crimes against persons involving the use of weapons and result in some level of bodily injuries to victims. The distinction between aggravated assaults and homicide is simply with the outcome for victims, injuries in the case of assaults and deaths for homicides. More serious and lethal assaults come close to homicides as the most dangerous types of all types of crimes. Firearm assaults are a more lethal type of assault having greater potential to result in serious injuries or death. The degree of lethality is greater for these types of offenses than those involving other weapons (knife and other weapon assault types) or no weapons (strong-arm assaults). In this regard, these offenses are similar to firearm robberies (not examined here). The use of firearms also suggests that these crimes result from disputes and conflicts where the use of force and injury to persons are vital to the disputants. Firearms are the most effective weapons in terms of the potential for serious damage to persons. Assaults in general and firearm assaults in particular are more common for lower-status groups. Higher-status groups and places are the least likely to be victims of these types of offenses and rates of firearm assaults should be very low for these groups and places. These are truly status-specific offenses.

Functional characteristics of places do not have any influence on these offenses except for the characteristics of the residential environments (i.e., housing stock). Lower value and older housing is more likely to house lower-status populations. However, assaults of all types tend to be situation-specific and status differences between places should be more consequential.

The 1980 model for firearm assaults confirms these expectations. Only two predictors emerged in this model, African American populations and the unemployment rate. Both of these explanatory variables differentiate suburbs on status characteristics. Both positively relate to firearm assault rates so that lower-status places have higher firearm assault rates. No functional employment variables are included in this model. This is different in the case of highway and commercial robberies- both these offenses are more common in urban and large city environments. The dummy coefficients for the regions' counties do not show easily understood relationships with the dependent variable.

The only model outlier was the city of La Puente. Located in Los Angeles County, this city's low Black population resulted in identification of this city as an outlier. The overall explanatory power of the model is quite high (R-square of .686), but lower than for highway robberies in 1980.

1990 Firearm Assaults

Spatial autocorrelation is less for firearm assaults than highway robberies. The Global Moran's I value is .3332, which is lower than that of highway robberies. Firearm assaults occur in greater frequency in some municipalities in the Inland Empire counties. This is different from highway robberies, which were more specific to large cities. There exist a few local clusters of municipalities with similar rates. The most significant is the cluster of high firearm assault cities in Los Angeles County neighboring each other. These include the cities of

Compton, Lynwood, and Paramount, all are lower-status jurisdictions. One other significant cluster of high rates in Los Angeles includes the cities of Pico Rivera and Santa Fe Springs. Spatial outliers that are high rate cities are more difficult to find with firearm assaults, but the most prominent is the city of San Bernardino. Two cities with low rates of firearm assaults are the cities of Loma Linda and Beverly Hills. Both have a neighbor with significantly higher rates. Thus, more affluent jurisdictions may neighbor cities with high rates. All of these give credence to the view that firearm assaults are more localized offenses with the status of each locale being important to the determination of its firearm assault rate.

Table 27 - Model Specification for Firearm Assaults (1980)

Variable	Unstandardized Coefficients (B)	Standardized Coefficients (Beta)	t	Significance Level	Collinearity Statistics	
					Tolerance	VIF
(Constant)	-12.98 (11.99)		-1.08	.281		
Orange	-17.02 (10.36)	-.091	-1.64	.103	.831	1.204
San Bernardino	-28.91 (14.29)	-.107	-2.02	.045	.902	1.109
Riverside	-.79 (14.15)	-.003	-.06	.956	.850	1.177
Ventura	-38.72 (15.31)	-.131	-2.53	.013	.944	1.059
Unemployment Rate	13.58 (2.05)	.402	6.63	.000	.688	1.454
African American Population	4.31 (.43)	.552	10.07	.000	.844	1.185
R^2	.686					

The 1990 model specification for the original 1980 jurisdictions finds that the unemployment rate and African American population concentrations positively relate to firearm assault rates. This is consistent with the 1980 model, but the coefficient for the African American population concentrations is smaller in magnitude than before (from .552 to .350).

We found this to be the case for highway robberies as well suggesting that the influence of Black population concentrations on violent crime rates declined in the 1980s as well as into the 1990s. Two outliers are identified by this model. Both cities are in Los Angeles County and have relatively high firearm assault rates. Santa Fe Springs has been identified earlier as neighboring another high rate city. Artesia has a mix of residential and commercial land uses, which have more to do with its assault rate than this model specification predicted.

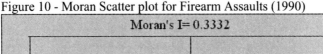

Figure 10 - Moran Scatter plot for Firearm Assaults (1990)

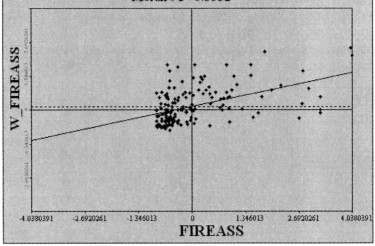

The 1990 model for all jurisdictions is similar to the other 1990 model. The overall explanatory power of the model has decreased significantly with an R-square of .485. All county dummy coefficients are significant and negatively related to firearm assault rates. One possible interpretation of this finding may concern the clustering of high rate cities in Los Angeles County, the absence of high rate cities in Orange and Ventura counties, and a much more limited number of cities in Riverside and San Bernardino that have high firearm assault rates.

Table 28 - Model Specification for Firearm Assaults for Original
Jurisdictions (1990)

Variable	Unstandardized Coefficients (B)	Standardized Coefficients (Beta)	t	Significance Level	Collinearity Statistics	
					Tolerance	Variance Inflation Factor
(Constant)	6.26 (25.13)		.25	.804		
Orange	-57.76 (25.44)	-.158	-2.3	.025	.825	1.212
San Bernardino	-45.49 (34.41)	-.086	-1.3	.189	.934	1.071
Riverside	-116.12 (34.12)	-.229	-3.4	.001	.878	1.139
Ventura	-80.36 (37.75)	-.139	-2.1	.035	.933	1.071
Unemployment Rate	35.62 (6.18)	.425	5.76	.000	.732	1.366
African American Population	6.25 (1.24)	.350	5.05	.000	.831	1.203
R²	.501					

In the later counties, these high rate cities may be more physically
isolated than in other counties.

2000 Firearm Assaults
The Global Moran's I value for 2000 firearm assaults is lower than that
for 1990. Cities that had high rates of firearm assaults in the previous
period continue to have higher rates of these assaults in this period. One
local cluster of high rate cities, Compton and Lynwood, still exists in
2000. The patterns of the same spatial outliers in 1990 reoccur. The one
exception of a high firearm assault rate spatial outlier is the city of
Needles. Located in San Bernardino County, this city is the
westernmost portion of the county and shares no borders with any other
municipality. This is a physically isolated city with its own internal
dynamics explaining its relatively high firearm assault rate.

Table 29 - Model Specification for Firearm Assaults for All
Jurisdictions (1990)

Variable	Unstandardized Coefficients (B)	Standardized Coefficients (Beta)	t	Significance Level	Collinearity Statistics	
					Tolerance	Variance Inflation Factor
(Constant)	16.88 (21.07)		.80	.424		
Orange	-58.01 (22.64)	-.164	-2.6	.011	.815	1.227
San Bernardino	-83.70 (24.30)	-.211	-3.4	.001	.886	1.129
Riverside	-94.46 (24.83)	-.233	-3.8	.000	.883	1.133
Ventura	-76.36 (33.80)	-.135	-2.3	.025	.928	1.078
Unemployment Rate	31.30 (5.24)	.396	5.97	.000	.756	1.322
African American Population	6.46 (1.14)	.359	5.66	.000	.823	1.215
R^2	.485					

The 2000 models for the original jurisdictions and all jurisdictions are
not much different from each other. Unemployment rate and African
American population concentrations continue to be significant
predictors. In both models, the dummy coefficients for the four
counties are insignificant. Additionally, for both 2000 models, the same
outliers are present. These are the cities of Needles, Compton, and
Lynwood. Such consistency suggests that model comparisons for the
same year with different jurisdictions is possible.

Comparisons for Firearm Assaults
The comparisons of models for three decades for firearm assaults
suggest that past models applicable to earlier decades are not applicable
to current environments. Even though the two predictors identified in
these models, the unemployment rate and African American
populations, remain significant, the overall explanatory power of the
model has declined. This is consistent with the case of highway

robberies. Violent crime rates have declined significantly since the early 1990s. The suburbanization of particular ethnic and status groups has accompanied these reductions. The best strategy to account for these significant trends is to use different sets of predictors for different years. Suburban diversity has increased substantially that limits using the same models for changing environments

Figure 11 - Moran Scatter plot for Firearm Assaults (2000)

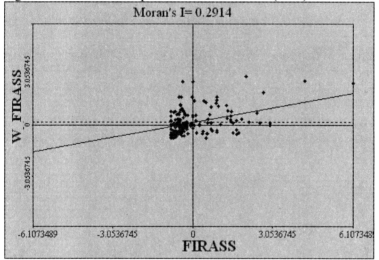

Nevertheless, firearm assaults do occur in greater frequency in lower-status environments, usually residential environments where the scarcity of resources leads to the greater prevalence of these offenses. These offenses are more lethal and the fact that they occur with greater frequency in particular environments (low-status residential areas) suggests that violent crimes are more status-specific than property crimes and offenses. A limited number of suburbs have a crime mix with greater rates of violent crimes than property crimes. However, this does not negate the importance of understanding that suburban crime problems vary by status differences between suburbs and require different prescriptions. These are real problems requiring more targeted policies and programs and do not derive from generalized theories and models.

Table 30 - Model Specification for Firearm Assaults for Original Jurisdictions (2000)

Variable	Unstandardized Coefficients (B)	Standardized Coefficients (Beta)	t	Significance Level	Collinearity Statistics	
					Tolerance	Variance Inflation Factor
(Constant)	-35.74 (12.06)		-2.9	.004		
Orange	-2.79 (10.75)	-.018	-.26	.796	.801	1.248
San Bernardino	1.79 (14.41)	.008	.12	.902	.923	1.084
Riverside	-8.42 (14.08)	-.040	-.60	.551	.893	1.120
Ventura	-16.07 (15.78)	-.067	-1.0	.310	.925	1.081
Unemployment Rate	11.10 (1.63)	.520	6.81	.000	.689	1.452
African American Population	2.36 (.59)	.287	4.03	.000	.791	1.264
R^2	.498					

Table 31 - Model Specification for Firearm Assaults for All Jurisdictions (2000)

Variable	Unstandardized Coefficients (B)	Standardized Coefficients (Beta)	t	Significance Level	Collinearity Statistics	
					Tolerance	Variance Inflation Factor
(Constant)	-29.61 (9.51)		-3.1	.002		
Orange	-4.82 (9.05)	-.034	-.53	.595	.792	1.262
San Bernardino	-14.11 (9.53)	-.089	-1.5	.141	.878	1.138
Riverside	-10.45 (9.47)	-.066	-1.1	.272	.890	1.124
Ventura	-16.83 (13.76)	-.071	-1.2	.223`	.924	1.082
Unemployment Rate	10.23 (1.32)	.514	7.74	.000	.715	1.398
African American Population	2.33 (.52)	.286	4.48	.000	.773	1.294
R^2	.483					

Table 32 - Firearm Assaults Model Comparisons for Three Decades (1980-2000)

	1980 Baseline	1990 Original Jurisdictions	1990 All Jurisdictions	2000 Original Jurisdictions	2000 All Jurisdictions
Variables	**Standardized Coefficients**				
Orange	-.091	*-.158*	*-.164*	-.018	-.034
San Bernardino	-.107	-.086	**-.211**	.008	-.089
Riverside	-.003	**-.229**	**-.233**	-.040	-.066
Ventura	*-.131*	*-.139*	*-.135*	-.067	-.071
Unemployment Rate	**.402**	**.425**	**.396**	**.520**	**.514**
African American Population	**.552**	**.350**	**.359**	**.287**	**.286**
R²	.686	.501	.485	.498	.483

Bold – significant at p < .01 level, Bold/Italics – significant at the p < .05 level

1980 Strong-arm Assaults

Strong-arm assaults are the last offenses examined in this study. These offenses are more common for lower status individuals and places, but the low levels of lethality of these offenses in comparison to other assault types and violent crimes suggests that they are not as concentrated in suburban places. These types of assaults are prototypical examples of disputes and conflicts of individuals that result in injuries, but do not involve the use of weapons. The outcomes are usually not lethal and have lower potential to result in lethal outcomes. Functional attributes of places should not be pertinent to explanations for these types of offenses as they concern more situation-specific disputes and conflicts between individuals.

Strong-arm assaults can be characterized as possible in many different types of environments, but usually involve individuals of the same status levels. Given the increased diversity of suburbs and the diversity in suburban status populations, strong-arm assaults are more likely to be diffused throughout the metropolitan region.

The 1980 strong-arm assaults model specification demonstrates the difficulty in explaining the variation in suburban strong-arm assault rates. Only one significant predictor emerges and this predictor is not easy to interpret. The proportion of housing units that are vacant is the predictor that has a positive relationship with strong-arm assault rates. Higher rates of vacancy imply either places have more seasonal housing serving tourists or have an older housing stock with many abandoned housing structures.

Table 33 - Model Specification for Strong-arm Assaults (1980)

Variable	Unstandardized Coefficients (B)	Standardized Coefficients (Beta)	t	Significance Level	Collinearity Statistics	
					Tolerance	Variance Inflation Factor
(Constant)	53.10 (14.95)		3.55	.001		
Orange	-73.36 (22.06)	-.256	-3.3	.001	.911	1.098
San Bernardino	-4.40 (32.96)	-.011	-.13	.894	.844	1.184
Riverside	-46.17 (36.46)	-.117	-1.3	.208	.638	1.568
Ventura	-35.51 (34.21)	-.079	-1.0	.301	.942	1.062
Vacant Housing	15.78 (2.59)	.558	6.09	.000	.643	1.556
R^2	.325					

The first scenario is characteristic of cities along the coast as well resort areas located in more inland portions of the region and in the mountains and desert. Inland areas tend to have a mix of low and high status places, while coastal areas in the Los Angeles region are generally of higher-status. The second scenario suggests an interpretation specific to lower-status suburbs. Abandoned housing is more common to poorer suburbs and suburbs of low-status.

Given that the dummy coefficient for only Orange County is significant and negative, an interpretation of the first scenario is less likely. However, support for an interpretation derived from the second scenario is also lacking. There are no other predictors to suggest poorer suburbs face higher levels of strong-arm assaults. The low overall explanatory power of this model also suggests that these offenses are not easily explained.

1990 Strong-arm Assaults

The global measure of spatial association suggests little spatial clustering of these offenses. There are many local clusters of various levels (low rate, medium rate, and high rate cities) of strong-arm assault with cities with low and medium rate cities being more common than clusters of high rate cities. Southeastern Orange County is the leading example of a low strong-arm assault cluster with multiple cities neighboring each other having low strong-arm assault rates. Another low-rate cluster exists in San Bernardino including the cities of Ontario, Upland, Rancho Cucamonga, and Chino. It is not clear what distinguishes these clusters from other suburban jurisdictions. There are some spatial outliers including the cities of San Jacinto, Desert Hot Springs, and Beaumont all located in Inland Empire Counties.

The 1990 model for original jurisdictions provides little help in explaining variation in strong-arm assault rates. In this case the one predictor aside from the dummy coefficients is insignificant and negatively related to strong-arm assault rates. The two model outliers are the cities of Beaumont and San Bernardino and it is clear that these cities do not have high housing vacancy rates.

The overall explanatory power of the model, not surprisingly, is dismal with a R-square of .116. Clearly, a strategy of using different sets of predictors for different decades is appropriate for the examination of strong-arm assault rates.

The 1990 model with all jurisdictions is not much better. The coefficient for vacant housing units is now positive as in the 1980 model but is insignificant. The dummy for Orange County remains significant and negative suggesting this county's municipalities have lower strong-arm assault rates than cities in other counties. A new model outlier, the city of Lynwood, is also present in this model. This is in addition to the cities of Beaumont and San Bernardino.

2000 Strong-arm Assaults

As in 1990, there is little evidence of spatial autocorrelation in 2000 for municipal rates of strong-arm assaults. One reason relates to the decline in overall rates of strong-arm assaults throughout the region from 1990. There are a similar range of local clusters as in 1990. The most prominent change with spatial outliers has been emergence of the city of Palm Springs as a distinctive outlier. This city has the second highest rate of assaults in 2000 with a rate of 640 assault incidents per 100,000 persons. Only Desert Hot Springs had a higher rate (991) and this city is a spatial outlier. The city of Palm Springs had a strong-arm assault rate of only 172 in 1990.

Figure 12- Moran Scatter plot for Strong-arm Assaults (1990)

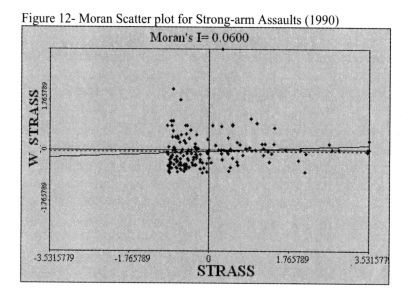

This large increase is symptomatic of reporting problems as in the years preceding 2000 Palm Springs had average strong-arm assault rates of about 200. One interpretation of the distribution of strong-arm assault rates focuses on the nature of these offenses. These offenses tend to be more situation-specific as well as location-specific. Local factors better explain these offenses than more general factors.

Table 34 - Model Specification for Strong-arm Assaults for Original
Jurisdictions (1990)

Variable	Unstandardized Coefficients (B)	Standardized Coefficients (Beta)	t	Significance Level	Collinearity Statistics	
					Tolerance	Variance Inflation Factor
(Constant)	260.20 (37.28)		6.98	.000		
Orange	-151.35 (53.42)	-.248	-2.83	.005	.915	1.093
San Bernardino	35.66 (77.93)	.041	.46	.648	.890	1.124
Riverside	170.97 (87.84)	.203	1.95	.054	.647	1.545
Ventura	-91.45 (82.46)	-.095	-1.11	.270	.956	1.046
Vacant Housing	-3.40 (5.98)	-.058	-.57	.572	.667	1.500
R²	.116					

Both 2000 models are essentially equivalent. Vacant housing units
has reemerged as a significant predictor. The dummy coefficients for
all counties are significant. Unlike other dummy coefficients, the
Riverside County dummy is now positive suggesting that jurisdictions
in these counties have higher strong-arm assault rates. The model
outlier in both 2000 models is the city of Desert Hot Springs, located in
Riverside County. Further, Palm Springs is also located in Riverside
County. An examination specific to Riverside County with regard to its
strong-arm assault rates may be appropriate.

Comparisons of Strong-arm Assaults
Model comparisons for strong-arm assaults demonstrate the importance
of using different sets of predictor variables over time as well as using
region-specific analysis for such offenses. The single predictor
variable, vacant housing units, was unable to explain the variation in
strong-arm assaults. No status variables emerged in 1980 as significant
predictors. Orange County jurisdictions had consistently lower rates of
strong-arm assaults and this is probably more true for its high-status
residential suburbs. Riverside County jurisdictions, particularly Palm

Springs and Desert Hot Springs, seem to suffer from high rates of strong-arm assaults. County-specific and more localized analyses are more appropriate given these findings.

Table 35 - Model Specification for Strong-arm Assaults for All Jurisdictions (1990)

Variable	Unstandardized Coefficients (B)	Standardized Coefficients (Beta)	t	Significance Level	Collinearity Statistics	
					Tolerance	Variance Inflation Factor
(Constant)	239.80 (27.45)		8.74	.000		
Orange	-162.85 (49.49)	-.261	-3.3	.001	.893	1.120
San Bernardino	-58.57 (56.69)	-.084	-1.0	.303	.852	1.173
Riverside	57.64 (64.06)	.081	.90	.370	.694	1.440
Ventura	-106.25 (76.54)	-.107	-1.3	.167	.947	1.056
Vacant Housing	3.35 (2.14)	.137	1.57	.120	.737	1.357
R²	.123					

Figure 13 - Moran Scatter plot for Strong-arm Assaults (2000)

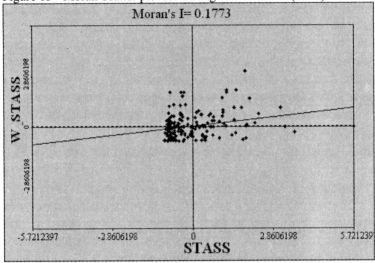

Table 36 - Model Specification for Strong-arm Assaults for Original Jurisdictions (2000)

Variable	Unstandardized Coefficients (B)	Standardized Coefficients (Beta)	T	Significance Level	Collinearity Statistics	
					Tolerance	Variance Inflation Factor
(Constant)	108.26 (17.62)		6.15	.000		
Orange	-66.94 (28.03)	-.186	-2.4	.018	.919	1.088
San Bernardino	-73.72 (42.49)	-.142	-1.7	.085	.828	1.207
Riverside	125.16 (47.14)	.251	2.66	.009	.622	1.608
Ventura	-65.97 (43.36)	-.116	-1.5	.131	.957	1.045
Vacant Housing	9.43 (3.15)	.286	3.00	.003	.613	1.633
R^2	.297					

210

Table 37 - Model Specification for Strong-arm Assaults for All
Jurisdictions (2000)

Variable	Unstandardized Coefficients (B)	Standardized Coefficients (Beta)	t	Significance Level	Collinearity Statistics	
					Tolerance	Variance Inflation Factor
(Constant)	131.87 (14.62)		9.0	.000		
Orange	-76.80 (26.42)	-.212	-2.9	.004	.886	1.128
San Bernardino	-69.82 (30.38)	-.174	-2.3	.023	.825	1.213
Riverside	82.98 (32.04)	.207	2.60	.010	.741	1.349
Ventura	-71.41 (41.98)	-.120	-1.7	.091	.946	1.057
Vacant Housing	3.29 (1.24)	.208	2.65	.009	.773	1.293
R²	.219					

Table 38 - Strong-arm Assaults Model Comparisons for Three Decades
(1980-2000)

	1980 Baseline	1990 Original Jurisdictions	1990 All Jurisdictions	2000 Original Jurisdictions	2000 All Jurisdictions
Variables	Standardized Coefficients				
Orange	-.256	-.248	-.261	-.186	-.212
San Bernardino	-.011	.041	-.084	-.142	-.174
Riverside	-.117	.203	.081	.251	.207
Ventura	-.079	-.095	-.107	-.116	-.120
Vacant Housing	.558	-.058	.137	.286	.208
R²	.325	.116	.123	.297	.219

Bold – significant at p < .01 level, Bold/Italics – significant at the p <
.05 level

Substantive Findings and Implications

The examination of multiple model specifications for six different offenses presents some consistent findings. Of the three property crimes examined, two of these showed the importance of functional characteristics on the distribution of these offenses across suburbs. These are shoplifting and nonresidential burglaries. Shoplifting was consistently higher in retail centers which is consistent with the existing literature. An additional status factor qualifies this finding by suggesting that shoplifting is by no means particular to high-status suburbs, but distributed across suburbs of varied status levels. Suburbs with higher unemployment rates tend to consistently have higher shoplifting rates. So both the interactive effects of place functional and status characteristics combine to create ripe conditions where targets and resource-deprived and motivated offenders exist together to create higher shoplifting rates in particular jurisdictions. The contributions of both the routine activities and anomie-and-opportunity structures perspectives are important for suggesting that the combination of the features of physical and nonphysical environments create conditions where resource abundance and resource deprivation meet to produce higher shoplifting rates. However, the stronger predictive power of functional variables suggest shoplifting is more of a target-specific crime than status-specific.

The other offense which is target specific and more closely tied to the functional characteristics of places is nonresidential burglaries. For this offense, both retail and wholesale specialization positively relate to higher rates. Again, the unemployment rate also suggested that place-status differences were critical in the distribution of burglary rates. Lower-status places tend to have a relatively larger number of resource-deprived actors who may encounter these targets in their daily routines and live close to and/or work near these targets. One should be careful in suggesting that motivations and targets are similar for all cases of nonresidential burglaries. This is clearly not the case. Rather, these are probabilistic relationships where certain conditions are more likely to result in particular events and outcomes. This is true for all offenses examined in this study.

Resource deprivation and status improvement considerations were apparent in the case of three violent crimes. Although commercial robberies were hypothesized to be a property crime and motivated by property values, the model specifications consistently found status characteristics of places to be significantly related to these offenses. Larger cities with high minority (Black populations) had higher rates of commercial robberies. Further, median household income consistently was negatively related to rates of commercial robberies. Violent crimes such as commercial robberies tend to occur near residential environments with a larger number of resource-deprived and status-motivated actors. Conversely, higher-status places tend to have environmental features (nonphysical mostly) and conditions less favorable for the occurrence of commercial robberies. These areas tend to be resource-abundant and are able to maximize status more readily than other places. This is particularly true for high-status residential suburbs. Actors in these types of places do not have the need for or consider crime adaptations and choices.

Status-specific offenses also included firearm assaults and highway robberies. The later offense was positively associated with the poverty rate whereby poorer suburbs tended to have higher rates of these offenses. As a violent crime, these offenses are more closely linked to the residential environments and their characteristics and less specific to physical environmental features. In the beginning of the study period, this offense distributed in a compact fashion so that more urbanized areas had higher rates of highway robberies, but the suburbanization of population groups of lower status decreased the concentration of these offenses solely in urbanized areas.

Lethal violence is also concentrated in places facing environmental conditions that offer fewer resources and probabilities to maximize status. Firearm assaults were higher in places with higher unemployment rates. The unemployment rate is a convenient measure of place conditions and correlated with other measures of resource deprivation including the poverty rate, median household income, rental housing stock, and ethnic status. This multicollinearity is also suggestive of the cumulative aspects of status and resources where an accumulation of disadvantages leads to more resource deprivation for actors and places. This is the reverse of the accumulation of advantages identified by Merton (1968) in status-dominated behavior (Zuckerman 1998). The same notion of resource abundance underlies the place stratification paradigm's assertion of higher-status groups being able to consolidate their advantages and resources. Resource abundance and resource deprivation coexist in most hierarchies and this is true for the suburban hierarchy as well.

The final offense examined was strong arm assaults. In this case, no status distinctions between places explained the distribution of strong-arm assaults. One clear finding is to use more localized and county-specific analyses to understand the particular distribution of the rates of strong-arm assaults across suburbs. As disputes and conflicts tend to be situation-specific behavior between individuals, these require more localized and context-specific explanations more closely attune to the particulars of the local situation.

Existing research on crime and violence has underemphasized the different etiologies of property and violent crimes. The notion of crime mix remains underdeveloped and requires specific attention. This study finds that suburban property crime rates within a large metropolitan region are better explained by the notions of resources and targets in combination. Existing research exclusively uses the notion of targets and assumes that status considerations through motivated offenders is not critical to the concentration and distribution of property crimes. Violent crimes are the product of conditions existing in the residential portions of suburban environments. Current research recognizes that violent crimes involve interpersonal conflicts between individuals and groups, but often only focuses on conditions immediate to individuals and groups and not with the overall conditions and resources in the broader environments shared with similarly located individuals and groups.

Conclusions

This study has contributed to the social science literature by demonstrating that a broader conceptualization of environments and their influence on human behavior is required for fuller explanation and understanding of many types of behaviors. Criminal and non-criminal behavior (not the object of examination here) result from the physical and non-physical features of environments. (Criminal and non-criminal behaviors link in complex ways that are poorly understood). All types of environments are created and distributed through the actions of human actors and the organization of these environments is critical to the distribution of conditions and resources across social and physical spaces. Human actors have different levels of access to resources and there is considerable consistency in the character of environments and the nature of crime and violence problems. While existing scholarship views environmental (including spatial) explanations within the scope of a limited set of criminological theories, the anomie-and-opportunity structures paradigm has found to directly incorporate environmental factors in explaining crime and violence across multiple social structures.

The context-specific approach used in the study is consistent with newer integrated micro-situational approaches (Miethe and Meier 1994; Miethe and McCorkle 1998) and supplements these approaches with more of a macro-situational perspective. Both macro and micro environmental approaches share an emphasis on the varying and interactive influence of motivations, targets, resources, and other situational factors on levels of crime and violence. Further, violent offenses differ from property offenses in terms of these elements. The utility of general theories of criminal events is found to be limited as particular settings differentiate on the frequency of different offenses with varied motivational, opportunity, and situational elements.

We have seen that the location of conditions and resources in different environments are critical aspects of both criminal and noncriminal behavior. The nonrandom patterning of both property and violent crime offenses needs to be further examined and analyzed. Both academics and practitioners need to stress contextual analyses that combine different theoretical as well as practical approaches to study human behavior.

This study has combined a wide range of theoretical approaches and provided a methodological approach to understand the nature and distribution of suburban crime and violence. Past theoretical approaches have not been particularly inclined to integrate theories, but any approach to study complex behavior such as crime and violence requires interdisciplinary theoretical and methodological orientations.

Multiple aspects of environments and contexts are found to be important to explaining crime and violence and theoretical approaches must seek to study the interactive and related aspects of these environments. Theoretical approaches must also be sensitive to the limitations of their theories and emphasize the context-dependent nature of human choices and behavior. Theoretical and empirical specification of contexts is the heart of research that aims to provide explanations for social problems and solutions to these problems. A multiplicity of suburban crime and violence problems plague metropolitan areas requiring different prescriptions and solutions guided by context-sensitive and crime-specific theories and analyses.

Resource Distribution & Crime and Violence

Resources and Crime & Violence

The major finding of this book concerns the importance of resources and the distribution of resources to differences in property and violence rates. Property crimes that are target-specific are higher in environments with an abundance of resources that provide targets for those wanting to increase their resources. The environments of resource abundance offer more attractive targets than those environments characterized by fewer resources. Resource distribution in the physical environments of suburban municipalities is an important criterion of differentiation of rates of target-specific property crime rates.

For violent crimes, which are status-specific, resource deficiencies and/or deprivation in residential environments increase the likelihood of increased conflicts between residents mostly at the same status level and sharing other social attributes including ethnicity. Shared statuses or status-sets in multiple structures and patterned exposure to particular residential environments either increase the likelihood of higher rates of violent crimes or alternatively in environments with resource abundance to lower rates of violent crimes.

Resource distributions are crucial in any explanation of the non-random nature of crime and violence. The theoretical implications of resource distribution through the theoretical focus on physical and non-physical environments, probabilistic theorizing, specifying context and looking at the specific etiologies of different property and violent offenses are explored below. The policy implications of resource distributions are apparent in municipal and county law enforcement through fiscal needs, the role of environmental factors on the presence or absence of crime and violence, and effective use of available resources for targeted crime and violence reduction policies and responses. More attention is required to study the organization and provision of policing services and its effectiveness for varied crime and violence problems as well as the presence of lethal violence in some suburbs and parts of U.S. metropolitan regions. The distribution of resources is a critical factor in both the prevalence of crime and violence and policy responses.

Theoretical and Methodological Implications

The theoretical implications of this study primarily concern the fields of criminology and urban studies. Urban studies benefits from the development of a typology sensitive to the stratification of suburbs and the diversity of suburbs as well as the provision of a methodology that recognizes the consequences of such suburban diversity. Criminological theories benefit from the approach used here to integrate theories and stress their inherent complementarities.

Most scholars view theories of crime and violence as competing with each other and scholars seek to develop single overriding general theories. The study challenges these existing perspectives. Theories examining crime and violence in any society seek to explain the causes and effects of such behavior. Most theories emphasize different facets and aspects of crime. For example, routine activities theorists emphasize the effects of physical environments on crime, the attractiveness and other features of targets. These factors undoubtedly play a role in crime choices and adaptations, but also influence and result from non-criminal behavior. Non-criminal behavior, for example status-seeking behavior, is also influenced by physical environments and the nature of targets, but the range of physical environments and adaptations are narrowly construed in routine activities theory. Different theories of crime and deviance consider generality and greater scope as valid goals and objectives by which comparison between theories be made. The view here is that theory competition does not lead to general theories, rather theories apply to different levels and aspects of crime and criminality. However, all theories are incomplete as their focus is limited. This highlights the conditional nature of theorizing whereby causal relations are conditional – some factors may only produce specific effects in the presence or absence of others (Miethe and Regoeczi 2004). General theories are of limited usefulness unless these theories are applied and tested in particular contexts and settings.

This study is interdisciplinary in that it combines theories from different disciplinary perspectives in explaining rates of crime and violence. This is accomplished by borrowing the concept of targets and the emphasis of physical environments from routine activities theory and placing these concepts in the anomie-and-opportunity structures paradigm. The later paradigm emphasizes social and economic environments, gives structure and agency equal balance, and is sensitive to context. By doing this, the framework used is broader and general in the sense of having a larger domain of study. The utility of integration is considerable as the study of property and violent crime rates locate in a single paradigm - which of course is a major challenge in crime theory. Further, the study applied the paradigm to explain these rates in real-life contexts with suburban crime and violence being the focus of this application. Although the level of analysis is metropolitan Los Angeles, the units of analyses are the appropriate policy decision units of municipalities. We found that Los Angeles's complex suburban environments differentiate in numerous ways and this differentiation is consequential to the types and distribution of crime and violence across the metropolitan region.

We also found that stratifying a metropolitan system by function and status provides information on distinct places and their characteristics so that different environments influencing the concentration of particular types of crime and violence are analyzed. The typology purposefully aimed to collect data on the characteristics of places; these place characteristics are analytically distinct from the characteristics of populations residing in these places and represent the multiple environments distinguishing places from one another. The data sources used in this study to represent the functional and status dimensions of places are accessible to other researchers seeking to explain different metropolitan environments. Purposefully, various model specifications instead of one model specification are required to derive context-specific, target-specific, and status-specific models of crime and violence. The academic use of this typology and methodological approach easily extends to use by policymakers and practitioners interested in reducing social problems in metropolitan regions in the United States.

Most importantly, this study stresses the probabilistic nature of social science theories. Most of the relationships between environments and behaviors are indirect rather than direct and probabilistic not deterministic. Multiple features of environments and actors, place characteristics and choices, interact to produce these relationships between place characteristics and rates of suburban crime and violence. One can view these as tendencies of these environments and actors so that certain environments and actors more closely relate with high or low rates of crime and violence. Much current theorizing ignores (albeit unintentionally) the limits of theories in being able to explain and predict in a definitive manner.

Policy Implications

Most crime prevention and reduction policies in the United States lend themselves to formulation and implementation at the municipal level. Municipalities are effective entry points for intervention in both understanding the mix of crime and violence problems plaguing jurisdictions in metropolitan regions as well as developing solutions to these problems. This study consciously takes a municipality focus and finds that multiple crime and violence problems exist. Local prevention and reduction of crime and violence benefits from the recognition that different solutions are required for these multiple layered problems. Property offenses are more characteristic of suburban employment centers and violent offenses are more likely to be greater in lower-status residential areas. Municipalities can identify the type of crime and violence problems through theories and methodological approaches examined and applied in this study. Depending on the particular offenses confronting jurisdictions, formal (policing mostly) and informal responses specific to each offense are possible.

Some of the findings in the study are relevant for municipal policy responses to crime and violence. Shoplifting and other similar property offenses are more prevalent in suburban retail and wholesale centers accessible to major transportation routes. Local policing services need to effectively target and coordinate with private security agencies as well as other relevant policing organizations in order to examine the particular characteristics of places that may contribute to higher rates of these offenses. Decisions on patrolling and community relations are better made with explicit attention to the particular characteristics of the built environment that lead particular jurisdictions to face greater risks of victimization.

An important limitation of current problem oriented policing and situational crime prevention approaches is their effectiveness is much greater for property offenses and for areas with greater resources. Property offenses involve physical targets and the features of these targets are relatively easier to control and secure than mobile and poorly identified personal targets. However, target hardening, access control, and crime prevention through environmental design require considerable amount of coordination and resources (monetary and otherwise) to ensure effectiveness. Businesses and organized actors in affluent areas have strong interests in garnering additional resources and in many cases can provide additional private security to fill gaps in public law enforcement services. The reality in lower-status areas is the lack of organization and interest in pooling resources to combat minor property offenses as well as limited concern that these and other serious offenses are community problems requiring community solutions. Interactions with public policing are not uniform and the diversity in experiences across numerous status dimensions have been identified as responsible for the difference levels of trust in police by individuals and groups across these same status dimensions. As police officers have considerable discretion in response to criminal encounters, police-citizen encounters differentiate by the type of actor and their status in local social, economic, and political structures. Despite these problems, local policing is better suited to provide more balanced and effective crime control than private security agencies. Democratic governance of policing is critical in helping to solve crime and violence problems through the assistance and support of citizens. The lead must be with local governmental law enforcement to bring together both citizens and businesses to effectively coordinate policy responses to crime and violence.

Policing in metropolitan areas fulfills several functions besides reducing crime and violence. These include order maintenance, peacekeeping, and response to citizen calls for service for non-criminal incidents. Estimates indicate that up to 80 percent of calls for service to the police involve order maintenance and community services (Skogan and Frydl 2004). Further, the legitimacy of the police and compliance is garnered mainly from non-law enforcement and crime control activities (Hahn and Jeffries 2003). Community policing, problem-oriented policing, and other related initiatives are developed to counter the lack of good police-citizen relations with the professional model of policing. Some have argued that police agencies must reorient their missions to focus on community service as this improves police-citizen relations and reduces conflict and violence in high-crime areas (Hahn and Jeffries 2003). However, changing police organizations and their culture towards meeting other goals is problematic for numerous reasons. Increased demands coupled with scare resources led to mostly symbolic, not, real changes in police practices.

It is difficult to balance these demands and policies and programs are subject to political and fiscal constraints. Much of the resources and manpower available to policing derive from bureaucratic and political considerations in local governments. In this regard, policing organizations and policing as an industry depend upon resources from external environments beyond their control, but often with the various actors and agencies in local governments. Research has also pointed to the bureaucratic and political culture of police departments leading to inflexibility and rigidity in the development and implementation of policies and programs. Much like other local governmental organizations, policing is fragmented with little coordination and planning with other agencies. However, the police and law enforcement are the only actors with authority and mandate to develop and implement policies to prevent and reduce crime. Their specialized knowledge and experience is critical to use of tools and techniques that more effectively reduce and prevent crime.

Local law enforcement requires considerable amount of monetary resources in particular environments. Existing research finds that poorer and lower-status residential environments and municipalities associate with higher and increasing costs in provision of policing services (Estrich 1984; Ladd and Yinger 1989). Estrich (1984) found that the differences in rates of crime between poorer and affluent cities in the state of Massachusetts far exceeded differences in expenditures for policing and the number of police officers. On a per index crime basis, "the poor pay relatively more (since police are financed primarily by the regressive property tax) for relatively less protection" (Estrich 1984, p. 216). Ladd and Yinger (1989) found higher costs of policing services for poorer jurisdictions with poverty concentration being the environmental factor having the greatest influence on cost of provision of these services. In particular, jurisdictions with greater employment activities and rental housing that are relatively poorer are more difficult to service cost-effectively. One classic study of fiscal and environmental differences of cities in Los Angeles County by Miller (1981) found increased poverty, a deteriorating tax base, and higher rates of crime and violence occurring simultaneously for some municipalities in the region. In contrast, other cities with low-crime rates had adequate policing and other public services with an abundance of fiscal resources. Fiscal disparities and relationships with policing remain understudied in crime and violence research.

This study suggests that particular residential environments face higher rates of lethal violence including highway robberies and firearm assaults. Greater awareness of the broader ecological contamination and stigmatization that occurs for poorer and lower-status neighborhoods and how these affect police responses to these areas is required (Terrill and Reisig 2003). If officers use more force in lower-status areas, then standardized punitive responses may require modification for effective crime prevention. Policy responses have paid relatively little attention to lethal violence, usually formulating responses on an individualized basis and treatment of each lethal offense. Without an understanding of the factors responsible for the concentration of lethal violence in particular jurisdictions, these reactive policies are not able to address deeper problems requiring coordinated action at the municipality level. Other non-policing agencies of local governments must be involved in identifying place characteristics and the environmental conditions of place contributing to higher rates of lethal violence. Planning and economic development agencies, for example, could coordinate community relation and mediation efforts by referring resource-deprived individuals and groups to suitable jobs and placing them in affordable housing units in a municipality. Various municipal level organizations could coordinate less formal and more preventive dispute-resolution mechanisms. Citizens may react more favorably to alternatives that are less punitive and feel involved in improving the collective status of their places.

One particular point of interest is the fact that most lethal violence and other violent offenses involve individuals and groups of similar status levels and/or racial-ethnic groups. Police officers need training on specific techniques to address the intra-status and intra-ethnic nature of these offenses. There is little evidence that current training is sensitive to the influence of social and economic environments on the frequency of lethal violence. The tendency to treat offenders and potential offenders through a single reactive policing approach existing in jurisdictions facing lethal violence problems appears not to be effective against the need for improving place conditions and increasing accessibility of residents to greater resources from more favorable environmental conditions.

The nature of local policing in many metropolitan regions necessitates further examination in formulating policy responses. Currently, Los Angeles County and even other counties in the region lead the nation in contract policing. Many cities in the region contract for policing services with the County Sheriff's Offices where the municipality has a contractual agreement with the County for police manpower, patrolling, and other functions. An informal count for 2000 finds that 41 out of 88 cities in Los Angeles County, 14 cities (out of a total of 24 incorporated municipalities) each in Riverside and San Bernardino Counties, 12 out of 32 cities in Orange County, and 4 out of 10 cities in Ventura County obtain all policing services from their respective County Sheriff's Office. County policing also serves the unincorporated areas of the region and a few cities (for example, the city of Santa Fe Springs contracts with the city of Whittier) obtain policing services from other cities. Clearly, this high reliance on county level policing providers, who also provide other services including managing jails and prisons and providing prosecution and court services, directly impacts crime policy formulation and implementation.

The effectiveness of contract policing on crime prevention and reduction is not clear and little current research in this area exists. The danger is that county providers may not be sensitive to local crime and violence problems and formulate standardized responses (Skogan and Frydl 2004). Some jurisdictions requiring additional policing and non-policing services only can pay within their fiscal capacities so that equity issues and disparities in fiscal resources are critical in current metropolitan regions. Scarce fiscal resources for policing and other services take away from other services and it is not clear whether these formalized approaches can truly address systemic and environmentally created crime and violence problems.

Suggestions for Future Research

There are many avenues for future research to extend the theoretical and methodological approaches used in the study. With the dataset of supplemental offenses used in the study, one of the more important extensions would involve analysis of temporal patterns with the supplemental property and violent offenses examined in the study. Offense data is available for many offenses since 1970 and since 1981 for some other offenses. Violent offenses have different temporal patterns than property offenses particularly the decrease in property offenses since the late 1970s in all counties (the notable exception to this pattern for a property crime is motor vehicle thefts). In contrast, violent crimes increased in some counties consistently until 1980, were stable until the mid-1980s, increased dramatically until 1992, and dropped dramatically after that period. These divergent patterns require further examination.

The nature of the offense data also necessitates detailed examination of the impacts of policing on offense rate across the metropolitan region. Given these data reflect crimes reported to the police and high levels of discretion in recording actual incidents held by the police, some of the increases over time and differences across space in offense rates is likely due to differences in policing and policing practices across the region. Clearance and arrest data for each municipality in the region on the same Index offenses examined here are available for the last three decades. These include clearances by type of offense, felony arrest data by gender for juveniles and adults, and misdemeanor arrest data by gender for juveniles and adults. Clearance data are helpful in gauging the effectiveness of police in solving crimes, while the arrest data also help in explaining the type of crime and violence problem confronting municipalities and the focus of policing by offense. A more complete picture of (formal) responses to crime and violence and integration of responses would also allow for the integration of theoretical approaches focused on examining these aspects of crime and violence.

Possibly the strongest extension would involve a closer examination of high lethal violence suburbs and areas in metropolitan regions. The macro-environmental approach would not suffice in this case, but would require more disaggregated data and approaches. Jurisdictions with consistently high rates of lethal violence are good candidates for detailed case studies using a mix of qualitative and quantitative methods. This would involve direct observational methods as well as micro-situational approaches to supplement macro-environmental approaches. An understanding of the situational dynamics and tendencies in resource-deprived and high lethal violence areas would be extremely helpful for policy interventions to reverse this long-standing problem of lethal violence in America.

This study offers some other suggestions of areas of future research including the need to pay attention to lethal violence and its concentration in parts of the metropolitan region, assessing the effectiveness of contract policing and its equity aspects, and the development of less formal crime prevention and reduction policies. Metropolitan solutions and the sharing of information and resources may better serve the collective good of municipalities in metropolitan regions. These collective solutions require collective understandings of the nature of metropolitan problems.

Refining Problem-Oriented Policing

The specialized knowledge about crime and violence problems and the ability to apply this knowledge is unique to local police departments. The philosophy of problem-oriented policing also puts considerable emphasis on the police role, but treats policing as one of the municipal functions of local governments. Further, the police and law enforcement are only one of the possible responses to crime and violence problems and other responses are encouraged in problem-solving approaches. For effective responses to localized problems, other municipal agencies should be involved and mobilized. One of the core functions of police departments is to gather and process information, but one of the concerns by police practitioners and scholars was the lack of and/or ineffective use of valuable information for crime prevention and reduction policies (Goldstein 2003; Mastrofski 1998). Data and methodological tools used in this study address the need to effectively understand unique and similar crime and violence problems in suburban jurisdictions. Problem-solving efforts are effective when they involve coordination between metropolitan criminal justice agencies including the police, but the challenge remains to involve non-criminal justice agencies in coordinated responses. Direct measures of function and status collected by other municipal agencies are valuable for police planners and municipal policy makers in developing coordinated and comprehensive solutions to crime and violence problems.

A recent report by the National Research Council Committee to Review Research on Police Policy and Practice (Skogan and Frydl 2004) states "there is a growing body of research evidence that problem-oriented policing is an effective approach" (p. 243). The Committee argues that 'hot-spots' policing approaches, geographically targeted and proactive strategies, were the most promising for crime prevention and reduction. Problem-oriented policing ultimately aims to develop and implement localized responses to specific (local) crime problems. Problems must be conceptually and practically disaggregated and specified so that definitions of problems are not general and limited for policy purposes (Brodeur 1998). A cluster of similar (related and recurring) events that are of concern to communities and local agencies define as 'problems'. Problems have behavioral and environmental components including the relationships between actors (e.g., victim-offender), actor motives, and the physical location of the problem (Skogan and Frydl 2004). Situational crime prevention approaches, which are similar to problem-oriented approaches, have tended to downplay motives and actor relationships and focused mostly on offender decision-making processes in the immediate situation such as target selection.

A major issue with current applications of problem-oriented policing is a tendency to emphasize micro-environmental components at the expense of macro-environmental components of crime and violence problems. Much research and practice depicts and construes environments in a narrow manner, mainly as the immediate physical location of crimes. The incorporation and consideration of nonphysical and broader environments is inadequate and incomplete in these approaches. Additionally, some police officers like situational crime prevention scholars tend toward an 'individualistic' orientation to analyzing and responding to crimes and there may be an overreliance on use of arrests in resolving disputes (Barlow and Barlow 2000). The rise of individualistic explanations in criminology, which highlight the differences in personal attributes between criminals and non-criminals and the rational choices made by offenders, is well established (Well 1995; Feeley 2003; Haggerty 2004a, 2004b). This may lead to incomplete knowledge about offender motivations and limited understanding of the causal factors behind crime and violence. Hahn and Jefferies (2003) stress this issue:

> In evaluating the origins of urban unrest and in viewing the other social problems, law enforcement officers usually tended to stress individualistic explanations. Police officers seldom considered either social and economic forces or deficiencies in existing institutions as a source of conflict or unlawful acts (p. 132).

With violent crimes that are mainly interpersonal disputes and conflicts, an understanding of the broader social and economic environments influencing motivations and condition-derived resources is critical for policing and other responses. For example, Glenn et al. (2003) in their analysis of training and curriculum issues for the Los Angeles Police Department state "we repeatedly heard expressions of strong interest in greater interpersonal skills training for officers, especially those skills for essential for deescalating conflicts." (p. 8). Training programs should include background information on the communities and cities including demographic, socio-economic, and ethnic profiles (Barlow and Barlow 2000). The status-specific nature of violence must be addressed in training and response formulation. Unfortunately, this is largely missing in current policing research and practice. Broadening the conceptualization of environments is a significant contribution to the fields of criminology and criminal justice. It has a large potential to invigorate local law enforcement policy and practice to address crime-specific problems with fuller knowledge and collaborative efforts.

Appendices

Supplemental Offense Data Definitions and Classifications
Source: FBI (1984)
Property Crimes
1). **Larceny-theft** – the unlawful taking, carrying, leading, or riding away of property from the possession or constructive possession of another.
Notes: It does not include motor vehicle thefts as there exists a great volume of thefts in that particular category. Under the Uniform Crime Reporting Program, this offense category does not include embezzlement, counterfeiting, confidence games, forgery, and worthless checks (these are included as Part II offenses).
Larceny Types
a). *Pocket-picking* – the theft of articles from a person by stealth where the victim usually does not become immediately aware of the theft. (If force is used, incidents are classified as strong-arm robbery).
b). *Purse-snatching* – the grabbing or snatching of a purse, handbag, etc., from the custody of an individual. (If force is used, incidents are classified as strong-arm robbery).
c). *Shoplifting* – the theft by a person (other than an employee) of goods or merchandise exposed for sale. (This violation assumes that the offender had legal access to the premises and this no trespass or unlawful entry was involved. The category includes thefts of merchandise displayed as part of the stock in trade outside buildings, such as department stores, hardware stores, supermarkets, fruit stands, gas stations, etc.).
d). *Thefts from Motor Vehicles (except theft of motor vehicle parts and accessories)* – the theft of articles from a motor vehicle, whether locked or unlocked. (Includes thefts from automobiles, trucks, truck trailers, buses, motorcycles, motor homes, or other recreational vehicles. It also includes from any area in the automobile or other vehicle including the trunk, glove compartment, or other enclosure. Some of the items included in this category of theft are cameras, suitcases, wearing apparel, packages, etc. Does not include items that are automobile accessories.).

e). *Theft of Motor Vehicle Parts and Accessories-* the theft of any part or accessory attached to the interior or exterior of a motor vehicle in a manner which make the part an attachment to the vehicle or necessary for the operation of the vehicle. (Thefts of motors, transmissions, radios, heaters, hubcaps and wheel covers, manufacturers' emblems, license plates, radio antennas, side-view mirrors, gasoline tape decks, etc., are included in this category. If items being transported in the vehicle are stolen, the offense should be classified as a theft from a motor vehicle.).

f). *Theft of Bicycles* – the unlawful taking of any bicycle, tandem bicycle, unicycle, etc.

g). *Theft from Buildings* – a theft from within a building which is open to the general public and where the offender has legal access. (Includes thefts from such places as churches, restaurants, schools, libraries, public buildings, and other public and professional offices during the hours when such facilities are open to the public. Thefts from a structure accompanied by a breaking or unlawful entry (trespass) without breaking are included as burglaries. Does not include shoplifting and thefts from coin-operated devices or machines within open buildings; these offenses are listed in their separate categories.).

h). *Theft from Coin-operated Device or Machine-*a theft from a device or machine which is operated or activated by the use of a coin. (Some examples of machines include candy, cigarette, and food vending machines; telephone coin boxes; parking meters; pinball machines; or washers and dryers located in laundromats where no breaking or illegal entry is involved – these would be included in burglaries if the later was involved).

i). *All Other Larceny – Theft Not Specifically Classified-* all thefts which do not fit the definition of the specific categories of larceny listed above. (Includes thefts from fenced enclosures, boats, and airplanes. Thefts of animals, lawn furniture, handtools, and farm and construction equipment are also included where no breaking or entering of a structure is involved. Includes illegal entry of a tent, tern trailer or travel trailer used for recreational purposes followed by a theft or attempted theft, as well as the stealing of airplanes, bulldozers, and motorboats, are counted. The taking of gasoline from a self-service gas station and leaving without paying is included.).

Larceny Value

Notes: Part of monthly supplements reported to the FBI. The determination of the value of stolen property is the obligation of the investigating officer. Guidelines for determination of methods include using fair market value for article which are subject to depreciation; use cost to merchant (wholesale cost – no markup or profit added) for good stolen from retail establishments, warehouses, etc.; use victim's evaluation of items such as personal items that are not subject to deprecation; use replacement or actual cost for new personal items; and if victim exaggerates the value of stolen property, the officer uses common sense and good judgment for determining fair market value.

a). Under $50

b). $50-199

c). $200-499 – new category beginning 1983 was included in over $200 category prior to this date.

d). Over $400 – new category beginning 1983.

2). **Burglary** – the unlawful entry of a structure to commit a felony or theft.
Notes: The use of force to gain entry is not required to classify an offense as a burglary. For UCR purposes, offense locally known as burglary (any degree); unlawful entry either intent to commit a larceny or felony; breaking and entering with intent to commit a larceny, housebreaking, safecracking; and all attempts at these offenses are counted. Mobile units that are fixed as offices, residences, or storehouses are considered as structures that may be included in burglaries. Burglaries of hotels, morels, lodging houses, and other places where lodging of transients is the main purpose are scored under provisions of the Hotel Rule.

Burglary Types

a). *Forcible Entry* – counts all offenses where force of any kind is used to unlawfully enter a structure of the purpose of committing a theft or felony. Includes entry by use of tools; breaking windows; forcing windows; doors, transoms, or ventilators; cutting screens, walls, or roofs; and where known, the use of master keys, picks, unauthorized keys, celluloid, or other devices which leave no outward mark but are used to force a lock. Also includes burglary by concealment inside a building followed by an exiting of the structure.

b). *Unlawful Entry – No Force* – counts all offenses where no force applies and is achieved by use of an unlocked door or window. The element of trespass to the structure is essential so that this category includes thefts from open garages, open warehouses, open or unlocked dwellings, and open or unlocked common basement areas in apartment houses where entry is committed other than by the tenant who has lawful access. If the area entered was one of open access, thefts from the area would not involve an unlawful trespass and is counted as a larceny. (Law enforcement experience is assessed as critical for deciding whether force or no force was used in gaining entry. A forcible entry or unlawful entry where no theft or felony occurs but where acts of vandalism, malicious mischief, etc., are committed is not included as a burglary provided investigation clearly establishes that the unlawful entry was not for purposes other than to commit a felony or theft.

c). *Attempted Forcible Entry* – this classification counts situations where a forcible entry is attempted. Includes unlawful entry- no force when a perpetrator is frightened off while entering an unlocked door or climbing through an open window. If trespass occurs, these are included as unlawful entry, no force.

Burglary Location (and Time)

The category includes times of day classification for both residential and nonresidential burglaries. The time categories are as follows: day (from 6 a.m. to 6 p.m.), night (from 6 p.m. to 6 a.m.), and unknown. It is noted that the time of occurrence of burglaries to sometimes difficult for law enforcement to determine. If a forcible or unlawful entry of a building is made to steal a motor vehicle, the offense is counted under burglary, not motor vehicle theft.

a). *Residential* – dwelling.

b). *Non-residential* – store, office, etc.

3). **Motor Vehicle Theft** – the theft or attempted theft of a motor vehicle.

Notes: A motor vehicle is defined as a self-propelled vehicle that runs on land surface and not in rails. Does not include farm equipment, bulldozers, airplanes, construction equipment, or motorboats. All cases where automobiles are taken by persons not having lawful access even though the vehicles are latter abandoned are included. Includes joyriding. The definition excludes the taking of motor vehicle for temporary use by persons having lawful access. One offense is counted for each vehicle stolen or for each attempt to steal.

Motor Vehicle Types

a). *Autos* – includes all sedans, stationwagons, coupes, convertibles, and other similar motor vehicles which serve the primary purpose of transporting people from one place to another. Also includes automobiles used as taxis.

b). *Trucks and Buses* – this breakdown includes those vehicles specifically designed to transport people on a commercial basis and to transport cargo. These include pickup trucks and vans regardless of their use. A self-propelled motor home is a truck and classified in this category.

c). *Other Vehicles* – all other motor vehicles not included in the above categories. Includes snowmobiles, motorcycles, motor scooters, trailbikes, mopeds, golf carts, etc.

4). **Arson** – any willful or malicious burning or attempt to burn, with or without intent to defraud, a dwelling house, public building, motor vehicle or aircraft, personal property of another, etc.

Notes: Only fires determined through investigation to have been willfully or maliciously set are classified as arsons. Attempts included, but fires of suspicious or unknown origins are excluded. If arson crosses jurisdictions, the jurisdiction where the fire originates (point of origin) counts the arson.

Arson Types

a). *Structural* – includes residential and nonresidential structures. (Follows guidelines for structures set forth in burglaries).

b). *Mobile* – motor vehicles (Same types of motor vehicles used in motor vehicle definitions).

c). *Other* – not classified as structural or mobile. (Includes willful or malicious burnings of property such as crops, timber, fences, signs, and merchandise stored outside structures.).

Violent Crimes

1). **Criminal Homicide** – the willful (nonnegilient) killing of one human being by another.

Notes: The classification is based solely on police investigation as police investigation as opposed to the determination of a court, medical examiner, coroner, jury, or other judicial body. Not included for this offense classification are deaths caused by negligence, suicide, or accident; justifiable homicides, and attempts to murder and assaults to murder, which are scored as aggravated assaults.

2). **Forcible Rape** – the carnal knowledge of a female forcibly and against her will.

Notes: Assaults or attempts to commit rape by force or threat by force are also included; however, statutory rape (without force) and other sex offenses are excluded.

Rape Types

a). *Rape By Force*

b). *Attempts to Commit to Forcible Rape*

3). **Robbery** – the taking or attempting to take anything of value from the care, custody, or control of a person or persons by force or threat of force or violence and/or putting the victim in fear.

Notes: Robbery involves a theft or larceny, but is aggravated by the element of force or threat of force. It is committed in the presence of a victim. Armed robbery includes with any weapon, firearms, knife or cutting instrument, or other dangerous weapon, and strong-arm robbery is not armed robbery.

Robbery Types

a). *Firearm* – firearm is used as a weapon or employed as means of force to threaten the victim or put the victim in fear.

b). *Knife or Cutting Instrument* – includes knife, broken bottle, razor, ice pick, or other cutting or stabbing instrument is employed.

c). *Other Dangerous Weapon* – includes club, acid, explosive, brass knuckles, or other dangerous weapon is used to threaten or employed.

d). *Strong Arm – Hands, Fists, Feet, etc.* – includes muggings and similar offenses where no weapon is used, but strong-arm tactics (limited to the use of personal weapons such as hands, arms, feet, fists, teeth, etc.) are employed or their use is threatened to deprive the victim of possessions.

Robbery Locations

a). *Highway* – includes offenses which occur on streets, in alleys, and generally in view of law enforcement patrol but outside of structures.

b). *Commercial House* – commercial establishments including supermarkets, department stores, restaurants, taverns, finance companies, hotels, motels, etc. (Excludes gas stations, convenience stores, and banking-type institutions, for which there are separate categories).

c). *Gas or Service Station* – pertains to all gas stations with the primary function of selling gasoline, petroleum, and related products.

d). *Convenience Store* – includes the neighborhood store that specializes in the sale of consumable items, is easily accessible, and generally has extended hours of operation.

e). *Residence* – robberies of dwellings utilized for human habitation. (Excludes which occur at hotels, motels, lodging houses, and places where lodging of transients is the main purpose, these are included in the commercial category.).

f). *Bank* – includes robberies of banks, savings and loan associations, building and loan associations, credit unions, and other such institutions. (Excludes lending institutions and finance companies where the function is lending, these are included in the commercial category).

g). *Miscellaneous* – encompasses all other categories. (Includes robberies occurring on or at waterways, houses of worship, union halls, school buildings, government buildings, subways, trains, airplanes, doctors' and lawyers' offices, wooded areas, etc.).

4). **Aggravated Assault** – an unlawful attack by one person upon another upon another for the purpose of inflicting severe or aggravated bodily injury. This type of assault usually is accompanied by the use of a weapon or by means likely to produce death or great bodily harm.
Notes: Attempts are included since it is not necessary that an injury result when a gun, knife, or other weapon is used which could and probably would result in serious personal injury if the crime were successfully completed. Include commonly entitled offenses such as assault with a dangerous or deadly weapon; maiming, mayhem, assault with explosives; and all attempts to commit the foregoing offenses. Simple assault is differentiated from aggravated as it does not involve use of weapons and in which there is no serious or aggravated injuries to the victims. The assault will be aggravated if the personal injury is serious, e.g., broken bones, internal injuries, or where stitches are required. Simple assault is counted if the injuries are not serious (abrasions, minor lacerations, or contusions). Coercion, assault and battery, injury caused by culpable negligence, intimidation, and all attempts to commit these offenses are included in the simple assault category.

Assault Types
a). *Firearm* – wherein a firearm of any type is used or its use threatened. (Includes assaults with revolvers, automatic pistols, shotguns, zip guns, rifles, etc.).
b). *Knife or cutting instruments* - assaults wherein weapons such as knives, razors, hatchets, axes, cleavers, scissors, glass, broken bottles, ice picks, etc., are used as cutting or stabbing objects or their use is threatened.
c). *Other Dangerous Weapon* – assaults resulting from the use or threatened use of any object as a weapon which does or could result in serious injury. (Includes, but not limited, to clubs, bricks, jack handles, tire irons, bottles, or other blunt instruments used to club or beat victims. Also includes attacks by explosives, acid, lye, poison, scalding water, burning, etc.).
d). *Hands, Fists, Feet, Etc.*- use of these means as personal weapons.

Supplemental Offense Temporal Coverage

1). Seven Part 1 Crimes
1970-1999
2). Supplemental Arson
Categories: Property - a). Structural; b). Mobile; and c). Other
1981-1999
3). Supplemental Rape
Categories: a). Rape By Force and b). Attempts
1970-1999
4). Supplemental Robbery
Categories: Weapon - a). Firearm; b). Knife or Cutting Instrument; c). Other
Weapon; and d). Strong-Arm.
1974-1999
Categories: Location – a). Highway; b). Commercial; c). Gas Station (1982-);
d). Convenience Store (1982-); e). Residential; f). Bank; and g). Miscellaneous.
1981-1999
5). Supplemental Aggravated Assault
Categories: Weapon – a). Firearm; b). Knife or Cutting Instrument; c). Other
Weapon; and d). Hands, Fists, Feet.
1970-1999
6). Supplemental Burglary
Categories: Means of Entry – a). Forcible and b). No Force
1970-1999
Categories: Location & Time – a). Residential – i). Night; ii). Day; and iii).
Unknown and b). Non-Residential – i). Night; ii). Day; and iii). Unknown.
1981-1999
7). Supplemental Motor Vehicle Theft
Categories: Type – a). Autos; b). Trucks & Buses; and c). Other.
1974-1999
8). Supplemental Larceny
Categories: Type – a). Pocket-Picking; b). Purse-Snatching; c). Shoplifting; d).
From Motor Vehicle; e). Motor Vehicle Accessories (1982-); f). Bicycles; g).
From Building; h). Coin Operated Machines; and i). Other.
1981-1999
Categories: Value – a). Over $400 (1983-); b). $200 Through $400; c). $50
Through $199; and d). Under $50.
1970-1999

APPENDIX B

Economic Censuses Kinds of Businesses By Sector

	1982 & 1992 Retail	1982 & 1992 Services	1997 Retail	1997 Services
Kinds of Business (SIC or NAICS Group No.)				
Building Materials (52)	Y		Included	
General Merchandise Stores (53)	Y		Included	
Food Stores (54)	Y		Included	
Automotive Dealers/Gas Stations (58)	Y		Included	
Apparel/Accessory (56)	Y		Included	
Furniture/Home Equipment (57)	Y		Included	
Eating & Drinking (58)	Y			Included
Miscellaneous Retail (59)	Y		Included	
Hotels (70)		Y		Included
Personal Services (72)		Y		Included
Business Services (73)		Y		Included
Auto Repair (75)		Y		Included
Miscellaneous Repair (76)		Y		Included
Motion Pictures (78)		Y		Included
Amusement (79)		Y		Included
Health (80)*		Y		Included
Selected Educational (823,824,829)		Y		Included
Social Membership (861-862,864.889)		Y		Included
Miscellaneous Services (89)		Y		Included
Finance and Insurance (NAICS 52)		N		Y
Real Estate		N		Y
	Wholesale		Manufacturing	
Kinds of Businesses			139 Industry Groups	
Durable Goods (50)	Y			
Miscellaneous Durable Goods (509)	Y			
Nondurable Goods (51)	Y			
Miscellaneous Nondurable Goods (519)	Y			

*Does not include hospitals

APPENDIX C
Function and Status Data Measures for Model Specifications

Employment Functional Measures

Identifier	Definition
Retail E/R	Number of employees in retail establishments divided by the residential working population in working in the retail sector
Wholesale E/R	Number of employees in wholesale establishments divided by the residential working population in working in the wholesale sector
Service E/R	Number of employees in service establishments divided by the residential working population in working in the service sector

Demographic/Socioeconomic/Population Measures

Identifiers	Definition	Base/Universe
Hispanic Populations	Percentage of Total Population of Hispanic Origin	Total Population
African American Populations	Percentage of Total Population that is African American	Total Population
Female Headed Persons	Percentage of Total Population Headed by Females	Total Population
Average Household Size	Number of households in family and non-family (excluding group quarters) arrangements divided by total occupied housing units	None
Foreign Born	Percentage of Total Population that is Foreign Born	Total Population
Median Household Income	Median Household Income in 1989	Households
Public Assistance	Percentage of Households Receiving Public Assistance Income in 1979 and 89	Households
College Degrees	Percentage of Total Working Population with College Degrees	Total Population 25 Years and Over
Female Headed Households	Percentage of Households that is with Female Householder with Children under 18 years	Households
Poverty Rate	Percentage of Total Population that Are in Poverty Status	Persons for Whom Poverty Status is Determined

Labor/Population Measures

Identifiers	Definition	Base/Universe
Work Outside Residence	Percentage of Working Population that Worked Outside Place of Residence	Working Population (Ages 16 and over)
Labor Force Participation Rate	Percentage of Working Population Participating in the Labor Force	Working Population (Ages 16 and over)
Unemployment Rate	Percentage of Persons in the Total Working Population That Are Unemployed	Working Population (Ages 16 and over)
% 35 Minutes	Percentage of Total Working Population With Travel Times Less Than 35 Minutes	Working Population (Ages 16 and over)
Industry Groups (Various)	Percentage of Total Working Population Employed in the Following Industries: Agriculture, Forestry, and Fisheries, Mining, Construction, Manufacturing (nondurable goods), Manufacturing (durable goods), Transportation, Communications and other public utilities, Wholesale trade, Retail trade, Finance, Insurance, and Real Estate, Personal Services, Entertainment and Recreation Services, Health Services, Educational Services, Other Professional and Related Services, and Public Administration	Working Population (Ages 16 and over)

Identifiers	Definition	Base/Universe
Occupation (Various)	Percentage of Total Working Population With the Following Occupations: Executive, Administrative, and Managerial Occupations, Professional, Specialty Occupations, Technicians and Related Support Occupations, Sales Occupations, Private Household Occupations, Protective Service Occupations, Service Occupations Other, Farming, Forestry, and Fishing Occupations, Precision, Production, Craft, and Repair Occupations, Machine Operations, Assemblers, and Inspectors, Transportation and Material Moving Occupations, and Handlers, Equipment Cleaners, Helpers, and Laborers	Working Population (Ages 16 and over)

Housing/Property Functional Measures

Identifiers	Definition	Base/Universe
Housing Value	Percentage of Owner-Occupied Housing Units in A Range of Housing Values in Dollar Amounts	Specified Owner-Occupied Housing Units
Vacant Housing	Percentage of Housing Units that are Vacant	Housing Units
Single Family Homes	Percentage of Housing Units that are One Unit (Detached and Attached)	Housing Units
Multiple Housing Units	Percentage of Housing Units that Have 5 or more Units	Housing Units

Housing/Population Status Measures

Identifiers	Definition	Base/Universe
One Person Households	Percentage of Households with One (1) Person in Household	Households
Renters	Percentage of Total Occupied Housing Units that are Renter Occupied	Occupied Housing Units
Homeowners	Percentage of Total Occupied Housing Units that are Owner Occupied	Occupied Housing Units

Bibliography

Adams, Richard E. & Richard T. Serpe. 2000. "Social Integration, Fear of Crime, and Life Satisfaction." *Sociological Perspectives* 43:605-629.

Agnew, Robert. 1992. "Foundation for a General Strain Theory of Crime and Delinquency." *Criminology* 30:47-87.

—. 1994. "Techniques of Neutralization and Violence." *Criminology* 32:555-579.

—. 1995. "Testing The Leading Crime Theories: An Alternative Strategy Focusing On Motivational Processes." *Journal of Research in Crime and Delinquency* 32:363-398.

Alba, Richard D., John R. Logan, & Paul E. Bellair. 1994. "Living with Crime: The Implications of Racial/Ethnic Differences in Suburban Location." *Social Forces* 73:395-434.

Alba, Richard, John R. Logan, Wenquan Zhang, & Brian J. Stults. 1999. "Strangers Next Door: Immigrant Groups and Suburbs in Los Angeles and New York." Pp. 108-132 in *A Nation Divided: Diversity, Inequality, and Community in American Society*, edited by P. Moen, Donna Dempster-McClain, & Henry A, Walker. Ithaca, NY: Cornell University Press.

Allen, James P. & Eugene Turner. 1996. "Ethnic Diversity and Segregation in the New Los Angeles." Pp. 1-30 in *Ethnicity: Geographic Perspectives on Ethnic Change in Modern Cities*, edited by C. C. Roseman, Hans Dieter Laux, & Gunter Thieme. Lanham, MD: Rowman & Littlefield Publishers, Incorporated.

—. 1997. *The Ethnic Quilt: Population Diversity in Southern California.* Northridge, CA: The Center for Geographical Studies, California State University, Northridge.

Altshuler, William M. Harold Wolman, & Faith Mitchell. 1999. "Governance and Opportunity in Metropolitan America." Washington, DC: National Academy Press.

Anselin, Luc and Arthur Getis. 1992. "Spatial Statistical Analysis and Geographic Information Systems." *The Annals of Regional Science* 26:19-33.

Ashton, Patrick J. 1977. "Toward a New Conceptualization of Suburbs: A Theoretical and Empirical Exploration." *Sociological Focus* 10:287-307.

—. 1984. "Urbanization and the Dynamics of Suburban Development Under Capitalism." Pp. 54-81 in *Marxism and the Metropolis: New Perspectives in Urban Political Economy*, edited by W. K. Tabb & L. Sawers. New York: Oxford University Press.

Baldassare, Mark. 1986. *Trouble in Paradise: The Suburban Transformation in America.* New York: Columbia University Press.

—. 1994. "Suburban Communities: Change and Policy Responses." Pp. 3-12 in *Suburban Communities: Change and Policy Responses*, edited by M. D. C. Baldassare. Greenwich, CT: Jai Press.

Banerjee, Tribid & Niraj Verma. 2001. "Sprawl and Segregation: Another Side of the Los Angeles Debate." in *Lincoln Institute Conference on Segregation and the City*.

Barbano, Filippo. 1968. "Social Structures and Social Functions: The Emancipation of Structural Analysis in Sociology." *Inquiry* 11:40-84.

Barlow, David E. and Melissa Hickman Barlow. 2000. *Police in a Multicultural Society: An American Story*. Prospect Heights, IL: Waveland Press.

Baumer, Eric, Janet L. Lauritsen, Richard Rosenfeld, & Richard Wright. 1998. "The Influence of Crack Cocaine on Robbery, Burglary, and Homicide Rates: A Cross-City Longitudinal Analysis." *Journal of Research in Crime and Delinquency* 35:316-340.

Baumgartner, M.P. 1984. "Social Control in Suburbia." in *Toward A General Theory of Social Control, Volume 2: Selected Problems*, edited by D. Black. New York: Academic Press.

—. 1988. *The Moral Order of a Suburb*. Oxford: Oxford University Press.

Bernard, Thomas J. 1983. *The Consensus-Conflict Debate: Form and Content in Social Theories*. New York: Columbia University Press.

—. 1984. "Control Criticisms of Strain Theories: An Assessment of Theoretical and Empirical Adequacy." *Journal of Research in Crime and Delinquency* 21:353-372.

—. 1987. "Testing Structural Strain Theories." *Journal of Research in Crime and Delinquency* 24:262-280.

—. 1990. "Twenty Years of Testing Theories: What Have We Learned and Why?" *Journal of Research in Crime and Delinquency* 27:325-347.

—. 1995. "Merton versus Hirschi: Who is Faithful to Durkheim's Heritage?" Pp. 81-90 in *The Legacy of Anomie Theory*, vol. 6, *Advances in Criminological Research*, edited by F. Adler &. W. Lufer. New Brunswick: Transaction Publishers.

—. 2001. "Integrating Theories in Criminology." in *Explaining Criminals and Crime: Essays in Contemporary Criminological Theory*, edited by R. Paternoster & R. Bachman. Los Angeles: Roxbury Publishing Company.

Bernard, Thomas J. & Jeffrey B. Snipes. 1996. "Theoretical Integration in Criminology." Pp. 301-348 in *Crime and Justice: A Review of Research*, vol. 20, edited by M. Tonry & A. Reiss. Chicago: The University of Chicago.

Bernburg, Jon Gunnar. 2002. "Anomie, Social Change and Crime: A Theoretical Examination of Institutional-Anomie Theory." *British Journal of Criminology* 42:729-742.

Besnard, Philippe. 1990. "Merton in Search of Anomie." Pp. 243-254 in *Robert K. Merton: Consensus and Controversy*, edited by J. Clark, & S. Modgil. London: Falmer Press.

Blau, Peter M. 1990. "Structural Constraints and Opportunities: Merton's Contributions to General Theory." Pp. 141-155 in *Robert K. Merton: Consensus and Controversy*, edited by C. Modgil, J. Clark, & S. Modgil. London: Falmer Press.

—. 1994. *Structural Contexts of Opportunities*. Chicago: The University of Chicago Press.

Bollens, Scott A. 1987. "Municipal Decline and Inequality in American Suburban Rings, 1960-1980." *Regional Studies* 22:277-285.

Brantingham, Paul & Patricia Brantingham. 1984. *Patterns in Crime*. New York: Macmillan Publishing Company.

Brantingham, Paul J., Delmar A. Dyreson, & Patricia L. Brantingham. 1976. "Crime Seen Through a Cone of Resolution." *American Behavioral Scientist* 20:261-273.

Brodeur, Jean-Paul. 1998. "Tailor-Made Policing: A Conceptual Investigation." Pp. 30-51 in *How To Recognize Good Policing: Problems and Issues*, edited by J.-P. Brodeur. Thousand Oaks, CA: Sage Publications.

Brown, Marilyn A. 1982. "Modeling the Spatial Distribution of Suburban Crime." *Economic Geography* 58:247-261.

Buck, Andrew J. & Simon Hakim. 1981. "Analysis of Suburban Crime - An Exploratory Data Analysis Approach." *Australian & New Zealand Journal of Criminology* 14:83-90.

Burns, Nancy. 1994. *The Formation of American Local Governments: Private Values in Public Institutions*. New York: Oxford University Press.

Bursik Jr., Robert. 1988. "Social Disorganization and Theories of Crime." *Criminology* 26: 519-551.

Bursik Jr., Robert & Harold G. Grasmick. 1993. "Economic Deprivation and Neighborhood Crime Rates, 1960-1980." *Law and Society Review* 27:263-283.

Burton, Velmer S., Jr. & Francis T. Cullen. 1992. "The Empirical Status of Strain Theory." *Journal of Crime and Justice* 15:1-30.

Cervero, Robert. 1989. *American's Suburban Centers: The Land Use-Transportation Link*. Boston: Unwon Hyman.

Chapman, Jeffrey I. 1981. *Proposition 13 and Land Use: A Case Study of Fiscal Limits in California*. Lexington, MA: Lexington Books.

Cion, Richard M. 1971. "Accommodation Par Excellence: The Lakewood Plan." Pp. 224- in *Metropolitan Politics: A Reader*, edited by M. N. Danielson. Boston: Little, Brown and Company.

Cloward, Richard & Lloyd E. Ohlin. 1960. *Delinquency and Opportunity: A Theory of Delinquent Gangs*. New York: The Free Press.

Cloward, Richard A. & Frances Fox Piven. 1990. "Why People Deviate in Different Ways." Pp. 71-100 in *New Directions in the Study of Justice, Law, and Social Control*, edited by A. S. U. School of Justice Studies. New York: Plenum Press.

Cohen, Albert K. 1955. *Delinquent Boys*. New York: The Free Press.

—. 1965. "The Sociology of the Deviant Act: Anomie Theory and Beyond." *American Sociological Review* 30:5-14.

—. 1985 "The Assumption that Crime Is a Product of Environments: Sociological Approaches." Pp. 223-243 in *Theoretical Methods in Criminology*, edited by R. E. Meier. Beverly Hills, CA: Sage Publications.

—. 1997. "An Elaboration of Anomie Theory." in *The Future Of Anomie Theory*, edited by R. Agnew & N. Passas. Boston: Northeastern University Press.

Cohen, Albert K. Alfred Lindesmith, & Karl Schuessler. 1956. *The Sutherland Papers*. Bloomington, IN: Indiana University Press.

Cohen, Bernard P. 1989. *Developing Social Knowledge: Theory and Method.* Chicago: Nelson-Hall.

Cohen, Lawrence and Marcus Felson. 1979. "Social Change and Crime Rate Trends: A Routine Activities Approach." *American Sociological Review* 44:588-608.

Cohen, Lawrence, James Kluegel, and Kenneth Land. 1981. "Social Inequality and Predatory Victimization: An Exposition and Test of a Formal Theory." *American Sociological Review* 46: 505-524.

Conklin, J. & E. Bittner. 1973. "Burglary in a Suburb." *Criminology* 11,2: 206-232.

Cook, Philip J. 1986. "The Demand and Supply of Criminal Opportunities." Pp. 1-27 in *Crime & Justice: An Annual Review of Research*, vol. 7, edited by M. Tonry & A. Reiss Jr. . Chicago: University of Chicago Press.

Crothers, Charles. 1987. *Robert K. Merton.* Chcichester, U.K: Ellis Horwood Limited.

—. 1996. *Social Structure.* London: Routledge.

Cruickshank, Justin. 2000. "Social Theory and the Underclass: Social Realism or Rational Choice Individualism?" Pp. 75-92 in *Rational Choice Theory: Resisting Colonization*, edited by M. Archer. London: Routledge.

Cullen, Francis T. 1983. *Rethinking Crime and Deviance Theory: The Emergence of a Structuring Tradition.* Totowa, NJ: Rowman & Allanheld Publishers.

—. 1988. "Were Cloward and Ohlin Strain Theorists? Delinquency and Opportunity Revisited." *Journal of Research in Crime and Delinquency* 25:214-241.

Danielson, Michael. 1976. *The Politics of Exclusion.* New York: Columbia University Press.

Dear, Michael & Steven Flusty. 1998. "Postmodern Urbanism." *Annals of the Association of American Geographers* 88:50-72.

—. 2002. "The Resistible Rise of the L.A. School." Pp. 5-16 in *From Chicago to L.A.: Making Sense of Urban Theory*, edited by M. J. Dear. Thousand Oaks, CA: Sage Publications.

Deflem, Mathieu. 1989. "From Anomie To Anomia And Anomic Depression: A Sociological Critique On The Use Of Anomie In Psychiatric Research." *Social Science and Medicine* 29:627-634.

Evans, Davis. 1995. *Crime and Policing: Spatial Approaches*. Aldershot, UK: Avebury.

Featherstone, Richard & Mathieu Deflem. 2003. "Anomie and Strain: Context and Consequences of Merton's Two Theories." *Sociological Inquiry* 73:471-489.

Felson, Marcus. 1987. "Routine Activities and Crime Prevention in the Developing Metropolis." *Criminology* 25: 911-931.

—. 1993. "Social Indicators For Criminology." *Journal of Research in Crime and Delinquency* 30:400-411.

Felson, Marcus & Ronald V. Clarke. 1998. "Opportunity Makes the Thief: Practical Theory for Crime Prevention." Home Office, London.

Findlay, Mark. 1999. *The Globalization of Crime: Understanding Transitional Relationships in Context*. Cambridge: Cambridge University Press.

Fong, Eric & Kumiko Shibuya. 2000. "Suburbanization and Home Ownership: The Spatial Assimilation Process in U.S. Metropolitan Areas." *Sociological Perspectives* 43:137-157.

Freidman, Judith J. 1994. "Suburban Variations Within Highly Urbanized Regions: The Case of New Jersey." Pp. 97-132 in *Suburban Communities: Change and Policy Responses*, vol. 4, *Research in Community Sociology*, edited by M. Baldassare. Greenwich, CT: Jai Press.

Frey, William H. & Alden Speare, Jr. 1992. "Metropolitan Areas as Functional Communities: A Proposal for a New Definition." Population Studies Center, University of Michigan, Ann Arbor.

Frey, William H. & Douglas Geverdt. 1998. "Changing Suburban Demographics: Beyond the "Black-White, City-Suburb" Typology." Population Studies Center, University of Michigan, Ann Arbor, MI.

Friedman, Judith. 1994. "Suburban Variations within Highly Urbanized Regions: The Case of New Jersey." in *Suburban Communities: Change and Policy Responses*, vol. 4, *Research in Community Sociology*, edited by M. B. D. A. Chekki. Greenwich, CT: JAI Press, Incorporated.

Fuchs, Stephan. 2001a. *Against Essentialism: A Theory of Culture and Society*. Cambridge, MA: Harvard University Press.

—. 2001b. "Beyond Agency." *Sociological Theory* 19:24-40.

Fulton, William, Rold Pendall, Mai Nguyen & Alicia Harrison. 2001. "Who Sprawls Most? How Growth Patterns Differ Across the U.S." Center on Urban & Metropolitan Policy, The Brookings Institution, Washington, D.C.

Glenn, Russell, Barbara R. Panitch, Dionne Barnes-Proby, Elizabeth Williams, John Christian, Matthew W. Lewis, Scott Gerwehr, and David W. Brannan. 2003. "Training the 21st Century Police Officer: Redefining Police Professionalism for the Los Angeles Police Department." Rand, Santa Monica, CA.

Goldstein, Herman. 2003. "On Further Developing Problem-Oriented Policing: The Most Critical Need, the Major Impediments, and a Proposal." Pp. 13-

in *Problem-Oriented Policing: From Innovation to Mainstream*, edited by J. Knuttson. Monsey, NY: Criminal Justice Press.

Goldthorpe, John. 2001. "Causation, Statistics, and Sociology." *European Sociological Review* 17, 1: 1-20.

Gottfredson, Michael R. and Travis Hirschi. 1990. *A General Theory of Crime.* Stanford, CA: Stanford University Press.

Haggerty, Kevin D. 2004a. "Displaced Expertise: Three Constraints on the Policy-Relevance of Criminological Thought." *Theoretical Criminology* 8:211-231.

—. 2004b. "From Risk to Precaution: The Rationalities of Personal Crime Prevention." Pp. 193-214 in *Risk and Morality*, edited by R. Ericson &. A. Doyle. Toronto: University of Toronto Press.

Hahn, Harlan and Judson L. Jeffries. 2003. *Urban America and Its Police: From the Postcolonial Era Through the Turbulent 1960s.* Boulder, CO: University Press of Colorado.

Hakim, Simon. 1980. "The Attraction of Property Crimes to Suburban Localities: A Revised Economic Model." *Urban Studies* 17:265-276.

Hakim, Simon, Arie Ovadia, & J. Weinblatt. 1978. "Crime Attraction and Deterrence in Small Communities: Theories and Results." *International Regional Science Review* 3:153-163.

Hale, David. 2003. "Introduction: The New York and Los Angeles Schools." Pp. 1-46 in *New York and Los Angeles, Politics, Society and Culture: A Comparative View*, edited by D. Hale. Chicago: The University of Chicago Press.

Hannon, Lance. 2002. "Criminal Opportunity Theory and the Relationship Between Poverty and Property Crime." *Sociological Spectrum* 22:363-381.

Harries, Keith. 1997. *Serious Violence: Patterns of Homicide and Assault in America.* Springfield, IL: Charles C. Thomas.

Harris, David R. 1999. "All Suburbs Are Not Created Equal: A New Look at Racial Differences in Suburban Location." Population Studies Center, University of Michigan, Ann Arbor.

Harris, Richard. 1999. "The Making of American Suburbs, 1900-1950s: A Re-Construction." Pp. 91-110 in *Changing Suburbs. Foundation, Form, and Function*, edited by R. P. L. Harris. London: E &FN Spon,

Heimer, Karen. 1997. "Socioeconomic Status, Subcultural, and Violent Delinquency." *Social Forces* 75:799-833.

Heitgerd, Janet L. & Robert J. Bursik, Jr. 1987. "Extracommunity Dynamics and the Ecology of Delinquency." *American Journal of Sociology* 92:775-787.

Henslin, James M. 1988. "Structuralism and Individualism in Deviance Theory." *Deviant Behavior* 9:211-223.

Hirschi, Travis. 1969. *Causes of Delinquency.* Berkeley, CA: University of California Press.

Hoch, Charles. 1984. "City Limits: Municipal Boundary Formation and Class Segregation." Pp. 101-119 in *Marxism and the Metropolis: New Perspectives in Urban Political Economy*, edited by W. K. Tabb & L. Sawers. New York: Oxford University Press.

—. 1985. "Municipal Contracting in California: Privatizing with Class." *Urban Affairs Quarterly* 20:303-323.

Lucy, William H. & David L. Phillips. 2000. *Confronting Suburban Decline: Strategic Planning for Metropolitan Renewal*. Washington, D.C: Island Press.

Lynch, James P. 2002. "Crime in International Perspective." Pp. 5-42 in *Crime: Public Policies For Crime Control*, edited by J. Q. Wilson & J. Petersilia. Oakland, CA: Institute for Contemporary Studies (ICS) Press.

Lynch, Michael J. & W. Byron Groves. 1995. "In Defense of Comparative Criminology: A Critique of General Theory and Rational Man." Pp. 367-392 in *The Legacy of Anomie Theory*, vol. 6, *Advances in Criminological Research*, edited by F. Adler & W. Lufer. New Brunswick, NJ: Transaction Publishers.

Marcuse, Peter. 1997. "The Enclave, the Citadel, and the Ghetto: What Has Changed in the Post-Fordist U.S. City." *Urban Affairs Review* 33:228-264.

—. 2001. "Enclaves Yes, Ghettoes, No: Segregation and the State." Lincoln Institute of Land Policy Conference Paper.

Massey, Douglas S. 2001. "Segregation and Violent Crime in Urban America." Pp. 317-344 in *Problem of the Century: Racial Stratification in the United States*, edited by E. A. a. D. S. Massey. New York: Russell Sage Foundation.

Mastrofski, Stephen D. 1998. "Community Policing and Policing Organization Structure." Pp. 161-189 in *How To Recognize Good Policing: Problems and Issues*, edited by J.P. Brodeur. Thousand Oaks, CA: Sage Publications.

Matsueda, Ross. 1988. "The Current State of Differential Association Theory." *Crime & Delinquency* 34: 277-306.

McNulty, Thomas L. 1999. "The Residential Process and the Ecological Concentration of Race, Poverty and Violent Crime." *Sociological Focus* 32:25-41.

Mehay, Stephen L. 1979. "Intergovernmental Contracting for Municipal Police Services: An Empirical Analysis." *Land Economics* 55:59-72.

Meier, Robert F. 1989. "Deviance and Differentiation." Pp. 199-212 in *Theoretical Integration in the Study of Deviance and Crime: Problems and Prospects*, edited by S. Messner, M. Krohn, & A. Liska. Albany, NY: State University of New York Press.

—. 2001. "Macro Models of Criminal Events." Pp. 47-60 in *The Process and Structure of Crime: Criminal Events and Crime Analysis*, vol. 9, *Advances in Criminological Theory*, edited by R. F. Meier, L. Kennedy, & V. Sacco. New Brunswick, NJ: Transaction Publishers.

Merton, Robert K. 1934. "Durkheim's Division of Labor in Society." *American Journal of Sociology* 40:319-328.

—. 1936. "The Unanticipated Consequences of Purposive Social Action." *American Sociological Review* 1:894-904.

—. 1938. "Social Structure and Anomie." *American Sociological Review* 3:672-682.

—. 1949. "Social Structure and Anomie: Revisions and Extensions." Pp. 226-257 in *The Family: Its Functions and Destiny*, edited by R. N. Anshen. New York: Harper & Brothers Publishers.

—. 1956. "The Socio-Cultural Environment and Anomie." Pp. 24-80 in *New Perspectives For Research on Juvenile Delinquency*, edited by H. L. W. R. Kotinsky. Washington, DC: Children's Bureau, U.S Department of Health, Education, and Welfare.

—. 1959. "Social Conformity, Deviation and Opportunity Structures." *American Sociological Review* 24:177-189.

—. 1964. "Anomie, Anomia, and Social Interaction: Contexts of Deviant Behavior." Pp. 213-242 in *Anomie and Deviant Behavior: A Discussion and Critique*, edited by M. Clinard. New York: Free Press.

—. 1968. *Social Theory and Social Structure*. New York: The Free Press.

—. 1976. "The Sociology of Social Problems." Pp. 5-43 in *Contemporary Social Problems*, edited by R. K. M. R. Nisbet. New York: Harcourt Brace Jovanovich, Incorporated.

—. 1987. "Three Fragments From A Sociologist's Notebooks: Establishing The Phenomenon, Specified Ignorance, and Strategic Research Materials." *Annual Review of Sociology* 13:1-28.

—. 1995. "Opportunity Structure: The Emergence, Diffusion, and Differentiation of a Sociological Concept." Pp. 3-78 in *The Legacy of Anomie Theory*, vol. 6, *Advances in Criminological Research*, edited by F. Adler & W. Lufer. New Brunswick, NJ: Transaction Publishers.

—. 1997. "On the Evolving Synthesis of Differential Association and Anomie Theory: A Perspective from the Sociology of Science." *Criminology* 35:517-525.

Messner, Steven & Richard Rosenfeld. 1997. *Crime and the American Dream*. Belmont, CA: Wadsworth Publishing Company.

Miethe, Terance D & Richard McCorkle. 1998. *Crime Profiles: The Anatomy of Dangerous Persons, Places, and Situations*. Los Angeles: Roxbury Publishing Company.

Miethe, Terance D. & Robert F. Meier. 1994. *Crime And Its Social Context: Toward An Integrated Theory Of Offenders, Victims, And Situations*. Albany, NY: State University of New York Press.

Miethe, Terance D. and Wendy C. Regoezi. 2004. *Rethinking Homicide: Exploring the Structure and Process Underlying Deadly Situations*. Cambridge: Cambridge University Press.

Miethe, Terance D., Mark C. Stafford, & J. Scott Long. 1987. "Social Differentiation in Criminal Victimization: A Test of Routine Activities/Lifestyle Theories." *American Sociological Review* 52:184-194.

Miller, Gary J. 1981. *Cities by Contract: The Politics of Municipal Incorporation.* Cambridge, MA: The MIT Press.

Orfield, Myron. 2002. *American Metropolitics: The New Suburban Reality.* Washington, D.C.: Brookings Institution Press.

Orru, Marco. 1987. *Anomie: History and Meanings.* Boston: Allen & Unwin.

—. 1990. "Merton's Instrumental Theory of Anomie." Pp. 231-240 in *Robert K. Merton: Consensus and Controversy,* edited by C. Modgil, J. Clark, & S. Modgil. London: Falmer Press.

Palen, J. John. 1995. *The Suburbs.* New York: Mc-Graw Hill, Incorporated.

Petersilia, Joan. 1992. "Crime and Punishment in California: Full Cells, Empty Pockets, and Questionable Benefits." Pp. 175-205 in *Urban America: Policy Choices for Los Angeles and the Nation,* edited by J. Steinberg, D. Lyon, & M. Vaina. Santa Monica, CA: RAND.

Pfohl, Stephen. 1985. *Images of Deviance and Social Control.* New York: McGraw-Hill, Incorporated.

Porpora, Douglas V. 1987. *The Concept of Social Structure.* New York: Greenwood Press.

—. 1989. "Four Concepts of Social Structure." *Journal for the Theory of Social Behavior* 19:195-211.

Reiss Jr., Albert. 1986. "Why Are Communities Important in Understanding Crime?" in *Communities and Crime,* vol. 8, *Crime and Justice: A Review of Research,* edited by M. Tonry & A. Reiss. Chicago: The University of Chicago Press.

Rubinstein, David. 1977. "The Concept of Action in the Social Sciences." *Journal for the Theory of Social Behavior* 7:209-236.

—. 1992. "Structural Explanation in Sociology: The Egalitarian Imperative." *The American Sociologist* 23:5-19.

—. 1993. "Opportunity and Structural Sociology." *Journal for the Theory of Social Behavior* 23:265-283.

—. 1994. "The Social Construction of Opportunity." *The Journal of Socio-Economics* 23:61-78.

—. 2001. *Culture, Structure & Agency: Towards a Multidimensional Society.* Thousand Oaks, CA: Sage Publications.

Short Jr., James F. 1998. "The Level of Explanation Problem Revisited - The American Society of Criminology 1997 Presidential Address." *Criminology* 36:3-35.

Skogan, Wesley and Kathlyn Freydl. 2004. *Fairness and Effectiveness in Policing: The Evidence.* Washington, DC: The National Academy Press.

Skogan, Wesley G. 1977. "The Changing Distribution of Big City Crime: A Multi-City Time Series Analysis." *Urban Affairs Quarterly* 13:33-48.

Sloan III, John J. & John M. Stahura. 1986. "Crime Rate Stability for 685 Suburbs, 1972-1980: Violent Crime Pattern More Stable; Property Crime, Less So." *Social Science Research* 70:308-309.

Stahura, John M. 1987. "Suburban Socioeconomic Status Change: A Comparison of Models, 1950-1980." *American Sociological Review* 52:268-277.

Stahura, John M. & C. Ronald Huff. 1979. "The New "Zones of Transition": Gradients of Crime in Metropolitan Areas." *Review of Public Data Use* 7:41-48.

—. 1981. "Persistence of Suburban Violent Crime Rates: An Ecological Analysis." *Sociological Focus* 14:123-137.

—. 1986. "Crime in Suburbia, 1960-1980." Pp. 55-70 in *Metropolitan Crime Patterns*, edited by R. Figlio, S. Hakim, & G. Rengert. Monsey, NY: Criminal Justice Press.

Stahura, John M. & John J. Sloan III. 1988c "Urban Stratification of Places, Routine Activities, and Suburban Crime Rates." *Social Forces* 66:1102-1118.

Stahura, John M. & Richard Hollinger. 1988. "A Routine Activities Approach to Suburban Arson Rates." *Sociological Spectrum* 8:349-369.

Stahura, John M., C. Ronald Huff, & Brent L. Smith. 1980. "Crime in the Suburbs: A Structural Model." *Urban Affairs Quarterly* 15:291-316.

Stinchcombe, Arthur. 1995. "Social Structure in the Work of Robert K. Merton." Pp. 81-95 in *Robert K. Merton: Consensus and Controversy*, edited by C. Modgil, J. Clark, & S. Modgil. London: Falmer Press.

Vold, George B., Thomas J. Bernard, & Jeffrey B. Snipes. 2002. *Theoretical Criminology*. Oxford: Oxford University Press.

Warr, Mark. 2001. "Crime and Opportunity: A Theoretical Essay." Pp. 65-94 in *The Process and Structure of Crime: Criminal Events and Crime Analysis*, vol. 9, *Advances in Criminological Theory*, edited by R. Meier, L. Kennedy, & V. Sacco. New Brunswick, NJ: Transaction Publishers.

Weiher, Gregory R. 1989. "Public Policy and Patterns of Residential Segregation." *Western Political Quarterly*:651-677.

—. 1991. *The Fractured Metropolis: Political Fragmentation and Metropolitan Segregation*. Albany, NY: State University of New York Press.

Williams, Oliver. 1971. *Metropolitan Political Analysis: A Social Access Approach*. New York: The Free Press.

Zuckerman, Harriet. 1998. "Accumulation of Advantage and Disadvantage: The Theory and Its Intellectual Biography." Pp. 139-161 in *Robert K. Merton & Contemporary Sociology*, edited by S. Tabbonia& C. Mongardini. New Brunswick, NJ: Transaction Publishers.

Index